COLETTE, BEAUVOIR, AND DURAS

Colette, Beauvoir,

GAINESVILLE
TALLAHASSEE
TAMPA
BOCA RATON
PENSACOLA
ORLANDO
MIAMI
JACKSONVILLE

University Press of Florida

and Duras

AGE AND WOMEN WRITERS

BETHANY LADIMER

04 03 02 01 00 99 6 5 4 3 2 1

Library of Congress Cataloging-in-Publication Data

Ladimer, Bethany.
Colette, Beauvoir, and Duras : age and women writers / Bethany
Ladimer.
p.   cm.
Includes bibliographical references and index.
ISBN 0-8130-1700-9 (alk. paper)
1. Colette, 1873–1954. 2. Beauvoir, Simone de, 1908–1986. 3. Duras,
Marguerite, 1914–1996. 4. Women authors, French—20th century—
Biography. 5. Authors, French—20th century—Biography. 6. Aged
authors—France—Biography. I. Title.
PQ149.L27 1999
840.9'9287'0904—dc21
[B]   99-033017

The University Press of Florida is the scholarly publishing agency for
the State University System of Florida, comprising Florida A&M
University, Florida Atlantic University, Florida International
University, Florida State University, University of Central Florida,
University of Florida, University of North Florida, University of South
Florida, and University of West Florida.

University Press of Florida
15 Northwest 15th Street
Gainesville, FL 32611-2079
http://www.upf.com

THIS BOOK IS DEDICATED TO | Michael G.
Edward K.
and John McW.
in friendship.

CONTENTS

ACKNOWLEDGMENTS

A book about aging writers is almost inevitably one that is written in middle age or beyond, one that draws on the accumulated resources of years of reading and interpreting. The French women writers in this book fascinated me even before it was professionally acceptable or desirable to write about them; in my twenties, I studied them with special attention to their childhood and youth. By the time I was in my thirties and forties, the full span of their lives interested me, and I began to write about the works of all their various seasons. But it is now, in my fifties, that I have seen how Colette, Beauvoir, and Duras actually chose to grow old and how much their late-life work owes to the choices they made. Now that I have lived with them for decades and have chosen to age in their company, I realize that they inspire me more at this time in my life than ever before.

It has not always been easy to write on a subject that is often considered unpleasant, if not actually taboo. Fortunately, an encouraging number of ground-breaking works on aging writers appeared in the early 1990s as I began work on this book, particularly *Aging and Gender in Literature,* edited by Anne Wyatt-Brown and Janice Rossen; *Safe at Last in the Middle Years: The Invention of the Midlife Progress Novel* by Margaret Morganroth Gullette; and *Aging and Its Discontents: Freud and Other Fictions* by Kathleen Woodward. Yet there is more work to be done. I often saw distinct uneasiness with the problematics of aging reflected in many faces at gatherings when I mentioned the subject I'd been working on. The fact that this reaction is still so widespread would be reason enough to write about it again, simply to overcome the taboo, much in the way Beauvoir herself wrote about it. But I also hope that readers will find these late-life writings meaningful, moving, and finally deeply comforting.

Inspiration originally came from the works of Joan DeJean, Nancy Miller, Michèle Sarde, and Marianne Hirsch, to whom I am most grateful. I am also indebted to Danielle Deltel at the University of Paris, to the Société des Amis de Colette in Saint-Sauveur-en-Puisaye, and in particular to Jeanne Contou for organizing a most stimulating colloquium on the late-life work of Colette in June 1997. I would also like to thank Kathleen Woodward at the Center for Twentieth Century Studies in Milwaukee for sharing her manuscript in galley form with me, and for organizing and inviting me to participate in an important colloquium on aging in 1996. I also thank Margaret Morganroth Gullette for corresponding with me about middle-aged writers and the way in which their mothers experienced middle age. The staff members of the Bibliothèque Marguerite Durand and the Bibliothèque Nationale in Paris generously gave me hours of help. Most of all, I am grateful to Middlebury College for funding my leave to work on this book and for allowing me to travel to France when necessary.

Several people have given me especially valuable criticism and encouragement along the way: my colleagues Chantal de Grandpré, Ed and Huguette Know, John McWilliams, Brigitte Szymaneck, and Paula Schwartz, and my assistant Theodora Anastaplo. And, of course, my family has endured with humor and patience all the vicissitudes of researching, writing, and preparing a manuscript.

Portions of this book have been published previously. Parts of chapter 3 appeared as "Moving Beyond Sido's Garden: Ambiguity in Three Novels by Colette" in *Romance Quarterly*, 36.2 (May 1989), "A Sick Child and a Cure: Mother-Daughter Relations in Colette" in *Genders* 6 (Fall 1989), and as "Colette: Rewriting the Script for the Aging Woman" in *Aging, Gender and Creativity*, edited by Anne Wyatt-Brown and Janice Rossen (Charlottesville: University Press of Virginia, 1993). Part of chapter 5 appeared as "The Space of a Woman's Autobiography in *Emily L.*" in *Dalhousie French Studies*, vol. 18, 1990. I gratefully acknowledge permission to reprint all the material listed here.

INTRODUCTION

Three Lives

Sidonie-Gabrielle Colette, Simone de Beauvoir, and Marguerite Duras all lived long lives. They were enormously productive writers who continued to write in advanced age and almost until death, each forging and refining a late style that continued to evolve up to the end. Colette's last work, *The Blue Lantern* (Le fanal bleu), was published when she was seventy-three. Beauvoir's last full-length work, *Adieu: A Farewell to Sartre* (La Cérémonie des adieux), was published in 1982; she died in 1986. Duras continued to write prolifically until her death in March 1996. In their late works, each offers a portrait of herself as woman and artist in old age.

They were great innovators in French literature, noted for crossing boundaries in their lives as well as in their writing. Their personal histories with respect to courtship, marriage, and childbearing, which are also the basic elements of the traditional literary plot for the novel, were quite unconventional for their times. Colette married at twenty for the first time, divorced by age thirty-two, lived for a time in a lesbian relationship, remarried, and had a daughter at age forty. She divorced again and, after a ten-year liaison, remarried at age sixty-two a man sixteen years her junior. She remained married to him until her death. Beauvoir, who never married and never wanted to be a mother, was attached to Sartre from the age of twenty-one until Sartre's death in 1980. But she had numerous affairs with other men, and with women as well. Two passionate hetero-sexual affairs occurred when she was in her forties. The first, with an American, was in some ways as formative to her conception of women's experience as was her relationship with Sartre. The second lover was a man seventeen years younger. In the late years of her life, after Sartre's death, she established an intimate bond with a younger woman. Duras's story differs from the others in that she had a lover while still a young girl in French Indochina. When she moved to France, she married at a con-ventional age, but after World War II she arranged to live together with two men: her husband, and a lover with whom she had a son. Much later, she developed a close relationship with a homosexual man much younger than she and stayed with him until her death.

A glance at these marital and sexual histories reveals that each woman, in her own way, privileged a kind of sexual ambiguity or undecidability in terms of traditional definitions of femininity and that this tendency in-tensified significantly as she aged. In the case of Colette, the intensifica-tion with age may seem less apparent, but I will show that her late works reveal a kind of redirected eroticism, away from the objects of genital sexual desire and towards a form of pleasure derived from writing. In all three cases, there seems to have been room for both femininity and mas-culinity, for heterosexuality and homosexuality, for an old and a new kind of eroticism—all contributing to a new construction and enactment of femininity.

It must be remembered in reviewing these women's lives that their stories were considered more extraordinary at that time than they would be in today's world of greater sexual freedom and frequent divorce. They represent a breaking away from received ideas in fiction and in life of how a woman "ought" to think and behave. This liberation found its way into the texts they wrote, both fictional and autobiographical, for like the established Anglo-American women writers of the 1920s and 1930s, they were all great autobiographers as they advanced in age. In sociological terms, one might say that they experienced the life cycle differently than other people did, and resisted definitions of their femininity that would have been imposed by common cohort behavior, or the behavior that is common to all members of a particular generation at a given moment in their lives. Instead of moving through the prescribed stages for their cohort, they experienced their lives as more fluid and were able to envision certain changes late in life as easily as in their youth.

All three were conscious of their own aging process and each discussed it in her autobiographical writing and made it a central theme of certain fictional works. For all of them, aging involved anxiety, which was eventually replaced by specific growth and change. After the difficult passage through the menopausal years, they found that age opened up a far broader range of possibilities for them as women and as writers than had been the case before. Their three examples stand as proof of the variability of the late-life femininity that women can and must create for themselves. Perhaps because they had been to some extent outside the prescribed bounds of womanly behavior all their lives, they were willing and able to let age take them all the way out of these bounds and into a newly defined place where the traditional economy of sexual difference was altered at last. It was their lifelong independence and originality that enabled them to negotiate the difficult potential contradiction of age and femininity: at the very time when a woman loses her youthful sexual appeal, she becomes aware, if she is conscious of her own process of maturation, of a greater need and desire for intimacy. In middle age, these three writers in fact underwent an experience in which solitude threatened, even if Beauvoir would not consciously acknowledge this phase. But all three found solutions to their loneliness in the loving company of someone much younger. Duras lived out her "impossible love" with Yann Andréa despite much negative public opinion. Beauvoir, who had refused to marry or have children during a time and in a milieu when such decisions cut her off from almost all of her cohorts, turned increasingly in her sixties to another woman, in whose company she became more productive and less depressed than she had been since childood. Colette's "best friend" and second husband, Maurice Goudeket, remained her closest relationship until her death. Colette, Beauvoir, and Duras were wise enough to deal constructively with the need to sustain bonds of intimacy and to create new ones in their late years, and to find ways to express their erotic impulses both within and apart from these bonds.

At the same time, all were also conscious of their gender in their works, even if this consciousness took a less explicitly feminist form in the work of Colette. But even Colette can be considered a feminist writer in several key texts. She was acutely aware of the power relations that accompany heterosexual passion and her signature as a woman called into question many of the conventions of plot and perspective that she had inherited. As Nancy Miller says, "The signature of the woman writer who is also a feminist writer is the mark of a resistance to dominant ideologies; for the feminist critic, the signature is the site of a possible political disruption" (17).

Colette, Beauvoir, and Duras all departed from the social milieu of their origin, and one could say of each that by mid-life she had no clearly defined location within the social class structure of twentieth-century France. Each was, though, responsible for defining and creating her own milieu and for popularizing it as a stylish fringe. In the tradition of George Sand, but from a humbler background, each had elected a situation of marginality. Colette, born in 1873, was a young woman in the Belle Epoque around 1900 and had developed into a mature, productive writer by the 1920s. A native of a small village in Burgundy, she became Parisian when she married but was never fully at home in any pre-existing Paris social milieu. After her divorce from Willy, she created her own circles there. In a way, the same vague sense of social estrangement had haunted even her marvellous childhood: her family was bourgeois but financially impoverished by the time of her adolescence, and she attended the village public school for girls with the daughters of peasants, a very different class origin from her own. Beauvoir was born in Paris in 1908 to a bourgeois, devout Catholic family of some standing but that similarly saw its resources dwindle away while Beauvoir was still a young girl. When her studies were completed and she was independent, she broke with her social class of origin (she had already renounced Catholicism) and lived in the intellectual margins of society with a group of friends whom she and Sartre called "the family." From this position, Beauvoir exerted great influence on the intellectual life of France and the rest of the world. Marguerite Donnadieu was born near Saigon in 1914. The daughter of French colonial schoolteachers, she lost her father at an early age and watched her mother struggle financially to raise three children. After earning her *baccalauréat,* she left for France, where she felt simultaneously at home and estranged and where no one in her entourage shared her background. Like Beauvoir, she affiliated herself all of her life with intellectuals of various different origins. Like George Sand or the women of the Sappho 1900 movement, Colette, Beauvoir, and Duras were considered at various points in their lives "scandalous" in their behavior, an epithet that apparently troubled none of them.

There is also much similarity in the configuration of their mother-daughter relationships. Each of these three women had a mother who, in very different ways, ways was omnipresent in the young daughter's life, whereas the father was either literally absent (as in the case of Duras), or emotionally relatively distant (as in the cases of Colette and Beauvoir). The presence of a strong mother-daughter connection, regardless of its affective coloration at different points in the daughter's life, is also characteristic of each woman's writing. Issues of individuation or merging with a symbolic mother are especially marked, even when the universality of these issues for women writers in general is taken into account. Perhaps this is the reason the question of late-life femininity, associated with the mother's femininity and with her death, was a preoccupation for them.

Texts and Methodology

This book is an attempt to bring together and articulate several areas of critical concern. While women's studies and French literary criticism are well established, it is a third approach, largely ignored until very recently, that I am seeking to foreground here: the study of aging and the dimension it confers on our understanding of the personal and creative development of writers. I define aging studies as a distinct part of the more general field of age studies. Whereas the latter encompasses all the ages of men and women, I focus specifically on the study of *advancing* age as a necessary category of experience to be taken into account in the same way as gender or race; for example, in the analysis of literature or other symbolic cultural representations. Reading the work of an author through time and over the life cycle allows for new and different interpretations, as a work is understood according to its place along the trajectory of a life, or as the creation of an artist writing from the widely differing perspective and assumptions of girlhood, maturity, menopause, or late life. In particular, this reading through time upsets the notion of an essential Colettian, Beauvoirian, or Durasian style that somehow reaches a fixed and final iteration by early middle age. Instead, one sees that the writing of late life continues to evolve and reflects the changed perspectives, both anxious and serene, of the end of the life course. Foregrounding the writing of advanced age illuminates the aging process itself, allowing us to confront at last a chapter of human experience that has too often been an object of dread and avoidance.[1]

This book is also an exploration of the differences between the aging experience of men and women writers. Women growing old are doubly marginalized as writers, and many older women pass through a phase in which they feel that they are invisible in their private lives when men, who once paid attention to them in part because they found them attractive, suddenly find them lacking in interest of any kind.[2] Colette, Beauvoir, and Duras all explicitly dealt with the issue of their own aging and the aging of women in general. To a great extent, the feeling of having few elderly antecedents is a modern dilemma for both men and women, in that the population of France is aging much as it is in the rest of Europe and the United States. Hence there are more writers of both sexes than in past centuries who arrive at middle and old age in good health and who continue to be productive.[3] But it is also a particular dilemma for women, whose intimate experiences of aging are even more unknown to us, as Simone de Beauvoir points out in *The Coming of Age* [La Vieillesse] : "Neither history nor literature has left us any valid account of the sexuality of older women. The subject is even more taboo than the sexuality of older males" [Ni l'histoire ni la littérature ne nous ont laissé de témoignage valable sur la sexualité des femmes âgées. Le sujet est encore plus tabou que la sexualité des vieux mâles] (371).

I also hope to provide an exploration of the three-way conjunction involving gender, age, and cultural heritage. I ask how a woman's linguistic and cultural heritage affects the way she experiences life when she has gone beyond the age when women are usually considered sexually desirable. What do modern French women write about when they are older and interested in writing truly personal accounts, not simply the same old stories that always sell copies?

The legacy of the French literary tradition has conditioned, though it has not determined, the late style and production of these otherwise very different aging women writers. Over the centuries since the Renaissance, the aging of French women as portrayed in writing by female and by male authors has been fraught with anxiety over declining sexual attractiveness. Although even this constant has been constructed and reconstructed, waxing and waning, it needs to be understood in the twentieth century in conjunction with the cult of youth and youthful beauty that flourished in the late nineteenth century and especially in the 1920s.

For a long time I have believed that the intersection of female gender and the literary tradition of French culture gave rise to an exceptionally difficult set of problems and resolutions for aging women in France, and that to consider the sharply delineated terms of their dilemma would shed light on the problematic relationship between femininity and aging in all Western societies, including our own. To understand how this has occurred, I have chosen, in the three chapters devoted to Colette, Beauvoir, and Duras, to engage the complexity involved in reading the life and the text together, admitting that both form part of a single weave, without disregarding the specificity of the literature. I have tried to "think in terms of individual life stories, but looking harder than biography usually does at the way a woman reads her own aging within the cultural contexts of her time" (Gullette 1993, 45). Basically, I share the belief expressed by Toril Moi in her work *Simone de Beauvoir: The Making of an Intellectual Woman* that "there can be no methodological distinction between 'life' and text," especially because the autobiographical self is inevitably fictionalized to some degree, whereas a writer's fiction constantly and inevitably refers to her autobiography. Moi is interested in examining the "intertextual network of fictional, philosophical, autobiographical, and epistolary texts" by Beauvoir because, taken together and read "with and against each other in order to bring out their points of tension, contradiction, and similarities," they constitute the complex and powerful set of evocations of "Simone de Beauvoir" as an intellectual woman and writer that are called up whenever we hear her name (Moi 1994, 4–5). The same kind of intertextual network exists for Colette in her memoirs, novels, and letters, and for Duras, who created these kinds of texts and also theater and film scripts. And both are presences in French culture in much the same way as Beauvoir: they are widely known and appreciated, although Beauvoir and Duras remain excluded from the prestigious and highly canonical "Editions de la Pléiade" even now, and Colette has only recently been admitted to that elite, in which the only other women ever to be the subject of an entire volume were Marguerite Yourcenar and George Sand.[4] In the case of Beauvoir, Moi reminds us, "It is particularly important to guard against the idea that Beauvoir's autobiographical texts somehow are 'truer'—closer to 'real life'—than the essays and the fiction" (119). Colette also warns us against trying to find her "real" self in the semi-autobiographical work *Break of Day* [La Naissance du jour] when she says that, despite appearances to the contrary, she is not painting her portrait but only attempting to model herself after her mother (297), and of course much of what she chooses to reveal about herself here as in other works may have been distorted or invented. In fact, *My Apprenticeship* [Mes Apprentissages] illustrates with unusual clarity the problem of taking too literally the autobiographical pact ("What I'm about to tell you really did happen to me") made by a writer in a work presented as autobiographical. In *My Apprenticeship*, Colette offers the purportedly true and complete account of her early years with her first husband, Willy, including her beginnings as a writer. But by the time of its writing, years of acrimonious dispute and silence had embittered Colette against him. Much of the information she offers about him, including his inability to write anything on his own and the conditions under which he obliged her to write, is contradicted by witnesses and by her own correspondence around 1900. Yet the complementary strands of biography and fiction, when read together with the autobiography, corroborate the degree to which she was disappointed and hurt in her marriage, and was ultimately frustrated in her need to become a writer independent of Willy. This part of *My Apprenticeship* emerges from a complex reading as the truest account.

These kinds of problems also arise in reading Beauvoir and Duras, both of whom enjoyed writing their life stories, and occasionally even contradicted themselves from one version to the next. In Duras's several accounts of her early life, of which *The Lover* is best known to the general public, the Chinese lover and the narrator's mother undergo several metamorphoses between their earliest presentation in *The Sea Wall* [Un

Barrage contre le Pacifique] and the last, *The Lover from the North of China* [L'Amant de la Chine du nord]. As they grew older, both Colette and Duras sometimes even engaged in a deliberate blurring of the boundaries of autobiography and fiction, inserting themselves as characters in texts that stand somewhere between the two genres. In this way, they seem almost to invite us to read these different kinds of texts together. The genre ambiguity generated by the mélange of verifiable and fictional characters in the late works of all three writers has everything to do with a certain sexual ambiguity these writers are suggesting as they attempt to redefine their femininity in advanced age.

Aging and the Reinvention of Femininity

As I examine the role of gender difference in French culture and the way it is transmitted from one generation to the next by means of the literary canon, of particular interest is the way older women writers dealt with what it meant to be a woman in advanced age, when their femininity was no longer as simple to define in terms of the ordinary system of masculine/feminine polarities. There were very few role models available to them for themselves or for their fictional characters. If women in general have sometimes felt invisible in late life, there had also been very few older women characters in French literature, at least in any form that a woman reader could recognize as corresponding to her own lived interaction with society and with her sexuality. The representation of older women was usually restricted to unhappy, abandoned, and unproductive characters by certain well established conventions of plot. It is true that a tradition of social initiation of a younger man by an older woman existed in France through the nineteenth century, but a close look at Mme de Bargeton in Balzac's *Lost Illusions* [Les Illusions perdues], Ellénore in Constant's *Adolphe,* or Mme de Rênal in Stendhal's *The Red and the Black* [Le Rouge et le noir] reveals that these "older" women are not yet forty, though they are troubled by growing older. Mme de Bargeton, Ellénore, and Mme de Rênal all believe that the young man's ultimate rejection of them is due to their age.

The virtual absence of women writers speaking as older women (over forty) is equally complete. Apart from a few legendary figures like Ninon de Lenclos or Diane de Poitiers, neither or whom was a writer but who distinguished herself respectively as a *salonnière* and a long-standing mistress of the king, very few older women even contributed to the formation of a coherent idea of what this time in a woman's life might be like. Only a very rare woman like Madame de Sévigné in the seventeenth century systematically wrote her perceptions in epistolary form, as an older woman observing society and communicating without pretense with a younger reader.

Since 1900, older, established women writers have dared to tamper with the system of gender-related genre and subject matter, as their own sexuality, their erotic stance towards the world, evolved in ways that could no longer be easily subsumed under the traditional concept of the heterosexual married couple. Advancing age, more than any other single factor, enabled Colette, Beauvoir, and Duras to establish a more complete feminine identity that could not be contained within, or lay *beyond,* French traditional definitions of femininity and the silence or echo of male desire that such traditional definitions enjoin. The latter are rigidly based on courtship, sexual relationships, and childbearing and are thus appropriate to *young* women. (Conventional definitions of masculinity have been equally youthful and probably equally damaging to men, but they have allowed for a voice in society and are not perceived as disappearing, or changing in their very essence, at age fifty.) And in each case the writing itself contributed to the redefinition of their femininity.

Within the terms and conditions dictated by their national heritage, these three writers left a strong testimony to the fact that the feelings and problems of aging women—as well as rich new possibilities for them— have already been eloquently explored and expressed. One might well say, with Carolyn Heilbrun, that they had found a way to stop being "female impersonators" or "heroines" of male fantasies, and that after they had mourned the closing of the door on youthful beauty, they were able to perceive that another door was opening before them. They accepted the challenge of seeing what lay beyond and out of bounds, knowing that opening the door "marks . . . the end of the dream of closure" (Heilbrun 1988, 126, 129, 130) and ushers in the infinitely various, open-ended plots of age.

THE FRENCH LEGACY
TO A WOMAN OF LETTERS

chapter 1

Traditional Relations: Gender and Writing in France

Almost from the beginning of what we now call French literature, literary aesthetics were intimately influenced, if not actually determined, by relations of power as "the ability to take one's place in whatever discourse is essential to action, and the right to have one's part matter" (Heilbrun 18). Gender in particular has figured throughout the centuries in France as a means of consolidating power and, to this end, of constructing literary representation.[1] Usually this power has belonged to men, as one might expect, but there have been moments of challenge on the part of women to that rule.

Traditional French definitions of femininity and masculinity have played and still play somewhat different roles in France, in the organization of the *polis* and in literary representation, from the ones that can be assumed for other cultures. The rigorous play of gender difference and the enormous value, in a sociological or anthropological sense, that the French have always ascribed to such difference were of key importance in the creation of French literary genres, the national French canon of what would be considered great works, and their subject matter. Gender differentiation has also been a primary factor in the protection and promotion of the established canon in schools and universities.

The difficulties of being a woman writer in this system of gendered hierarchy have been well described by Martha Noel Evans in her work *Masks of Tradition: Women and the Politics of Writing in Twentieth Century France.* Evans demonstrates that written language is hierarchically placed above speech and is the powerful domain of men. Woman is thus by definition already estranged from language and writing, in a language whose "cultural inheritance includes a valorization of language that at once differentiates it from that of other Western nations and makes it their epitome"(15). In her study of several modern French writers, Evans explores the notion that, for women, literary language and literary plots are simultaneously theirs and not theirs, that in order to be acceptable within the French tradition to a French reading public, these women have both dramatized this situation in a series of self-referential moves within their works yet also felt the necessity to disguise certain aspects of their lived experience.

A Classic Plot for Women

The influence in France of one plot in particular for the stories of women's lives has been long and extraordinarily pervasive. I was struck again by this not long ago when I began *Les Hommes et les femmes,* a transcribed series of discussions on the subject of love and eroticism between two prominent intellectuals on the Paris scene today, Françoise Giroud and Bernard-Henri Lévy. (Translations herein are mine.) In the first chapter, which bears the interesting title "The Liberation of Women as a Subject of Derision" [De la libération des femmes comme sujet de dérision], Giroud argues against Lévy's point of view, maintaining that women today strive for greater self-realization and happiness, whereas Lévy cannot see that much has changed in this regard. This issue is one of the subjects of disagreement between them throughout the discussions.

Yet in this introductory chapter they also lay a certain groundwork for what is to follow by agreeing on a few basic assumptions. One of the first is that women have traditionally been represented in literature according to a certain plot that inevitably involves their lack of fulfillment in love. Giroud claims that now that she herself is older, she is no longer "operational" as a woman with respect to men; rather, she is observant. She states: "François Mauriac, who didn't like women, said, 'In any case, they are unhappy. It's their vocation'" [François Mauriac, qui n'aimait pas les femmes, disait: 'de toute façon, elles sont malheureuses. C'est leur vocation'] (11). She goes on to say that this image is changing, but Lévy reacts to this phrase, calling it "beautiful but terrible," and then saying about a novel by Balzac: "That's the whole history of literature, you know. That poor Henriette de Mortsauf, in love with her Félix but obliged to hide her love, to dream about it in secret—and then finally to declare it, but too late, in a letter that was overwhelming but also, one has to admit, rather pathetic: desire, for her, is something horrible, guilty, somewhat shameful" [C'est toute l'histoire de la littérature, vous savez. Cette pauvre Henriette de Mortsauf, amoureuse de son Félix, mais contrainte de cacher cet amour, de le rêver en secret—et puis de l'avouer enfin, mais trop tard, dans une lettre bouleversante et, il faut bien le dire, pitoyable: le désir, pour elle, est quelque chose d'horrible, fautif, vaguement honteux] (11).

Giroud's answer is revealing of the self-perpetuation of this literary tradition and its influence on women's expectations not only of literature but of their lives as well: "And all that [Henriette] knows about [desire]—and this is what is most incredible—is what she has read in books! A kind of ignorance, in fact. An interdiction on the very idea of happiness" [Et dont elle ne sait guère, c'est même le plus incroyable, que ce qu'elle a lu dans les livres! Une sorte d'ignorance, en fait. D' "interdit" sur l'idée même de bonheur] (11). The hold of the academic canon over the national imagination would be difficult to overestimate, and although in the above exchange Giroud and Lévy are aware of the pitiable plot that has governed the representation of women, they do not go so far as to challenge that such representation has been made by male writers and promoted by national institutions of learning that have also excluded women and not consulted them on the choice of texts to be taught.[2] Lévy notices that only men have written about female sexuality, but he actually suspects that women may have wanted things this way, saying: "How it is that the job or the privilege of recounting feminine sexuality fell to men? Why this silence on the part of women? This excess of modesty? This resignation? By virtue of what modesty or—who knows—what calculation have women handed over the task, in an obviously strategic move?" [D'où vient que ce soit à des hommes qu'échurent, en effet, ce soin, ou le privilège, de raconter la sexualité féminine? Pourquoi ce silence des femmes? Cette pudeur? Cette démission? en vertu de quelle prudence ou, allez savoir! de quel calcul s'en être remises à d'autres de cette tâche évidemment stratégique?] (29) Giroud is more sensitive to the fact that women writers before the twentieth century, with very rare exceptions, would have considered it impossible to talk about certain subjects of intimate concern to them: "Where would they have spoken? To whom? Can you imagine a woman daring before this century to confess such things? Even to herself? It would have been strictly inconceivable. On the subject of themselves, they never spoke about anything, ever. All through history, women have been silent. So you can imagine how it's been on the subject of sexuality!" [Où auraient-elles parlé? A qui? Vous imaginez une femme osant, avant notre siècle, se livrer sur un tel sujet? L'osant même vis-à-vis d'elle-même? C'eût été proprement inconcevable. S'agissant d'elles-mêmes, elles n'ont parlé de rien, jamais. A travers toute l'histoire, les femmes sont muettes. Alors sur la sexualité!] (30)

In all the history of what we now call France, the Renaissance was certainly the time of greatest defeat for women in terms of their rights and status, although intellectual opportunities were constantly opening for men, as classical and Italian art and literature were rediscovered. Women spent their time doing housework, locked for life into marriages that were almost all arranged without consulting them; only renunciation through convent life, or adultery, which was no longer really acceptable, were available to them outside of these marriages. Female beauty, their only possible source of influence as already defined by their culture, was represented in the art and literature of the sixteenth century as ephemeral before all else. Petrarchism flourished in France as a source of literary inspiration. Its lyrical insistence on idealized women inaugurated the reign of the patriarchal gaze in Western literature and contained a latent tendency to objectify the woman's body. With its euphoric poetry there coexisted various minor works by well-known poets, such as Saint-Amant and Henri de Régnier, in which the appearance of older women was vilified (Beauvoir, *La Vieillesse* 160). The latter tendency continued into the seventeenth century, until finally the prescriptions of French classicism purged the poetic genre of these grotesque and burlesque evocations. Only Brantôme, at the height of the Renaissance, undertook the defense of older women in his *History of Galant Women* [Histoire des dames galantes]. He is still widely read today and provides information on the intimate lives of members of the royal court. However, his writing is probably mingled with his own fantasies about these women and masks the despair over aging and consequent loss of self-esteem that women increasingly experienced.

In the seventeenth century, the austere teaching of the Jansenists recommended abstention from sexual relations and encouraged celibacy for women. *The Précieuses,* or Precious Women *salonnières* of the seventeenth century, were a woman's literary movement advocating purely spiritual love. Thus they also reflected the generalized libidinal repression of the times and appear to the modern observer as a sort of impoverished version of courtly love, though they were certainly seeking, not without some success, to impose the woman's point of view on literature and manners. The consequences of this enforced abstention, despair, and finally repression were finally internalized by women themselves, who thus stood at the brink of the seventeenth century—the great century of Louis XIV and French neoclassicism—in a particularly weak posture.

The seventeenth century was above all the century of neoclassicism and French classicism. This body of texts, written mostly between 1660 and 1700, drew on or claimed inspiration from ancient Greek and Roman texts, which had again begun to circulate at the beginning of the Renaissance, a century earlier. It finally came to include the novel, a newly developing genre that incorporated from its beginning a vision of woman as the male authors of the time wanted and believed her to be, an image that corresponded to the unhappy situation of women described before and that also enshrined a very particular reference to the aging woman. These texts had become the official canon of French literature by 1700, and for several centuries afterward it was scarcely modified. The term "official" must be taken in the case of France somewhat more literally than elsewhere, for the seventeenth century also posited rules of classical usage with respect to French language and literary expression, enforceable by the Académie française, newly founded under Cardinal Richelieu and regarded quite literally by Louis XIV as safeguarding this discourse, which he considered inseparable from the social and political order of his absolutist rule.

Joan DeJean describes the singular and perhaps unexpected relationship of the French of this period to the ancient Greek poet Sappho, a female contemporary of Homer's who had been considered his equal. Practically no biographical facts about her can be ascertained, and her poetry today exists in fragments, only a few of which are nearly complete. It was first translated into Latin in the sixteenth century, but the French became "obsessed" with creating fictions about Sappho's life when Ovid's *Héroïdes* were disseminated in French in the seventeenth (DeJean, 12). It was as if French authors felt the need to fill the vacuum of ignorance about Sappho the woman, to understand, classify, and if possible subordinate this great woman of letters who had preceded and influenced them all. In the fifteenth epistle of this collection of fictional love letters from well-known abandoned women of the ancient world, Ovid imagines a letter Sappho might have written to her legendary lover Phaon. DeJean characterizes this letter as "quite simply the most influential Sapphic fiction ever: fictions of Sappho begin when Ovid and Sappho intersect in the early modern imagination" (12). In this epistle, Sappho, an older woman, has fallen in love with a younger man, Phaon, after a lifetime of writing poetry in the company of women. When he rejects her, she finds she can no longer create, and she finally throws herself into the sea in the famous (though strictly legendary) leap from the Leukadian cliffs. Thus Heroinism, following an overwhelming and immediate acceptance of Ovid's creation as the true story of Sappho, involves "a longing for love both lost and treacherous, limiting therefore its territory to tales of betrayal and abandonment. Because of Ovid's founding influence, a novelistic heroine, unlike her male counterpart, traditionally was almost always unhappy and unlucky in love" (45–46). This suffering woman corresponds to a seventeenth-century vision of women that male poets could share, bonding with each other in the exchange of competing works about such a character. It might not have been so at another time, or rather it would surely have taken a somewhat different form, but the intersection of Ovid's epistle with the ever more confining norms for political and literary behavior that were being put in place by 1660 meant that this Sapphic fiction shaped the new novelistic form and associated it with the heterosexual female imagination and experience.[3] Fictional works about Sappho as an abandoned older woman were a seemingly unending source of literary inspiration in France from the seventeenth century until the twentieth.

Boileau and his fellow founders of the Académie Française also inaugurated a final separation of the woman's *body* from her artistic *voice*; that is, women were allowed to write and their works could be published, but only if they wrote in prescribed ways and remained within the boundaries of certain established forms, and not if they wrote specifically as women. As Joan DeJean points out, this radical and tenacious split between a masculine account of passion within prescribed forms and a womanly expression of desire often deemed unruly and lacking in formal artistic merit was another salient characteristic of classicism. It complicated still further the dilemma of any woman writer who had been heir to this national tradition when she attempted any direct expression of her feelings or experience.

Jean Racine's tragedy *Phèdre* (1677) is one of the best-known plays of French classical theater and is a good example of the influence of Sapphic preoccupation in the creation of French canonical masterpieces. Racine identified closely with the woman author of fragment 31, borrowing her terms and images from that poem for the celebrated speech in which Phèdre confesses her passion for her much younger stepson. She claims to be hot and cold, red and pale, and above all driven mad by the force of her passion itself as much as by the pain of rejection, much like the observer/narrator of fragment 31. One has only to compare Racine's verse with a part of Sappho's fragment 31:

Racine

I saw him, turned red, turned pale at the sight;
A storm arose in my frantic soul;
I could no longer see, I could no longer speak;
I felt my whole body freeze and burn.

[Je le vis, je rougis, je pâlis à sa vue;
Un trouble s'éleva dans mon âme éperdue;
Mes yeux ne voyaient plus, je ne pouvais parler;
Je sentis tout mon corps et transir et brûler.]

(*Phèdre I. iii.*724–27)

Sappho 31

. . . For when I look at you a moment, I have no longer the power to
   speak,
But my tongue keeps silence, straightway a subtle flame has
stolen beneath my flesh, with my eyes I see nothing, my ears are
   humming,
A cold sweat covers me, and a trembling seizes me all over,
I am paler than grass, I seem to be not far short of death. . . .

(Translated by Lobel and Page, 1955)

The gaze of this female narrator had to be brought back under control as
a male prerogative. This meant that French classical interpretations of
Sappho's material simply chose to interpret the feminine adjective
("paler") that identifies the narrator at the end as of indefinite gender.
There remained the reconstruction of the triangle, in which Sappho/
Phèdre is abandoned by the man for another woman. Racine accom-
plishes this feat by reconstructing the Phaedra plot with the introduction
of the *younger* woman Aricie with whom Hippolyte falls in love.

The influence of *Phèdre* on subsequent generations would be difficult
to overestimate. Henri Peyre sees it as an example of the initiation tradition in France, according to which a young man's first experience of love
occurs in relation to an older, passionate woman: "French males of every
generation, like Proust's enraptured hero watching La Berma in the part,
have dreamed for years of the great actress who had impersonated Phèdre
in their youth. It would be no exaggeration to say that . . . the play and its
burning picture of jealousy have done much to frame the French conception of love"(80). Phyllis Banner, author of *In Full Flower: Aging Women,
Power, and Sexuality,* believes this practice of initiation confers sexual
desirability on the older woman and is thus proof of a certain acceptance
of her sexuality in France. But I would urge caution in accepting this

view of the initiation story as evidence of a reassuring prestige for the older woman. Her fate is not a happy one here, and I mentioned above that in Romantic novels, where she reappears, she is not really an older woman yet, and her story usually has a dysphoric closure there too. The point is that these are texts written by men, creating fictions of feminine desire, and hence they are not talking about the woman's own point of view.

It clearly follows that after the Ovidian Sapphic plot for novels was put in place, it could be problematic for a woman writer, especially an older one, simply to adopt for her characters or for herself the Phaon/suicide/silencing plot for women. The feminocentric genre that Ovid had unwittingly launched was in fact challenged in the seventeenth century by those who wished to impose other plots, designed by women, on both the epistolary and historical novels. These new plots were countered in turn by reassertions of the Ovidian plot, in a brief but decisive battle. The most significant challenge came from Madeleine de Scudéry, a *Précieuse* and the first modern biographer of Sappho. Scudéry found a way to exert a lasting though limited influence on the evolution of French prose fiction in *Famous Women*, where Sappho appears again as a character in *Artamène*, the last volume. This Sappho rereads the Phaon/suicide plot and finds it totally implausible; together with Phaon, she travels to the country of the Amazons, where she controls her destiny and retains Phaon's respect and love. Like other French women writers who over the centuries protested against the institution of marriage, Scudéry has Sappho and Phaon live together without marrying. Thus she reappropriates Sappho to describe the life a woman might create for herself outside marriage and the usual novelistic plots, just as Mme de Staël was to do in the early nineteenth century, or Simone de Beauvoir in our time.

The only other option for a woman writer concerned with love, marriage, and eventual abandonment in this ascetic seventeenth-century climate was the novel of renunciation, of which the finest example is of course *The Princess of Cleves* [La Princesse de Clèves] by Madame de Lafayette. The heroine of this historical novel denies herself and her lover the fulfillment of their love, even when she has become a widow, out of her unshakable conviction that the passing of time will bring unbearable pain to her if she should yield to her desire. For she will age, and he, like all men, will be unfaithful to her and ultimately abandon her, even if they are married. There is a kind of triumph for the princess in her refusal, but the woman whose tragic pathos and beauty are celebrated in this novel is a woman who finds no fulfillment in love and dies young, even if she avoids a certain kind of suffering and disgrace. Female renunciation of love and work became a pattern and was so well internalized by women themselves that the theme of abstention, for example, is still very much present in the works of Colette in the early twentieth century. Thus the objectives of patriarchal canon formation had been accomplished according to another definition of power cited by Carolyn Heilbrun: "Power consists to a large extent in deciding what stories will be told; . . . male power has made certain stories unthinkable" (105).

Like Scudéry's plot in the country of the Amazons, Germaine de Staël's *Corinne* [*Corinne ou l'Italie*] (1807) takes place in a novelistic space outside the country of the father, that is, outside the space of patriarchy, which is in this case England. By the Napoleonic era, when Staël was writing, the canonical objectives of Boileau and other classicists had been put in place so firmly that even the political upheavals of the nineteenth century would not have the power to shake them. Nor would they have the power to improve women's political status either, as we shall see. In *Corinne*, there is a condemnation of the family-oriented ideology of Napoleon, according to which all women should have as many children as possible, but *Corinne* also attempts to undo certain other consequences of the Ovidian plot: the radical split between the productive woman artist and the unproductive woman whose creativity has been ravaged by the catastrophe of love, as well as the cleavage between the woman who creates *as a woman,* usually in a way considered spontaneous and uncontrolled because disrupted by passion, and the woman artist who has learned to write *not* as a woman, that is, with a maximum of detachment and artifice. Corinne goes from England to Italy in order to be able to practice her art of spontaneous, oral, poetic improvisation. There she meets and falls in love with the English Oswald, who loves her but ends by marrying her considerably younger half sister. How to be both a performing artist and a woman, both objects of the masculine gaze, becomes her central concern after she has begun to love Oswald. There are limitations to Staël's imagination of solutions to this problem, and in the end the abandonment plot wins out, and Corinne dies alone. But the preceding struggle obviously turns on the impossibility for Corinne as for Sappho of living as both productive artist and woman in love.

Nancy K. Miller describes Corinne's goals in coming to Italy to perform her art: "She imagines a more complicated form of existence for herself, beyond the exclusive, either/or models of the fathers: 'Thanks to the rare combination of circumstances that had given me a dual education and, if you will, two nationalities, I could think myself destined for special privileges'" (Miller, *Subject to Change* 176; Staël 14.3:264–5, 379). Miller believes Corinne's sense of being "double," of having "differences within" (176) may also be Staël's way of trying to express a more complex femininity, a position outside the confines of conventional gender, such as we have already seen in several instances. But Staël, at the beginning of the nineteenth century, is not yet able to incorporate the consequences of such a life into her plot, though the record of the attempt is there.

Seduced and Abandoned in the Century of Revolution

The educational disparity between the sexes caught up with women in time, and in the eighteenth century the *salonnières* created far fewer original works but served as protectresses, women in the wings of the national drama of ideas that was taking place among the *philosophes* in preparation for the French Revolution. They again occupied their special space in society within bounds, from which they could offer only indirect influence, but at this point this role represented a real loss of status for women. Considered intellectually inferior by all prerevolutionary thinkers except Poulain de la Barre, women saw no improvement in their political or civil rights and no promise of any specific amelioration for them in the various utopian imaginings about the future. As for Rousseau, he was willing to allow his women characters to express their own desires, but only in renunciation and defeat. This is the case for Julie de Wolmar, the heroine of his *La Nouvelle Héloïse*. Women writers are largely absent from the scene, with the notable exceptions of Madame de Tencin and Julie de Lespinasse,[4] as though the available plots had left them no way to write their own feelings and desires, sign their own names, and be taken seriously as writers and simultaneously as women.

As the century advanced, and through the Revolution and the Napoleonic period, the role of the woman was increasingly seen as domesticated and contained within the sentimentalized nuclear family. Among other motivations for this ideological shift was the masculine desire to regenerate an older, heroic, domineering form of masculinity. But there was undoubtedly also the wish to protect a wife or daughter from the potential dangers of eroticism, a cultural current best exemplified by the writings of the Marquis de Sade. The totally objectified woman, victimized by love, became in this literature the prisoner of the male gaze and was sometimes a literal prisoner as well. Her own desire was completely eliminated from the scene of seduction. These writings, including less overtly sadistic but nonetheless pitiless examples of unmitigated gallantry like the epistolary novel *Dangerous Alliances* [Les Liaisons dangereuses] by Choderlos de Laclos, became a prominent and permanent element in the sexual fantasies of the French, and they convey a distinct message to women about aging. Madame de Merteuil herself, the villainess of *Dangerous Alliances,* sees aging as occurring abruptly with a sudden lack of physical charm rather than as a gradual process. Such a view of aging is implicit in the very terms of eroticism, in which women are valued for their sexual attractiveness rather than for skills, knowledge, or other characteristics they might possess. In the context of this plot for their sexuality, many real women actually began to view their own aging as a time of relief from the increasingly exploitative and explicitly sexual aims of male gallantry. Colette, whose unhappy first marriage brought her a century later into the somewhat smaller circles of that unbridled gallantry, often expressed similar feelings as she aged.

The Nineteenth Century

Balzac, Zola, Stendhal, Flaubert, and Maupassant all adored women, most particularly their own literary creations. The *idea* of woman was adulated as in no other country, but the reality of a woman's lived experience was carefully controlled, and if an individual woman chose to write about it, her work was either not taken seriously or quickly occulted. This situation obviously stands in marked contrast to the significant presence of women writers in nineteenth-century England. The schism between an idealized, protected, privileged status for women and a lack of interest in her own account of reality was always typical in modern times of French society, but it reached its epitome in the nineteenth century.

More than ever, a certain male consensus about women determined the kinds of fictions that were written.

Along with the adulterous, bourgeois Emma Bovary, the courtesan emerges as a source of fascination mingled with fear for male writers. In this age of chastity for the bourgeois wife, Emile Deschanel reworked the legend of Sappho and the Lesbians in 1847. DeJean remarks, "It is the first fiction in any tradition in two centuries that reembodies Sappho with a decidedly unconventional sexuality. So powerful is Deschanel's vision that it alters the entire course of Sappho's history in nineteenth century France." (239) Sappho's subsequent influence on French literary production then became greater than it had ever been, inspiring Baudelaire, Daudet, and Louÿs, to name only the best known, to write about Sappho in her new incarnation as courtesan/lesbian/prostitute.

This change in the available images of Sappho's sexuality was in turn of importance to the Sappho 1900 movement. Two women at the turn of the century, Nathalie Clifford Barney and Renée Vivien, both native English speakers, tried to revise still further the standard French vision of Sappho, insisting that there was no bisexuality in the work, only homosexuality. A number of women writers came into their own in the context of this movement, though, as Susan Gubar notes in comparing English speaking writers and the French writer Marguerite Yourcenar ("Sappho, or Suicide" in *Fires* [Feux], 1936), many women writers ultimately rejected Sappho as a model because of what they perceived as her extreme vulnerability. After 1900, there were fewer fictions of Sappho in France, but the introduction into French literature of a deviant voice for an older woman's sexuality was not without importance for the women writers to come, as we shall see in the case of Colette. It marked a desire to take exception with a prescribed sexuality and a prescribed plot for women, and even a willingness to accept the considerable scandal that greeted this kind of writing.

Writing and the Body

The split between a woman's body and her capacity to write like, or as well as, a man had been consecrated by Boileau, but in fact belonged to an even older, deeply rooted separation of social spheres along gender lines, often accompanied by a celebration of gender difference. Perhaps this essentialist view of the difference between male and female cultural production, on which the literary canon and many other social institutions were founded, had long been acceptable to French women because of a compensatory power that had been associated with it since the time of the courtly love tradition in the Middle Ages. Although the feminine language of power and desire expressed by the poetry of *La Courteoisie* is today relegated to a secondary status, if not to silence, in official histories of French literature, many of its notions, metaphors, and symbols were to find their way back into writing in later centuries, usually as part of a self-consciously secondary and subversive tradition that is nevertheless codified in other areas of French society. According to this tradition, much of women's power to influence social and political decisions was based on youthful physical attractiveness and the ability to inspire passionate love. This occult feminine power is sometimes called *la coquetterie* in French, and as Michèle Sarde puts it in her study of French women entitled *Regard sur les Françaises* [About French women], "In the France of Romanticism as in courtly Occitania, beauty and love are the great leveling forces in one of the most statified societies in the world" [Dans la France romantique comme dans l'Occitanie courteoise, la beauté et l'amour sont les agents niveleurs d'une des sociétés les plus stratifiées du monde] (81).[5]

The notion of a separate space from which women might exercise an occult power, rather than a common social space in which women might contest masculine power on its own grounds, was thus in place by the end of the Middle Ages and has remained very much in place through the twentieth century. One of its most striking features is the degree to which both sexes believe in its power and efficacity. In the discussions between Françoise Giroud and Bernard-Henri Lévy in *Les Hommes et les femmes,* Lévy is persuaded throughout the first chapter that female submission to men has been only a matter of appearance and that in their power of seduction women exercise a "symbolic power" that is "at least equal" to that which men exercise (23). Both sexes considered the silent space of women's influence to be a real source of social stability. It proved to be much more concrete to the imagination than the gains that would presumably accrue with the vote, for example, for if the French shared with the rest of the Western world most of the values of the Enlightenment tradition, even older French traditions prevented the benefits of that tradition from becoming available to all. (British women won the vote in 1918 but the French not until 1946, when former women Resistance fighters and implicit pressure from the Allies finally made enfranchisement inevitable.) It was with the Enlightenment and the culmination of humanist values that man, the male, fully came into his own and in the same moment the woman was "denied access to the universal" (Moi 209). The major texts and historical events of the twentieth century merely made more explicit what had long been true. It henceforth became clear to what extent women's sexual difference, so widely celebrated in France, was a deviance from a norm of personhood and thus would be used against women in the realm of citizenship and political rights.

It is difficult for the Anglo-American feminist observer of today to consider the compensatory nature of the privilege and influence that French women had been offered and that they had usually accepted as adequate. Or at the very least, one is left perplexed: while the American, along with Simone de Beauvoir, foregrounds the need and possibility of simultaneously founding both equality *and* a specific female identity, the history of women writers in France suggests that cultural insistence on difference, especially coupled with a long absence of societal concern for equality, has led either to denial of any specificity or—more often—to obsessive attention to it. And the literary legend that generically enshrines sexual difference as determining a perilous but inevitable life course corroborates and heightens anxiety about difference, even as it encourages women to seek refuge in the privileges afforded by the cult of femininity.[6]

Aging as a Solution

When we look back over the articulation in France between gender and genre, between sexual difference and decisions about what stories will be told about women, it seems clear why it has been harder for French women, necessarily bound by the values of their culture to a great extent, even if simultaneously excluded from it, to break away from the hegemony of masculine discourse in both literature and politics. The few women writers who transgressed the bounds, i.e. the boundaries of this space of prescribed social and sexual roles for women in their lives and/ or their work, necessarily felt that they were not only writing different stories but were also threatening received ideas about what it meant to be a woman within French society. They quite understandably felt a need to assert that they were women despite their refusal to subscribe to certain traditions. Thus we find in the work of Colette and Duras, despite other differences on the matter of feminism itself, a persistent emphasis on female gender identity outside the bounds of the original paradigm of their society. In the case of Beauvoir, writing seemed to her to protect her from certain attributes of femininity until her last years, when she was ready to accept her womanhood and claim it as a writer.

And this is exactly where the question of aging comes in, as a solution to what has otherwise often been a paralyzing dilemma: How does one remain a French woman and write one's own story in one's own voice? What a French woman needs is a position outside the *traditional* play of gender difference, a position that nevertheless does not deny the "dissymmetry of difference" (Miller 17). I have come to believe this gender position became available to certain women writers with advancing age, precisely when their traditional feminine role was partially altered, when they were considered to be and felt themselves to be somehow standing outside the traditional economy of sexual difference as defined for both sexes in their youth. Aging may have been more difficult for French women for one of the very reasons that makes the adaptation required by aging easier for women than for men in the United States: the absence of an influential woman's movement, first or second wave, has meant that most women have not been called upon throughout their lives, as they often were in the United States, to adapt to roles they had not been raised to anticipate. Yet at the same time, aging has been experienced as a liberation by more than one French woman, precisely because her feminine role as she aged was no longer so carefully circumscribed and she felt free to redefine it.

RECONCILING FEMININITY AND AGING

chapter 2

Images of Aging Women

From an historian's perspective, Phyllis Banner expresses a general truth about aging women in her book *In Full Flower,* which is corroborated by anthropologists and psychologists. Assimilating Chaucer's aging woman character Alison of Bath from *The Canterbury Tales* to a long tradition of "wise goddesses as mentors" who are "knowledgeable about life," she says: "In the European past as in the American present, aging women have exhibited more powerful personalities as they have aged. This power has given them authority and rendered them suspect. Alongside Chaucer's Alison of Bath existed both the shrew and the witch; these ancient stereotypes of aging women were still extant and were easily applied to actual assertive women" (128, 133). Even when the obsession with witchcraft ended in a time of greater rationality, new restrictions on the sexuality of older women were put in place. In the eighteenth century and into the nineteenth, prevailing definitions of women's sexuality as contrasted with men's meant that married women were considered more spiritual than sexual; no longer sexually voracious, the married woman became a maternal figure, contained and controlled within the domesticated family: "Women became the creators of hearth and home, not its destroyers. The aging woman living alone, even in contention with her community, was no longer dangerous. For her sexuality was under control by virtue of its being nonexistent" (Banner 248). This vision became a stereotype still well known to us today. Variants of it include the grandmother figure, or the aging married woman who has no further interest in sex. None of the writers I propose to examine was willing to accept this image of aging for herself.

If the aging woman was no longer "automatically denigrated" in the nineteenth century, she was nonetheless considered as "outside the bounds of male desire" (252). By the end of the century, this view had overtaken the benign notion of the older motherly woman when a new emphasis on youth, the burgeoning cosmetics industry, and heterosexual appeal defined in youthful terms took hold throughout Western Europe and the United States. It was to culminate in the shift from a valuation of spirituality to the sexual revolution of the 1920s. The definition of this female sexuality was an exclusively youthful one; the thin young body of the flapper became the vogue, as Gullette and Banner discuss at length, and menopause acquired the status of a deficiency disease from which it has even now not entirely emerged. Speaking of the fear of aging that inevitably accompanied these developments, Banner comments: "The 'sexual revolution' of the 1920s, enshrined in new dances and styles of dress, had ambiguous impacts on the prospects of women more generally. Once again, as in the past, defining women as sexual beings was problematic for them" (236).

The 1890s for Colette, then the 1920s and 1930s for Beauvoir and Duras, were the decades of their youth, when initial attitudes and feelings about aging were formed. Colette and Beauvoir in particular retained the lesson that the loss of youth was painful, but each emerged after her forties from that preoccupation to develop, like Duras, a stronger, more individuated personality and way of writing in her late years. The traditional view of women in France was in many ways not favorable to such an outcome. If women in general develop "more powerful personalities" as they age, Pauline Bart's cross-cultural study of the status of older women found only a few cultures in which this status did not improve: those which "focused on sexual attractiveness rather than on women's craft abilities or technical knowledge. When such was the case, young women were invariably the cultural lodestars and aging women's status was downgraded" (Bart 1–18). As long as educational and professional opportunity for girls was limited in France, this description undoubtedly fit French society. But as educational opportunity opened, and life span increased, greater and longer professional experience became available to women writers and to women generally, and this in turn led to greater status and more individuation.

Twentieth-Century Changes

The twentieth century, by offering the possibility of less constricting social mores, also permitted French women to write more freely. In the twentieth century it became possible as the decades advanced to create a marginal personal style of life, even if one was not a wealthy member of the aristocracy, and still be taken seriously as an artist. Colette was perhaps the first fully to exploit this plot for her own life story. To an extent this liberation was probably helped along by the presence of expatriate American and British women who had chosen since the beginning of the century to live in the margins of conventional society in Paris. The older professional woman character finally emerged in the writings of Colette (as Renée Néré in *The Vagabond*), Beauvoir, and Duras, just as she had finally emerged in the Anglo-American world of letters with Willa Cather's heroine Thea Kronberg in *The Song of the Lark* in 1915. Just as Thea, a singer, found her "true voice" (Gullette 30) at age forty (a late age in 1915), so our three French writers learned at last how to speak in their own voices and present their own plots and the objects of their own gaze.

However, French women were slowed in their progress by lack of access to even basic elementary education, not to mention university, until the late nineteenth century, and by a much slower entry in the twentieth century into the professions of writing and journalism in large numbers than was the case in the United States. During all the years of First and Second Wave feminism in the English-speaking world, French women could not derive the same benefits of intellectual work that the movement made possible for Anglo-Americans, and—perhaps more important still—they did not develop habits of reflection upon their status and upon the possibility of experimentation and change. In the Anglo-American world, as Gullette points out in "Creativity, Aging, Gender," a paradox existed: feminism was on the rise, but so was the "subversive force of agism" (44). Despite the negative images of aging that were put in place between 1910 and 1935, by the 1920s and 1930s, Mary Austin, Gertrude Stein, Edith Wharton, Charlotte Perkins Gilman, Elizabeth Robins, Edna Ferber, Mary Roberts Rinehart, and others were writing their autobiographies, having already entered the star system. Gullette goes on to say that "the mere published presence of so many autobiographies suggests the establishment of the older woman as literary success—some might say, her apotheosis. . . . Insofar as the fame and wealth and publicity of individuals can elevate a 'class,' older women writers were elevated—into the empyrean indeed" (33). This picture stands in striking contrast to the situation of women intellectuals in France of the same period, although the fact of *older* women's being able to rise above the constraints of either sexism or agism or both appears to be common to both cultures and to many others as well.

In France, interventionist governments at the end of the nineteenth century were responsible for a series of protective measures that sought to make working and childbearing conditions easier for women. Here as in so many other contexts, women were well protected within the sphere that was considered their own. Yet despite the increase in numbers of salaried women in the workforce, there still exist important inequalities in the areas of job qualification, professional training, and access to employment ("Les Femmes en France"). These are all, of course, dependent upon the educational system, which is certainly egalitarian today but was slow in accepting the *baccalauréat* degree for women. This diploma is the sine qua non of a professional career in France. Most secondary lay boarding schools for girls did not officially confer the *baccalauréat* until 1908 and in many cases not until after World War I. Instead, girls in state schools followed a shorter program, one that did not include Greek or Latin and that allowed them to sit for a diploma of secondary education that was specifically feminine. In 1900, there were still only 21,200 young girls in secondary school, compared with 84,500 boys (Sarde, *Colette libre* 81).

The same slow progress can be seen at the university level. Until 1914, there were more foreign than French women enrolled there. Several important but difficult victories, led by individuals such as Marie Curie, opened the way by 1930 for Beauvoir and her generation. Yet even Beauvoir did not enjoy a situation like the one we know today. She was one of the very few women first to be admitted to the qualifying examination of the Ecole Normale Supérieure. Women students increased dramatically at university level only in the 1960s and afterward.

The difficulty in obtaining the *baccalauréat* also illustrates the slowness with which some of these gains for girls were accepted into French mores. This fact and these new opportunities are important to my discussion of Colette, Beauvoir, and Duras, each of whom had a different story, and to the imagining and living of stories for women generally. Without the possibility of higher education or professional activity, the standard plot of the nineteenth century could not be modified, nor could a woman's life follow a different trajectory from the love, marriage, adultery, or courtesan stories with their implications of abandonment and empty later years. Unless, of course, the woman was independently wealthy, and indeed earlier women writers—Scudéry, Staël, Sand—were all wealthy members of the aristocracy.

The question of free public education at higher levels takes on its full importance when we consider the fate of young women without dowries, including Colette, Beauvoir, and Duras. Colette's story was literally determined by her marriage to Willy Gauthier-Villars and her move to Paris. In fact, whatever her feelings may initially have been, she had no choice in the matter of her first marriage: she was considered unmarriageable in her Burgundian village for lack of a dowry. With only an elementary school education, her employment opportunities there were extremely limited. In Beauvoir's case, almost thirty years later, access to the university had become possible, and she learned very early in her life from her father that her only salvation, socially and economically as well as intellectually, lay in her studies. These accidents of Colette's and Beauvoir's lives ensured that they were writing at an early age, as was Duras at a slightly later date, and were important in that the full measure of these women's success as writers only became apparent over time and with age. Their lengthy careers coincided with a time when educational opportunity had at last become available to other women as well, and this fortuitousness alone made it more likely than before to glimpse a different story for women and to live a different life themselves.

Articulating Notions of Aging and Gender

There is clearly a privileged relationship between aging and sexuality, and in particular between aging and female sexuality: both are culturally constructed, but both are simultaneously chosen and assumed according to an individual's view of herself/himself. Betty Friedan offers a sensitive analysis in *The Fountain of Age* of the parallels between the "feminine mystique" and what she has diagnosed as a mystique of aging. The alienation that women have felt is related to the alienation of aging in that both are consequences of a social mystification, and this basic similarity holds true despite certain obvious differences between gender and aging: "The image of age as inevitable decline and deterioration, I realized, was also a mystique of sorts, but one emanating not an aura of desirability, but a miasma of dread" (41).

I shall return to the question of the *construction* of gender, but for the moment I want to endorse Phyllis Banner's basic assumption in *In Full Flower,* that sexuality has also always been the key element in European and American cultural definitions of women's aging. Like Banner, I believe it is necessary to emphasize sexuality when discussing aging from the point of view of the individual aging woman or fictional character, because all stages of a woman's life in societies governed by patriarchy are determined by the way she is perceived in terms of desirability and the childbearing role.

In the epilogue to *Aging and Its Discontents: Freud and Other Fictions,*[4] Kathleen Woodward reminds us of the connection that existed for Freud between the "exhausting work" of becoming a woman and aging, as he expressed it in *The Interpretation of Dreams* and later, more elaborately, in his lecture on "Femininity" in 1933.[1] In the latter text, which Freud wrote at age seventy-seven, he makes the startling observation that women reach old age by thirty:

A man of about thirty strikes us as a youthful, somewhat unformed individual, whom we expect to make powerful use of the possibilities for development opened up to him by analysis. A woman of the same age, however, often frightens us by her psychical rigidity and unchangeability. Her libido has taken up final positions and seems incapable of exchanging them for others. There are no paths open to further development; it is as though the whole process had already run its course and remains thenceforward insusceptible to influence—as though, indeed, the difficult developments to femininity had exhausted the possibilities of the person concerned. (*SE* 22:134–35)

Woodward discerns the underlying connections here between femininity and aging: becoming a woman is so "exhausting" that it absorbs all mental energy and makes other normal developments impossible; in addition, Freud himself expresses *fear* in the face of this phenomenon. Woodward argues that "analytically, Freud is afraid of old women. Theoretically, he relegates the problem of female sexuality to the gray continent of old age, demeaning both women and the elderly in the process. As he puts it in 'Female Sexuality,' published in 1931, 'Everything in the sphere of this first attachment to the mother seemed to me so difficult in analysis—so grey with age and shadowy and almost impossible to revivify'" (193; *SE* 21:226). Throughout her work, Woodward stresses the absence or repression of aging from Freudian theory, which is in fact a "construction of a powerful discourse of subjectivity and generational relations . . . firmly anchored in infancy and early childhood" (9).

Yet where it is a question of early childhood, we already know from the work of feminist revisions of Freudian theory to what extent gender affects early childhood development. It is time to ask the same question about how gender affects aging, as recent theorists like Betty Friedan as well as researchers in the social sciences have been doing. Their findings suggest that women don't experience the aging process in the same way as men and that analysis of women's aging is necessarily a different enterprise from the analysis of aging in general or of men's aging. Beauvoir herself unintentionally provided a clear example of this in her work *The Coming of Age,* in which, as we shall discover, she limited her discussion almost entirely to aging men and leaves the reader wondering about how to generalize her observations to women.

At the same time, I also want to ask the question the other way around: How does aging affect gender, both as a cultural construct and as an individual experience? In France, as we have seen, gender difference takes on special importance in the organization of society and its representations of women. But this is difference as defined for and by *young* men and women, when both—but especially women—are considered desirable and hence part of a system of exchange. What happens to the perception of difference when the woman has gone beyond this age? And how does a woman experience her own womanhood?

Woodward would like to maintain a fundamental distinction between analysis of gender and analysis of aging, as she explains in her discussion of "Youthfulness as Masquerade": "We all have a stake in representations of old age and the aging body. Age necessarily cuts across all our lives and our bodies in a way that other differences fundamentally do not. . . . If we are white, we will never be black. If we are Native American, we will never be Irish Catholic. Similarly the analysis of age must be different from the analysis of gender" (156). In the various games of "masquerading" as either stereotypically feminine or as young, the two most common forms of artificial self-presentation in our society, there is an essential difference: aging involves confronting death, and thus "at bottom our resistance to old age may be *unconscious*," even if "we can resist and . . . destabilize social constructions of old age" as we can the constructions of gender (156). Psychoanalysis has indeed always assumed that "in terms of age, identification is not as clear-cut a phenomenon as it is . . . in terms of gender" (156).

Certainly there is no disagreement over the fact of a universal resistance to death and/or perhaps of a universal death wish. And it is also obviously true that we do not always feel completely identified with our physiological age. What I question, as I have been suggesting, is the notion implicit in the above distinction that the *gender* of a subject is identical to itself through time and throughout life. Instead, it needs to be understood in its *intersection* with age rather than as something that can be assumed as fixed, once and for all, by early adulthood and as existing in a category apart from age. Woodward corroborates that aging studies can be considered as part of a poststructuralist discourse according to which "the subject is not identical to itself through time" when she refers to the work of Jean-François Lyotard in *Just Gaming*.[2] In adding age to the ongoing debates on difference, it is of vital importance to the understanding of gender, ethnicity, race, or culture, as well as to the understanding of age, that these sources of difference and desire be considered in their articulation with one another. In this way we may come to understand how the femininity of older women may differ from the femininity of the young.

Constructing Gender

What does it mean to speak of constructing one's gender? In what sense is such an expression meaningful, given the fact that we are born male or female, and are immediately assigned a gender role by society that fits this physiology? The question was first posed by Beauvoir in *The Second Sex* [Le Deuxième sexe]: "One is not born, but rather becomes, a woman." [On ne naît pas femme; on le devient] (301). This original statement of the problem contains a certain ambiguity in the verb "become," as Judith Butler points out in her article "Sex and Gender in Simone de Beauvoir's *The Second Sex*" (35–49). If gender is imposed on male and female bodies by culture and language, then is the subject entirely passive in the process? Butler challenges this notion, which is assuredly not Beauvoir's, by stressing that if the subject were entirely passive, it would be impossible to account for the variations in individual gendered behavior that are observable in even the most rigidly traditional societies. Butler asks: "What is the role of personal agency in the reproduction of gender? In this context, Simone de Beauvoir's formulation might be understood to contain the following set of challenges to gender theory: to what extent is the 'construction' of gender a self-reflexive process? In what sense do we construct ourselves and, in that process, *become* our genders?" (36–37).

Beauvoir's word *become* was intentionally ambiguous. Her central argument throughout *The Second Sex* turns on this very point: although our point of departure is always that of an *embodied* subject, and even our transcendent consciousness cannot escape the physical aspect of our identity, it is nevertheless true that our gender is *also* a choice. There is no one, pre-existent feminine identity. Gender is an "incessant project, a daily act of reconstitution and interpretation," and femininity in particular is characterized by the absence of a fixed nature or meaning (Butler

40). The subject interprets "a cultural reality laden with sanctions, taboos, and prescriptions" according to her/his free choice of values and in the process reorganizes the givens of the culture in a personal variation. Of women, Beauvoir writes in *The Second Sex:* "Now, what specifically defines the situation of woman is that she—a free and autonomous being like all human creatures—nevertheless discovers and chooses herself in a world where men compel her to assume the status of the Other" [Or, ce qui définit d'une manière singulière la situation de la femme, c'est que, étant comme tout être humain, une liberté autonome, elle se découvre et se choisit dans un monde où les hommes lui imposent de s'assumer comme l'Autre] (xxxiii; Parshley trans. 34). Toril Moi identifies this statement as "perhaps the single most important passage in *The Second Sex,* above all because Beauvoir here poses a radically new theory of sexual difference." Moi continues, "While we are all split and ambiguous, (Beauvoir) argues, women are *more* split and ambiguous than men. . . . The specific contradiction of women's situation is caused by the conflict between their status as free and autonomous human beings and the fact that they are socialized in a world in which men consistently cast them as Other, as objects to their subject" (155). Thus the ambiguity and conflict inherent in their situation make each woman's definition of femininity under patriarchy a more difficult but more imperative and absorbing set of choices than the individual definition of masculinity.

Yet Beauvoir is also aware of the existential burden implicit in such freedom of choice. We can infer this from many of her works, including *Memoirs of a Dutiful Daughter* [Mémoires d'une jeune fille rangée], in which she describes her own youthful struggle to break free of a certain widely received construction of femininity that her family milieu sought to impose upon her. I shall return in more detail to the question of Beauvoir's process of gender reconstruction in the chapter devoted to her. But with reference to all three writers, it is worth remembering how difficult it is for an individual to construct a gender identity that is in any way ambiguous. Judith Butler says, "The fall from established gender boundaries initiates a sense of radical dislocation which can assure a metaphysical significance" (41). This is because the notion of choice is systematically denied in subtle ways by the social institutions that seek to impose conventional roles. One of Beauvoir's favorite examples of this bias is the widely held assumption that motherhood must be instinctual and physiologically determined (and hence not subject to choice) because it is so nearly universal. This type of assumption is not, as Butler points out, an innocent one: "The desire to interpret maternal feelings as organic necessities discloses a deeper desire to disguise the choice one is making. If motherhood becomes a choice, then what else is possible?" (42) This kind of invisible pressure is incessantly exerted on the individual subject. We have seen in the case of femininity as interpreted by the French that women themselves have internalized much of this pressure, to the point where they have almost all refused to question the gender arrangements imposed by their culture's definition of difference. Butler's last observation on this point seems to fit French women very well: "This kind of questioning often engenders vertigo and terror over the possibility of losing social sanctions, of leaving a solid social station and place" (42).

The effect of aging on their understanding of their femininity was, in a general way, different for Beauvoir and Colette than for Duras. Both Beauvoir and Colette knew anguish and crisis in their forties, when they began to leave physical youth behind. Ultimately convinced of their loss of desirability, both were conscious in the end, though in quite different ways, of a sense of relief at being excluded from the economy of heterosexual desire. A certain ambivalence persisted in both writers, but their latest works reveal in each case a kind of resolution and surpassing of anxieties. For Beauvoir, her own femininity was always problematic, identified in her mind with fear of abandonment and death. This problem, which originated early in life, was aggravated by her idealized and often painful relationship with Sartre. As part of this deep fear of the female body, Beauvoir always felt repulsed by all the physical functions connected to the woman's reproductive role. Intellectually and philosophically, this fear translated into the conviction that maternity condemns women to sacrifice of self and servitude to the species. Thus, while she regards menopause as a painful and depressing crisis in both her autobiographical and fictional texts (*Force of Circumstance* [La Force des choses], *The Mandarins* [Les Mandarins], *The Woman Destroyed* [La Femme rompue]), in writing *The Second Sex* at age forty-one she saw a potential source of new strength for aging women as a consequence of their bodily changes: "Woman is now delivered from the servitude of the female species, but she is not to be likened to a eunuch, for her vitality is unimpaired. And what is more, she is no longer the prey of overwhelming forces; she coincides with herself" [Alors la femme se trouve délivrée des servitudes de la femelle; elle n'est pas comparable à un eunuque car sa vitalité est intacte; dependant elle n'est plus la proie de puissances qui la débordent: elle coincide avec elle-même] (35; 63). By the end of her life, Beauvoir had come to accept her own femininity in her own way, largely by means of a love for another woman which was not unrelated, I believe, to a resolution of a long-standing conflict in her relationship with her mother.

Colette, like Beauvoir, felt enormous ambivalence about femininity in advanced age. Her fictional works present many characters, including Léa in Chéri and The End of Chéri [La Fin de Chéri] and Marco in "Le Képi," whose aging bodies are portrayed in harshly negative, even obsessional language. Her own sense of impending age was a source of anxiety even in her thirties, when her twelve-year marriage to Willy Gauthier-Villars ended in open hostility. Willy's subsequent strategies for humiliating his ex-wife included transparent literary references to her as an aging, ridiculous woman. Some of the fear of aging that she experienced as she simultaneously assumed her own professional and financial independence is expressed in her first full-length independent piece of writing, The Vagabond [La Vagabonde]. But Colette went on to establish her autonomy, literary reputation, and a more positive feeling about her aging body and femininity. In Break of Day [La Naissance du jour], when she is in her fifties, a fictionalized Colette looks at her weathered hands, which look older than her face, and claims to like them very much [C'est une bonne petite main, noircie, . . . et je n'ai pas honte d'elle, au contraire] (BD III:298); while she is represented as still desirable to younger men, she self-consciously turns away from them without regrets. At the same time, the real Colette was consolidating the early, passionate phase of her relationship with the much younger Maurice Goudeket. One gets the feeling that she is rehearsing in Break of Day a way of existing as a woman that she was not yet ready to assume in life, in order perhaps to dispel the anxiety she still felt about it, and to explore its possibilities; in any case, the feelings of confidence and control over her life that she had gained as a writer were clearly enabling forces in her assumption of her late life femininity.

Marguerite Duras presents herself as a radically different kind of aging woman on the first page of her autobiographical work, *The Lover* [L'Amant]. Here, there is real acceptance of the aged woman (Duras was in her seventies) as sensually beautiful; in fact, it is this promise of the fulfillment of age and experience that opens the book as an admiring man tells her he finds her "devastated" face more beautiful than the conventionally beautiful face of her youth. A few years later she wrote the semiautobiographical, semifictional *Emily L.*, a text she creates in the presence of and for the younger man she lived with, in order to be able to give him the gift of her own feminine voice as an experienced author, as well as a story that will increase his understanding of the gift and the gesture of making it. The text is an act of love, as *The Summer of 1980* [L'Eté 80] had already been, and as *Yann Andréa Steiner* was to be. In the chapters devoted to these writers I will return to these and other late-life, self-conscious reconstructions of gender.

"Successful Aging": Findings from the Social Sciences

My arguments have focused on the way aging functioned as an empowering force in the lives of French women writers, but in drawing this conclusion and in providing the historical, literary, and social background specific to France, I do not mean to describe the situation for older French woman as unrelated to a broader spectrum of problems experienced by women. On the contrary, much evidence from psychologists, anthropologists, and sociologists supports the notion that a woman's older years can be a time of liberation and power.[3] This view is true in so many cultures that part of the emergence of the older woman writer in France must be seen as stemming from more universal causes, even if the precipitating factors were specific to French literary and social history. Proceeding in this way, from a general, cross-cultural perspective is always a double move, so to speak: it sheds light on the particular situation of older women in one place by relating them to a general condition, even as it points up particularities and puts them into relief.

David L. Gutmann, a developmental psychologist who is widely read among theorists of aging, stresses the universality of the invigorated older woman:

Culturist explanations, which emphasize causes that are unique to each society, ignore an outcome that is found in all postparental female transitions. Whether old women become matriarchs or witches, a common factor underlies all these sundry transformations, namely, the general increase in their powers. . . . Finally, it is this protean potency of the older woman, notable precisely because it invigorates so many disparate roles, that signals the presence of a unitary endogenous phenomenon. (206)

Elsewhere in his article, Gutmann has said that these comparative data point to a pattern most evident in societies characterized by "stable, patrilocal, extended families" (201). In other words, the transition in women's roles that comes with age is most evident under patriarchy, a fact which modulates what might otherwise appear as a physically based essentialism.[4] Perhaps these observations point to a nearly universal difference in women's evolution because they reveal a reaction to the experience of early life under patriarchy, and this reaction is made possible when the woman is beyond the age of sexual definition according to the conventional terms of youth.

Other anthropologists and psychologists have also been aware that, as Judith K. Brown states in her introduction to *In Her Prime: A New View by Middle-Aged Women*, "there is no such thing as the 'status of women' in any particular society" because "age modifies the position of women, just as gender modifies the position of the aged" (7). Anthropologist Claude Meillassoux, in *Maidens, Meals and Money*, adds to the evidence: "Marx is . . . right to believe that women probably constituted the first exploited class. All the same, it is still necessary to distinguish different categories of women in terms of the function they fulfill according to age, by which they are not in the same relations of exploitation and subordination" (76). Most interesting perhaps is the counterpoint that Carl Jung brings to the Freudian notion that a woman ceases to develop psychically after her thirtieth year: "There are many women who only awaken to social responsibilities and to social consciousness after their fortieth year. . . . One can observe women . . . who have developed in the second half of life an uncommonly masculine tough-mindedness which thrusts the feelings and the heart aside. . . . Intelligent and cultivated people live their lives without even knowing of the possibility of such transformations" (Jung 398).

These writers and many others have long been saying, in voices often obscured by a more dominant, medicalized discourse of women's inevitable depression and the universal decline of old age, that aging brings women new roles which allow for greater individuation and self-definition, even in nonindustrialized societies. In fact, many of these studies focused on a sampling of cultures including the nonindustrialized. Judith K. Brown, writing in *In Her Prime* on gains made by older women in Western societies, claims that if these gains have been less than those suggested by the cross-cultural data, this is probably because restrictions on the behavior of younger women have been "negligible in the first place" (5). I think this conclusion is contestable. These lesser gains may rather be due to the absence of positive, empowering role models. As Gutmann points out, whether women in nonindustrialized societies become invested with "good" power as matriarchs after menopause, or with "bad" power as witches, in any case their power increases and they assume a fixed role (206). Gutmann implicitly corroborates what we have already had occasion to observe: these preconceptions of older women are dependent upon patriarchal perceptions of their sexuality after menopause.

In the West, things were not so different, in that two prevailing images of older women held sway for a long time: the wise woman, endowed with the power of experience and knowledge, who, like Alison of Bath, was not an asexual figure; and the witch, a sexually threatening woman. In modern times, as we have seen, older women's sexuality began to be denied but was not replaced, at least in France, by other clear, powerful roles, especially when the the youthful ideal of attractiveness made older women feel not only undesirable but invisible. The repression of women's self-expression in France and the polarization of sex roles, further aggravated these problems. It was up to women finally to invent new roles that would enable them to express whatever sexuality they chose and to assume the necessary power to do so.

Betty Friedan substantiates these claims by citing the work of Jane Loevinger on ego development and Bernice Neugarten on transcending polarized roles. She shows that "midlife rather than childhood or adolescence represents the pivotal time of individuation, autonomous self-definition, and conscious choice" (113). Here we have returned to Beauvoir's notion of individual choice, which Friedan agrees is most feasible for adults who are beyond the predefined roles of sexual partner and parenthood. She demands that age be regarded as a time of greater *choice* rather than simply as a time that is not youth: "The problem is, first of all, how to break through the cocoon of our own illusory youth and risk a new stage in life . . . to step out into the true existential unknown of these years of life now open to us, and to find our own terms for living it" (69). Perhaps without knowing it, Friedan has here cast both of the terms of Beauvoir's own struggle with aging, both her existentialist belief in the necessity of self-creation, but also the anguish of breaking out of "the cocoon of our illusory youth," which was all the more difficult in a culture that highly prized young, eroticized, feminine attractiveness. Friedan is clear and, to my mind, convincing in her realization that this personal struggle is inevitable in some form for all people: "It takes a conscious breaking out of youthful definitions—for man or woman—to free oneself for continued development in old age" (115). The key word is, of course, *conscious*, and as we shall see, this idea was a conscious and thematic preoccupation of our three writers.

Active identification with one's own aging rather than a rigid "clinging to the values of youth, denying age . . . " is thus one of the necessary ingredients to what Friedan calls "successful aging" (120). Other phenomena also appear necessary. The ability to sustain "an intact and supportive intimate social environment [is an] important factor in resisting assaults of old age and thus a significant factor in survival" (82). It is also essential to have acquired feelings of control over one's existence.

Friedan takes Gutmann's seminal notion of the gender "crossover" of age as a point of departure for her meditation on "personhood" (186). It is not merely the case that each gender comes to resemble the other with age. Friedan examines a hidden problem in the symmetry of Gutmann's analysis for both sexes (though it is certainly true that he has focused much more attention on the development of women); her thoughts about the "crossover" are worth quoting in full:

Where cultural values elevate young men's dominance to an overarching value, the repressed "passive" male potential is more likely to emerge as the basis of "mid-life crisis," illness, and the disengagement that precedes death. And yet these same studies showed that the same shift . . . increased the "authority and freedom" of older women. Brooding about this paradox, I suddenly realized that a "crossover" is not a sufficient explanation. For in our own society, women's greater strength in age—and their increasing edge in longevity—does not seem to be based on young men's power of dominance and possession, but rather on the ties of intimacy and social bonds which women are more able to sustain and re-create than men . . . How do we move beyond a mere "crossover" to new ways of loving and working? How do we *live our age* as simply a new time of our life, a new period of humanness, a new stage? The clue lies in those individual differences that increase with age . . . the clue is the personhood of age. (178;186)

Not simply reversal, in other words, of the old feminine and masculine roles of our youth, but going beyond dichotomization: this inevitably means finding new ways of loving and being loved, new forms of intimacy to sustain us in age that go "beyond the dreams of youth" (Friedan 256). Friedan, like Colette and Beauvoir, feels these were somehow insoluble dilemmas earlier in life because of "the male/female imbalance, the youth obsession, the pressures and terrors of middle-aged sex" (257). Now, in this new and final stage of life, women have the greatest chance of reaching "personhood" in France as elsewhere if they possess the fundamental characteristics of "successful aging" as presented by Friedan and as explicitly illustrated in their female characters and their lives by Beauvoir, Colette, and Duras: "Trust, risk-taking, adaptability, non-conformity, and the ability to live in the present" (160).

If Beauvoir discusses the problem of adaptation to her own aging, it was only very late in her life that she was able to overcome her resistance to change. As we shall see, she refused to the extent possible any kind of discontinuity in her personal life, which theoretically should have excluded her from the category of those who had aged "successfully." On the issue of adaptability, Friedan theorizes that those women who have lived through the Second Wave of American feminism have had to adapt to new situations throughout their lives and have therefore faced the changes brought by aging with greater equanimity than earlier generations. She goes so far as to say, "If the study of age had begun with women—my generation of women, moving and growing through changes we ourselves were continually creating, that dread mystique of age as drastic decline might never have embedded itself in the national psyche" (136). In this she joins Margaret Morganroth Gullette who, in addition to describing the ways in which a negative view of aging was put into place in the 1920s and 1930s, has also written *Safe at Last in the Middle Years,* in which she shows that male and female contemporary novelists are discovering middle age as a time of greater happiness than youth.

But if Beauvoir's resistance to change worked against her, there were other ways in which she broke through the accepted restraints on what should be "left out of an older woman's biography or autobiography" (Heilbrun 30). There are several striking examples of this refusal to be contained within the old limitations, to which I shall return. For the moment, I would like to note that in particular, "in the old style 'autobiography,' women never told of their love for other women," and friendship between women "had never been depicted in an autobiographical work was a major focus of a woman's life before the work of Audre Lorde and her generation" (72,75). Yet in *All Said and Done* [Tout compte fait], Beauvoir precisely does focus on her love for Sylvie Le Bon in the first section, in a move that reveals the special role of autobiography for a woman writer, who may be using it and re-creating it in order to write in her own authentic voice for the first time: "Other researchers have noted this increased self-awareness, this freeing ease and comfort with one's self, which leads to new, sometimes startling frankness and lessened conformity to the expectations and sanctions of others" (Friedan 151). It is this *shift* into a more authentic mode of self-description that gives autobiography a potentially more subversive role for older women than it has had for older men and may be the reason autobiography has been such a frequent practice among older women writers in all languages in the twentieth century.

Autobiography as a preferred genre is also undoubtedly related to new experiences of intimacy. If the aged person who has transcended the traditional masculine/feminine role definitions has truly attained a more integrated form of personhood, this change is invariably accompanied by a need to communicate, to create bonds of intimacy between author and reader as well as between friends and lovers. Women may have a greater ability to maintain an intimate environment for themselves even if it is not traditional remarriage, and indeed Colette, Beauvoir, and Duras did surround themselves with intimate relationships in old age, both conventional and highly unconventional. They were all keenly aware of their own need for intimacy and for nurturance in old age, and each arranged her life in order to ensure that she would be nurtured and enjoy truly intimate connections at the end of her life. The willingness to disclose one's feelings, the "ability to share feelings, the presence of a confidant . . . seems to constitute the essential intimacy"(Friedan 261). The older woman becomes a "truthteller" about herself, her feelings, her long-buried anger (151). This is another reason autobiography needs to be seen as fulfilling a special function in the case of older women. This intimacy is a matter of self-disclosure or exposure, which are at once, and paradoxically, the gestures that had been denied to women writers *and* were a necessary factor of productive old age. So it was hardly surprising that new forms of autobiography became central to the writing projects of all three authors as they aged and broke free of conventional restraints.

A particular way in which they chose to innovate was a deliberate blurring of distinctions between fiction and autobiography. All three to varying degrees, but especially Colette and Duras, placed a largely verifiable self as author in the center of an otherwise fictional work. It is true that "Colette" in *Break of Day* is not exactly identical to the author, but she is tantalizingly close, including her name, age, status as a writer, etc. Duras includes herself in *Emily L.* along with the real-life Yann Andrea and a fiction based on her imaginings about a couple seen in a bar. In her case, her self as character enters her work only when she is a distinctly older woman: older than Gérard Depardieu in her film "Le Camion," older than Yann Andréa, older than her younger self in *The Lover*. Whatever details of difference are observable among the three, what seems clear is that this deliberate blurring of boundaries between fiction and autobiography is a statement about designated plots or literary conventions for women and a desire to move beyond them. It is almost as if they were saying: "*I* want to be in this story; I want this story to be about me as *I really am*." This truth is present even though there is always a degree of fictionalization in the written presentation of the self, even in work that pretends to the status of autobiography, and certainly in the more hybrid genres.

Another aspect of this positive writing about the self, whether as autobiography or in fiction, is the notion of "healing fictions," or the "cure" story, as Gullette describes it: "What seems undeniably personal, autobiographical, is a writer's decision to repeat, for a time, among all the possibilities, stories of a particular conflict . . . the existence of different *versions* of the psychic situation over time forces us away from the typically static analytic statement about a writer's unresolvable problem: instead, we are urged outward toward the bigger and ultimately more useful hypothesis that for some writers, whether they know it or not, writing fiction *over time* helps to solve problems" (*Safe at Last* 50). Gullette's distinction between those writers who produce "progress narratives" in middle age and beyond, and those who produce "decline narratives" because they see aging only in terms of inevitable decline, relates as well to the characteristics of "successful aging." Accepting change, but also trust, is revealed in the literary strategies of progress novels: "How do writers . . . manage to maintain trust in the face of this last extremity [death]? All have narrative techniques that reveal how they have come to terms with this contradiction. Maintaining faith in the processes that accompany aging may be the crucial common factor . . . The first amounts to appreciating change ('strangeness')." (56)

In the lives and works we are about to examine, I believe it will be clear that writing the self for these women meant redefining what it was acceptable to say, appropriating a genre, and curing themselves of certain life-long obsessions. This process could obviously only have been accomplished at the end of a long writing career. Finally, each writer not only wrote about the way she was aging but aged as well in the way that she was writing. The way we perceive our own aging is to a great extent the result of the cultural representations that surround us. Writing about new gains in aging for women may well have changed their own experience still further. As Kathleen Woodward puts it, "All . . . bodies are themselves reflected through the prisms of personal phantasms and cultural representations. The aging body as imagined and experienced and the aging body as represented structure each other in endless and reciprocal reverberation" (*Aging* 5).

COLETTE: INVENTING
THE WAY BACK

chapter 3

The life of Sidonie-Gabrielle Colette (1873–1954) spanned an era of unprecedented change in the personal and professional lives of women. Even more than Beauvoir or Duras, Colette was situated at the crossroads of two centuries: of a world in which women stayed within the domestic sphere and one in which they went to work; of a time of extremely limited educational opportunities and a time of freer access to higher education; of Paris and the provinces. Colette was a newly married woman of twenty in 1893, during the Belle Epoque, the time of a new valorization of feminine youthfulness and fear of the loss of attractiveness with age. At the beginning of World War I, Colette had been recently married for the second time and was the mother of a new baby; by the end of the War she was a mature woman in her forties facing her second divorce. In the 1920s, her time of greatest productivity, her reputation as a writer was consolidated around the themes of aging and youth, as Western postwar society for the first time made a veritable cult of the youthful female body. By the beginning of World War II, Colette was an aged woman, writing serenely about her own aging. Though her relationship to her aging was conditioned by the era and its events, in this as in everything she refused to accept uncritically the widely held view of either the aging woman or her sexuality. She found her material in earlier and contemporary traditions but proceeded to revise it thematically and structurally. In old age, Colette was able to find an original way to exercise her influence and her sensuality. In this she was greatly helped by her long-held belief that gender roles are far from immutable.

Reading Colette's Life and Work

Much has been written about Colette's life, not least by Colette herself, and biographies continue to appear. The two published in 1997—Régine Detanbel's *Comme une flore, comme un zoo* and Claude Francis and Fernande Gontier's *Colette*—prove that Colette still fascinates biographers, whose accounts abound in contradictory interpretations, in particular of Colette's early relationship with her mother, Sido, the reality of her professional, sentimental, and erotic life in her first marriage to Willy (Henry Gauthier-Villars), and her affair with Bertrand de Jouvenel, the young son of her second husband, Henri de Jouvenel, which occurred when she was still married to the father. These are the issues that articulate the very real scandal that surrounded Colette both during and after her life. Most recently, Francis and Gontier have focused on the thirteen years spent with Willy in their attempt to revise the portrayal of Colette as Willy's passive victim. Colette sketched this portrait of herself as victim as early as *The Vagabond* in 1910 and reiterated it as autobiography in *My Apprenticeship* in 1936. Michèle Sarde, in *Colette Free and Fettered* [Colette libre et entravée], remains close to Colette's own account of this and other issues, relying primarily and uncritically on Colette's writings, though Sarde also uses the correspondence and historical evidence. Francis and Gontier, in contrast, eschew any reading of Colette's work and focus exclusively on biographical data. They show Colette in possession of considerable agency from the start of her first marriage, emphasizing that she was more than willing to engage in the lesbian affairs that

Willy arranged for his own gratification. Herbert Lottman's version of these years, *Colette*, similarly emphasizes biography to the exclusion of the fiction or autobiography, but he depicts both Colette and Willy as victims of a painful situation, stressing the role of work in the conflict and pointing out that Colette in particular was frustrated as a young woman writer.

Claude Pichois, whose biographical material included in the three volumes of the Edition de la Pléiade of Colette's works should be considered a highly judicious source of information and interpretation, restores a sense of proportion to the role of relationships with women and other scandalous behavior in Colette's early life, pointing out that her most basic problem was a need to assert herself and the extent to which marriage to Willy impeded her from doing so. Pichois doesn't deny Colette's lesbianism, but he makes room in his work for Colette's feelings of betrayed heterosexual love and the larger questions of emotional involvement with men, which shaped her life. More fundamentally, Pichois points the way towards a reading of Colette that accommodates both the biographical data and the work, navigating between a life that simultaneously involved much public display, but also discretion and even reticence on matters of feeling, and an oeuvre that never ceases to probe the most intimate feelings of its female protagonists. Because Francis and Gontier avoid reading Colette's work and her life together, the consequence is a biography that fails to illuminate the author's work in any way.[1]

The larger question here, as in the case of Beauvoir and Duras, is one of knowing how to read. As stated earlier, I have chosen to read both life and work as part of a single weave. It is also important to listen to Colette's autobiographical voice, for although she is not an entirely reliable source of information on her own past, her interpretations of that past are part of her work. If *My Apprenticeship* reviews Colette's early experience through the distorting lense of time and the desire for revenge against Willy, it remains essential that she felt it necessary to present herself as the victim of a Sapphic fiction for women in order to justify her youth to her readers in 1936. As Francis and Gontier point out, the decadence of the Belle Epoque was no longer fashionable by the 1930s, and Colette may have felt the need to attribute her scandalous sex life to

Willy alone. But by the same gesture, she invites us to admire her repudiation of that servile life and to contrast the independent older woman she has become with the submissive young wife of 1900.

A Provincial Girlhood

Gabrielle, as she was called for the first twenty years of her life, was born in Saint-Sauveur-en-Puisaye in Burgundy and spent her entire childhood in this very small village far from the sophistication of fin de siècle Paris, although her parents were well educated and had social connections in Paris. "Free and fettered," as Sarde describes her in *Colette libre et entravée* with respect to her love for Sido, Gabrielle grew up in a world in which girls and women, within the restricted sphere of activity available to them, experienced themselves as subjects. Sido herself was the center of activity and attention and the decision maker within the Colette family, the arbiter of values for her four children, the love of her husband's life. Jules Colette, a former army officer, had lost a leg in battle and had retired to provincial life as a tax collector with some political and literary pretensions. Passive and perhaps somewhat mesmerized by his love for his wife, his library contained volumes he was presumably writing but which were found at the time of his death to be totally blank, apart from a passionate dedication to Sido.

Gabrielle attended a girls' school, which offered only an elementary-school diploma. After graduating, she was sent neither to the lycée in the county seat nor to a convent school. Nevertheless, as Sarde points out in *Colette libre et entravée*, her attendance in this rural girls' school had its advantages, in that sexual discrimination played no part and, because no special thought was given to these peasant girls' future role as "ladies," their education, however brief, was pedagogically the same as the one dispensed to boys at this same time (83). Sarde, relying on Colette's own accounts, emphasizes the tomboy aspect of these girls' amusements, their very down-to-earth mastery of womanly skills in preparation for genuine work, and the virtual absence from their universe of concern with matters of love or *coquetterie*. The only girl to subscribe to the myth that she would attract a desirable husband by means of beauty and sensual attraction was Nana Bouilloux, "La Petite Bouilloux" of *My Mother's House* [La Maison de Claudine], who wastes her entire life in Saint-Sauver waiting for the man who never arrives.

In the "Claudine" series, as well as in her memoirs, what is striking is the sense of *autonomy* conferred on the young Gabrielle in her early experience of this gyneceum. With the later loss of this autonomy in her relations with men, Colette repeatedly described her early self, as in *Tendrils of the Vine* [Les Vrilles de la vigne] and *The Vagabond*, as having existed in an androgynous phase *before* gender: "But what I lost . . . is . . . the secret certainty that I was a precious child, the feeling that I had within me the extraordinary soul of an intelligent man, of a woman in love, a soul that would burst my little body. . . . Alas! . . . I lost almost all of that to become in the end just a woman." [Mais ce que j'ai perdu . . . c'est . . . la secrète certitude d'être une enfant précieuse, de sentir en moi une âme extraordinaire d'homme intelligent, de femme amoureuse, une âme à faire éclater mon petit corps . . . Hélas! . . . j'ai perdu presque tout cela, à ne devenir après tout qu'une femme] (*The Vagabond* I:1032). Most interesting from the perspective of gender construction over the life course is this equivalence of the loss of an early autonomy and subjecthood and the acquisition of conventional femininity. Suzanne Relyea discusses Gabrielle's sense of losing her identity when she discovers the more overtly patriarchal society of capitalist Paris: "In giving up her girlhood, she also gives up the maternal line, the symbol set where woman and full being coincide, to enter a whole new set of power relations within which she holds no title to existence except with respect to men. While restoring her to the world of Saint-Sauveur . . . her own ultimate choice [of name], 'Colette,' reflects the degree to which she viewed the loss as irreversible" (Relyea 285). What seems essential to my point about gender and aging is the sense conveyed by the early texts that the more conventional femininity assumed by Gabrielle after her marriage and move to Paris was at least partially experienced as an arbitrarily constructed gender role that was imposed upon her and therefore always remained subject to scrutiny and reservation.

Paris

When Henry Gauthier-Villars became her husband, he was fourteen years her senior and one of the most notorious libertines in Paris. He initiated her not only into sexuality but also into the sophisticated Parisian world of journalists and novelists, poets and playwrights. The shock of this initiation quite literally almost killed Gabrielle, normally a robust woman; she fell ill, the doctors despaired of her, and Sido came to nurse her back to health. She had lived through the coming true of prevailing romantic fantasies of sexual initiation by an older man and been introduced at the same time into the most potentially limiting aspects of the standard Sapphic plot for a woman's life, as Willy began almost at once to betray her sexually and to encourage Colette to engage in lesbian relationships. At first, she was without independent means of survival and thus—whatever the realities of her own participation in these sexual exploits—was necessarily bound to the marriage. During those thirteen years, as she recalls in *My Apprenticeship,* she suffered but never imagined leaving. She adds that in 1900, provincial girls, if not Parisians, regarded with terror the idea of "conjugal desertion" (III:1065). Unable for the moment to imagine an afterwards, a different outcome for her life, she compares herself to certain animals who struggle to open their cages, but then, once the cage is opened from the outside, withdraw into it, immobilized (1064–65).

Yet these conventional aspects of the story were soon modified, ironically by Willy himself. Willy had organized a business to produce many popular volumes of amusing prose by hiring writers, sometimes quite talented, in workshops and in exchange for meager pay. This arrangement suited a number of aspiring young writers looking for a living, but it did not suit Colette quite as well when he decided she would lend a hand with a rendition of her schoolgirl diary. The Claudine stories, perhaps the most important commercial literary success of the century, were thus largely written by Colette and signed by Willy alone. Over the course of the years, Willy unknowingly developed in her the skills and the desire to write, which would one day make of her a popular, successful writer after he had been forgotten. He also introduced her to the world of the theater and music hall, which was to guarantee her income in the years following the separation. Thus she acquired the professional and financial means and the discipline she would need to create a life after Willy. This conjunction of circumstances was to mean that writing would always be set in her mind against the experience of servitude and annihilation of self that marriage had brought.

Little of the actual subject matter of the Claudine novels was entirely chosen by Colette. But already one can discern in the language of certain descriptions some of the strategies by which Colette was struggling to regain her lost sense of herself as a subject. In particular, there is the question of who is doing the looking. Claudine in her rural village of Chatillon recapitulates not only Gabrielle's childhood but also a secondary myth of Sappho as rendered in minor prose works by men in the eighteenth and nineteenth centuries, that of the girls' school or convent ruled by a seductive female teacher. Following Willy's orders, Colette reproduces the titillating aspects of the gyneceum expected by his readers, but nevertheless inaugurates a significant departure, precisely because she is the first female narrator to write in this sub-genre. As Elaine Marks puts it: "In 1900, for the first time since Sappho, the narrator Claudine in *Claudine at School* [Claudine à l'école] looks at another woman as an object of pleasure and without any excuses describes her pleasure (Marks, "Lesbian Intertextuality" 362). A great revolution had begun:"

> She is like a cat caressing, delicate and sensitive, incredibly winning. I like to look at her pink little blond's face, her golden eyes with their curly lashes. Beautiful eyes that are always ready to smile! They oblige the young men to turn around when she goes out. Often, while we are chatting at the door of her excited little class, Mlle Sergent walks past us to go to her room, without a word, staring at us with a jealous, searching gaze. Her silence tells her new friend and me that she is furious at seeing us get on so well together.

> [Nature de chatte caressante, délicate et frileuse, incroyablement câline, j'aime à regarder sa frimousse rose de blondinette, ses yeux dorés aux cils retroussés. Les beaux yeux qui ne demandent qu'à sourire! Ils font retourner les gars quand elle sort. Souvent, pendant que nous causons sur le seuil de la petite classe empestée, Mlle Sergent passe devant nous pour regagner sa chambre, sans rien dire, fixant sur nous ses regards jaloux et fouilleurs. Dans son silence nous sentons, ma nouvelle amie et moi, qu'elle enrage de nous voir "corder" si bien.]

(*Claudine at School* I:12; Marks trans., "Lesbian Intertextuality" 363)

Marks goes on to observe that Claudine's voyeurism is different from the masculine version in that it is unabashed, public, and "directly related to her appetites" (363). This kind of appropriation of the gaze that yields expansive descriptions of the body, whether male or female, is found throughout Colette's oeuvre, and it was equally revolutionary in another way when a man became the object of a female narrator's gaze.[2]

A Wandering Freedom

This "unsetting of the problematics of the gaze," this need to see for herself, is developed thematically in Colette's first full-length independent work written after Willy finally left her (Miller, *Subject to Change* 229–64). At age thirty-seven, Colette experienced not only a fear of attachment but of solitude, a fear that would never again be so acute. In 1910, Colette in *The Vagabond* (1910) was just beginning to work through the issues of autonomy and connection that she would more explicitly explore eighteen years later in *Break of Day*. The beginning of her independent career as a writer also coincided with the beginning of middle age. This theme, too, is present in this novel about a working woman's decision to refuse an offer of marriage from a highly suitable and wealthy man in order to remain in control of her own destiny. Looking ahead to the rest of her life, the aging heroine Renée Néré is aware that her solitude may last forever. She is alarmed when her lover Max, who is her age, sends her a photo of himself playing tennis with a young girl.

Colette began as soon as she was free to create her own material and to refuse the standard plot: in her life as she went to work as a mime in the music hall, supporting herself by means of a highly unconventional and sometimes scandalous occupation, and by her writing. In both of these professions Colette, like her character Renée Néré, took pleasure in exposing herself to the male gaze, even as she changed the terms of that specular economy. In *The Vagabond,* Renée looks at her lover Max as an object of desire to be evaluated but also talks to the reader about other things, thereby giving weight to her subjective experience of her work in the music hall in such a way as to make believable her decision to leave Max in the last pages of the novel, despite the unconventionality of this open ending. Renée has no specific goal when she leaves, other than to pursue her wandering and her difficult, badly paid career. But, as Miller notes in *Subject to Change,* she chooses to construct a new female identity through her work and the comradeship of her fellow workers (252). Like Renée, Colette was to continue this independent construction of her feminine self until the end of her life, even when her solitude with respect to men was no longer a problem.[3]

Renée understands the power that accrues to the woman who sees and evaluates in order to write and sets this autonomy in *opposition* to her connection with Max: "You offer a young, ardent, jealous companion, who is tenderly in love? I know: he is called a master, and I want no more of that" [Tu me donnes un ami jeune, ardent, jaloux, et sincèrement épris? Je sais: cela s'appelle un maître, et je n'en veux plus] (*Vagabond* I: 1226); "I refuse to contemplate the most beautiful countries on earth reduced in size in the amorous mirror of your gaze" [Les plus beaux pays de la terre, je refuse de les contempler, tout petits, au miroir amoureux de ton regard] (1232).

As Reneé travels, she begins to feel a tension between her erotic love for Max and the pleasure she derives from seeing for herself and recreating in writing the objects of her gaze. She begins by becoming aware of the "true, and very limited role of love in a woman's life" (Ladimer, "Colette" 151–65). The fact that she is a mature woman who has already lived through the youthful courtship and marriage plot and observed its outcome is essential to making this perception: "If giving myself were the only thing at stake! But there is more than pleasure. . . . In the boundless desert of love, the burning fire of passion occupies only a small place, but it glows so brightly that at first one can see nothing else: I am not an innocent young girl, to let myself be blinded by its blaze" [S'il ne fallait que me donner! Mais il n'y a pas que la volupté . . . La volupté tient, dans le désert illimité de l'amour, une ardente et très petite place, si embrasée qu'on ne voit d'abord qu'elle: je ne suis plus une jeune fille toute neuve, pour m'aveugler de son éclat] (*Vagabond* I: 1211).

The compensation provided by writing is a physical one, rich in sensual potential. In her description of her feelings while writing, which follows immediately her recollection of her pain in the marriage, Renée recapitulates Colette's relationship to language as a means of exploring her own sensory reality and to deriving satisfaction from the writing of it. Words are physical beings: "And yet I had savored, in giving birth to [this book], the voluptuous pleasure of writing, the patient struggle against the sentence that becomes supple, curls itself up like a tamed animal, the motionless waiting, the lying in wait that finally *charms* the word" [Pourtant j'avais savouré, en mettant celui-là au monde, la volupté d'écrire, la lutte patiente contre la phrase qui s'assouplit, s'assoit en ronde comme une bête apprivoisée, l'attente immobile, l'affût qui finit par *charmer* le mot] (*Vagabond* I:1084). Miller's comment on this is pertinent as well to later developments in Colette's work: "This very bodily account of the mating of words and sentences as a negotiation between pleasure and struggle in which both agent and material are animated and animal may be seen to constitute the specificity of Colette's language about writing: a modern(ist) insistence on the agency of the letter, the physicality of language, the material force of its signifiers" ("Woman of Letters" 238). In *The Vagabond*, the writerly "pleasure and struggle" that recall all attempts at erotic possession enter into explicit conflict with the erotic pleasure offered by Max towards the end; Renée wonders: "For how long had I been forgetting Max, for the first time? Yes, forgetting him, as if I had no more urgent task in my life than to seek the words, the words to say how yellow is the sun, how blue the sea" [Pendant combien de temps venais-je, pour la première fois, d'oublier Max? Oui, de l'oublier, comme s'il n'y avait pas de soin plus impérieux, dans ma vie, que de chercher des mots, des mots pour dire combien le soleil est jaune, et bleue la mer] (*Vagabond* I:1220–21).

As Colette advanced in age, this pleasure became an alternative form of sensuality in both life and literature. Here, as in several other works, her female protagonist announces in advance a course that Colette herself will later follow. It is important to understand that this sensory and sensual pleasure that rivals the overtly sexual is not a simple recording of what the writer sees around her. Colette has often been misread as a painter of the natural, whereas in fact almost all of her descriptions express an implied rejection of the natural, the received idea or cliché, in favor of a paradox, by far the most prevalent figure in her works on the descriptive, thematic, and even narrative levels.[4] Hence the "yellow sun" and "blue sea" in the above quotation are finally set in contrast with the "salt in a fringe of *white jet*" [. . . et brillant le sel en frange de jais blanc] (*Vagabond* I:1220, emphasis mine). The paradox and contradictions that afforded her so much pleasure were undoubtedly expressions of her recognition that the sensual possession of the world effected by writing is as complicated as other attempts at sensual possession, even if it is ostensibly more innocent: things are not what they seem to be, they always surprise us, and they may disappoint or delight, according to our degree of autonomy with respect to them.

Postwar Maturity

As *The Vagabond* was appearing in serial form, Colette's divorce from Willy became official and, while continuing her stage career, she also began working for the newspaper *Le Matin*. There she met the director, Baron Henry de Jouvenel, who was to be her second husband and the father of her child. During World War I Colette remained in Paris, engaged in the war effort but frequently visiting Jouvenel at the front. By 1918, at the age of forty-five, Colette had changed. Because of her then-unconventional career changes, divorce, and late childbearing, in retrospect the period before the war seemed a time of several new beginnings in her personal life, which had kept alive in her the sense of being young. By the end of the war, Jouvenel had begun to tire of the passion that had united them and to betray her with other women, and physically she changed in a way that was to put her at odds with the 1920s ideal of slender, youthful feminine beauty: she had become heavy and visibly older. By age fifty she was legally separated from Jouvenel and two years later had met Maurice Goudeket, who was to become her third and last husband.

Never at home in the aristocratic world of Jouvenel's new political career and feeling excluded after their estrangement from the staff of *Le Matin*, where she had been a literary editor, she ceased her collaboration there and began to write regularly instead for several other major Paris daily papers. Despite an occasional return to the stage for the production of one of her own works, Colette devoted most of her time in the 1920s to her own writing. It was this decade and the next that saw her most prolific and innovative. Her works between ages forty-five and fifty-five are marked by her attempts to come to terms with growing old and her relations with men, by her increasing attachment to the memory of her mother, and by a probing investigation of what kinds of plots might lie beyond the conventional heterosexual plot already refused by Renée Néré. Colette's identity as a writer was well established by the beginning of this period, since *The Vagabond* had received three votes for the prestigious Prix Goncourt. By the time Colette was forty-nine in 1922, her mother, Sido, had entered her work for the first time. But Sido really came into her own as a fully developed character in *Break of Day,* when Colette was fifty-five. It is in this latter work that Colette makes her most explicit criticism of the ordinary plot for women's lives, by incorporating a secondary (and devalued) heterosexual love story into this meditation on how to grow old and renounce love. But first there were problems to resolve.

Chéri: First Portraits of the Aging Woman

The plot and setting of *Chéri* brought Colette a *succès de scandale* in 1920. Older men in particular were offended by this story of Léa, a forty-nine-year-old demimondaine from a fast-disappearing society of courtesans, and her lover "Chéri," a wealthy young man of twenty-four. Chéri and Léa must separate when Chéri's mother arranges his marriage to a very young woman, but after a period of some months both realize that the other had been their greatest love. Chéri returns one evening to Léa's rose-colored room, and in the next morning's light he is struck by the irremediable fact that Léa is old; at the end of this volume he returns to his young wife. Sarde astutely points out that this plot, when recounted from the point of view of the young man rather than the aging woman, is in fact quite acceptable and even canonical: it is the plot of Benjamin Constant's *Adolphe,* a standard French novel of the Romantic period (Sarde 390). The young Adolphe struggles with his pity for his aging mistress, Eléanore, whom he wishes to leave and who then dies when she realizes the truth of the situation. But here Léa does not die; she goes on to live a full life in her late years, in *The End of Chéri,* a sequel written in 1926. It is Chéri who dies instead, unable to forget his love for an early incarnation of Léa. Many women readers appreciated these works, according to Colette in *The Evening Star* [L'Etoile vesper], even if male reviewers violently reproached her for tampering with the "natural" order of youth and age and for portraying a social milieu that was unacceptable. (*Adolphe* had taken place among the high aristocracy).

Male critics also responded to the objectification of the male as the object of Léa's gaze and of his demythification as hero. Some were unwilling to accept that these characters bore any resemblance to real men. Jean Larnac, in an early critique on Colette and her work, exclaimed: "Can we really call these creatures men, who are only distinguished by their physical appearance and their value as lovers?" (200). It is in fact older women who do most of the looking and evaluating. Léa in *Chéri* is encouraged by Chéri himself, who spends considerable time parading before the mirror, as does Alain in *The Cat* [La Chatte]. Throughout Colette's work the gaze remains the act of only one partner and marks his/her power over the other at the same time as desire. Communication between two members of a heterosexual couple is all but impossible in this oeuvre, where the gaze is evaluative and always involves issues of subjugation, even when one woman looks at another, and some degree of sexual objectification.[5] What is also unusual in this rewriting of the love affair between an older woman and a younger man is that here the older mistress is sexually active and is seen as the stronger and more dominant of the two. Léa was the first fully middle-aged woman to "take her prey," "freely admitting as she lets fall on Chéri her glance of voluptuous con-descendence that she is reaching an age when she can grant herself a few pleasant rewards" [elle avouait volontiers, en laissant tomber sur Chéri un regard de condescendance voluptueuse, qu'elle atteignait l'âge de s'accorder quelques petites douceurs] (*Chéri* II: 722) In a later novel, the title character, Julie de Carneilhan, despite her enduring love for her ex-husband, Herbert, also dominates two younger men at the age of forty-five: her lover Coco Vatard, for whom she has a certain condescension or even contempt, and Herbert's son by a previous marriage, who is only an adolescent. The latter tries to commit suicide because Julie refuses him, and when called upon to disculpate herself, Julie simply points out that her appetites don't incline her towards the very young: "I don't like veal, I don't like lamb or kid, and I don't care for adolescents" [Je n'aime pas le veau, je n'aime pas l'agneau, ni le chevreuil, je n'aime pas l'adolescent] (117). Her ex-husband's fury in the face of this response reflects somewhat belatedly the angry confusion of Chéri's reception: "'Get out of here!' he cried in a low voice. . . . 'I cannot tolerate that here, before me . . . you talk about a male individual as if you could freely dispose of him! . . . your freedom doesn't extend so far as to come here and right under my nose evaluate the attractiveness of young Hortiz'" ['Laisse-moi!' cria-t-il à voix basse. . . . je ne tolère pas qu'ici, que devant moi . . . tu parles d'une créature masculine comme si tu pouvais délibérer d'en disposer! . . . ta liberté ne va pas jusqu'à venir sous mon nez supputer les avantages du petit Hortiz'] (118).

By the end of her life, the voluptuousness of writing first suggested in *The Vagabond* was able to replace sexual voluptuousness in a manner that allowed Colette to remain sensually engaged with the world. But during her middle years, writerly and sexual voluptuousness were indissociable, as she trained her gaze on the male or other object of desire. The "evaluative" look that Claudine had first given spontaneously and naturally to Aimée Lathenay in *Claudine at School* evolved into an assertion of her self against the standard conventions of narrative and of life in which it is the woman who is seen. It is interesting to compare this aspect of her revision of narrative to the remarks of some recent French women critics of Colette. Although Marcelle Biolley-Godino is highly sensitive to the revolution produced in literature by the woman narrator describing the object of her pleasure, she explains its originality in terms that are anything but original:

> Since the beginning of time, women have hidden their arms behind their apparent submissiveness, and have pretended to enter into the game of their partner in order to control him. . . . while preserving all the appearances of slavery, they finally manipulate the master as they please . . . by presenting themselves as human beings, but of the female gender, who have their own way of perceiving things, they make a claim for their specificity, and their originality, which goes much further than a claim of equality (89).

According to Biolley-Godino, these characters would be playing the historic game of manipulating male power from their special place of privilege rather than gaining a genuine autonomy and independence of their own. I cannot agree with this description, which fits neither Léa nor Julie de Carneilhan, who do not in the end manipulate the master or the tragic passing of time as they wish they could. In the painful accounts of their aging bodies and their inevitable loss of a Chéri or a scheming, unfaithful Herbert, there is a clearly implied need for a new position of equality as well as for specificity or difference. They try to employ their autonomy to find another script when their age makes the original one impossible, and their new story is certainly specific to them as women but quite different from what is expected of them by men.

Women readers of the 1920s responded sympathetically to the pain that Léa feels in *Chéri* when she must face, on the morning after, the loss of her beauty despite her lifelong efforts to preserve it. In her life, and only after the publication of *Chéri*, Colette herself engaged in an affair with her adolescent stepson, Bertrand de Jouvenel, without apparently experiencing the same tragic feelings of loss and the ravages of time, although the affair did contribute to ending her marriage to Henry. Perhaps she was able to render these feelings less debilitating precisely by writing about them. One must turn to her literature to find these powerful evocations of what she considered the inevitable loss of female attractiveness.[6] Léa has a real nobility of character that enables her to face the truth and generously to release Chéri. There is nothing ridiculous about her, unlike some of Colette's later aging characters, like Marco in "Le Képi." She actually helps Chéri formulate his own statement of the "truth": "Sitting up very straight now, [Léa] showed him in the full light her face, noble and ruined, glazed by her bitter tears. An invisible weight was pulling down her chin and her cheeks. . . . In this wreckage of her beauty, Chéri could retrieve, intact, her lovely strong nose, her eyes as blue as a flower" [Assise très droite à présent, elle lui montrait en pleine lumière son visage noble et défait, ciré par de cuisantes larmes sèches. Un poids invisible tirait en bas le menton et les joues. . . . Dans ce naufrage de la beauté, Chéri retrouvait, intacts, le joli nez dominateur, les prunelles d'un bleu de fleur bleue] (825) Chéri then says: " 'So, Nounoune . . . I arrive here, and . . . ' He stopped, frightened by what he had almost said. 'You arrive here, and you find an old woman,' said Léa in a weak and tranquil voice" ['Alors, n'est-ce pas Nounoune, j'arrive ici, et . . . ' Il s'arrêta, effrayé de ce qu'il avait failli lui dire. 'Tu arrives ici, et tu trouves une vieille femme,' dit Léa d'une voix faible et tranquille] (825).

She renounces him, and with him all men and indeed all sexuality, for when we see her again a few years later in *The End of Chéri*, her portrayal is full of the Colettian irony that is so singularly lacking in *Chéri*, simply because in the later novel it is no longer Léa who *sees*. The older Léa has not found a satisfactory solution to the question of late-life gender identity.

Throughout Colette's works, one finds in more or less explicit form the notion that as a woman's body ages, it is appropriate and necessary for her to renounce a certain youthful feminine sexuality and, by extension, love relationships with men. Léa's body is repeatedly described in *The End of Chéri* as grotesque, betraying the narrator's fundamental ambivalence towards the aging woman's body: "She was not monstrous, but vast, and weighed down by a lush development of all of her body parts. Her arms, like rounded thighs, stood away from her hips . . . The solid colored skirt, the long impersonal jacket . . . announced the normal abdication and disappearance of femininity and a sort of sexless dignity" [Elle n'était pas monstrueuse, mais vaste, et chargée d'un plantureux développement de toutes les parties de son corps. Ses bras, comme de rondes cuisses, s'écartaient de ses hanches . . . La jupe unie, la longue veste impersonnelle . . . annonçaient l'abdication, la rétraction normales de la féminité, et une sorte de dignité sans sexe] (214–15) Although Léa has proved to be a survivor and illustrates the inestimable virtue in Colette's universe of adapting to changed reality, I think we must read descriptions like this one as revealing obsessive fears and fantasies rather than as evidence of resolution. *The End of Chéri* is one of a series of "cure stories" in Gullette's sense. Léa is a frightening spectacle who lacks self-discipline and has let herself go, ballooning out of all proportion, as Marco will do in "Le Képi." Despite Léa's uprightness and real wisdom in *Chéri*, qualities so paradoxical in her world of demimondaines, there is a certain lack that makes her transition to old age both cataclysmic and genderless. She has wisely renounced the attempt to remain youthful and sexually active, but she has not altogether found the missing pieces of the puzzle of what might follow.

Late-Life Femininity: The Path Back

The themes of the need to renounce and to abstain from passion, re-worked by Colette, and the need to reestablish her connection to her mother were indispensable both to her late-life revision of plot and to finding what she considered an appropriate expression of her late-life femininity. But in order to find the path back to Sido's inspiration and wisdom, Colette had not only to come full circle, as critics have often pointed out. She also had to go forward along other routes that were sometimes tortuous and difficult, in order to arrive at an identity sufficiently differentiated from her mother's.

Sido had died in 1912, but Colette, like other writer-daughters of the early twentieth century, was only ready to write about her mother after Sido was deceased, when Colette as the daughter had acquired her own brand of mature wisdom that was inseparable from her identity as a writer, so that memory and desire could be allowed to play their transformative roles of reconnection and reconciliation. Thus Colette also resembled the Anglo-American female modernists, whose "family romances differ radically from those that predominate in the Victorian period. Female *Künstlerromane* of the 1920s feature young and middle-aged women who renounce love and marriage in favor of creative work, who renounce connection in favor of self-affirmation. This rebellious choice is intimately bound up in their relationships with their mothers but often is in great conflict with the choices their mothers themselves have made" (Hirsch 96). The question for such daughters of returning to connection with their mothers later in life was also made more difficult not only by historical changes, which had radically transformed the lives of the daughters' generation, but as well by the changes they themselves had made in order to avoid their mothers' conventional femininity.[7]

Stories of Ambiguity: Separation from the Mother

In the 1920s and early 1930s, in a few important texts that appear to be charged with ambivalence about connection to the mother or mother figure, Colette seems to have written her urgent need for individuation. The first were *The Ripening Seed* [Le Blé en herbe] (1923) and *The End of Chéri* (1926), but *The Cat* [La Chatte] (1933), written even after *Break of Day* (1928), has the same structure. And finally, in a less well-known story, "The Sick Child" [L'Enfant malade], published in a volume with "Gigi" when Colette was seventy-one, she seems to have provided the key to these novels of languishing young men which are simultaneously stories of a need to separate from the mother and of a coming to language/writing. The question of Sido's role as an inspiration for her daughter's writing has been treated by many scholars, and some have noted that the mother is absent from the early works, but only rarely has Sido's benign image as a goddess of nurturance been called into question in favor of a more complex, ambiguous relationship between mother and daughter. Marianne Hirsch is one of the few to have taken issue with the notion that Colette's writing came simply out of "plenitude" and "comfortable connection"(103). Hirsch refers to *Break of Day*, in which the mother-daughter plot coexists with a heterosexual plot in a narrative that is a hybrid in many ways. But I also think that Colette conflated these two kinds of plots in the three novels mentioned above, by creating triangular relationships involving a young man, a young woman, and an older woman.

In these works, conflicting parts of the narrator's self are portrayed by means of an aesthetic of ambiguity. The three novels are striking in their departure not only from any recognizable traditional plot but from the other works in Colette's corpus as well.[8] They form a class apart: the principal character within whom the narrative point of view is most often located is the man. They also share a particular kind of ambiguity connected to the older woman/mother figure. In terms of the narrative, Alain in *The Cat*, Chéri in *The End of Chéri*, and Phil in *The Ripening Seed* find themselves in similar situations. They are poised at a decisive moment early in life between two women who represent the mother figure and a young wife or lover. In Alain's case, the maternal role is shared by the cat and the mother; the cat stands between Alain and Camille. In Chéri's case, the memory of Léa prevents Chéri from joining Edmée in a new postwar life. Phil's attachment to his sexual initiator, Madame Dalleray, interferes with his feelings for his fifteen-year-old girlfriend and future wife, Vinca. The young men's dilemma represents not only a rite of passage, as critics have seen in the case of Phil, but also a less banal moment of decision for the self between two modes of existence.

The ambivalence felt by the reader towards the three young men is unusual because at the same time, she/he is invited constantly to share in their thoughts and feelings by means of narrative point of view and filtering techniques. Yet their point of view often conflicts with the impression created by the textual realities of the young man and woman, the set of descriptive elements considered in their relationship to one another. Thus in *The Cat*, Alain does his best to persuade the reader that Camille is insensitive and even cruel towards the cat, and because we see everything from his point of view, we are also made to share Alain's longing for the garden in which he grew up with his beloved cat. Yet a close look reveals that Camille's "negative" qualities may only be "reprehensible when measured against a certain ideal of passive femininity" (Ford 363). We are left feeling ambivalent about the breakup of the marriage and Alain's return to his mother's house and the company of his cat. In *The End of Chéri*, Chéri and Edmée create a similar puzzle in that Chéri's nostalgia for the Léa he loved is understandable to anyone who has read *Chéri*. There is less ambiguity in *The Ripening Seed*, because Phil regards his childhood friend, Vinca, with affection in the early chapters, although as the story develops he becomes increasingly fearful and estranged.

In fact, the three men and women are defined by several sets of opposite characteristics. The women are active, healthy, well adapted to change and to the present, and they communicate in an open and articulate way. The men are passive, physically weak, resistant to change, and unable to adapt. They flee from exposure and communication by protecting themselves and dissimulating. Compared with the young women, they are relatively silent and inarticulate, and they prefer to remain in dark, enclosed spaces.

My interpretation of these texts relies on the ubiquitous connection in Colette's work between textual space and the textual body of the person who inhabits it, usually a woman. As Yannick Resch puts it, "The comparison of the body at different moments of the day illustrates one of the principles that govern the construction of the female character: the woman's body is above all a milieu, an atmosphere. It is situated in space as well as in time. The body is that space which it inhabits" (23).[9] The textual space of the characters in these novels belongs to them by virtue of their characteristics and contains a key to their interpretation as works of Colette's middle age.

The men's spaces of predilection are claustral, secret, and dark. In each case, this intimate space is inhabited by the male narrator and by the mother or a mother figure and is informed by the young man's feelings about her. It excludes the younger woman, who is representative of adult connections in the present, and it appears to the young man to be a refuge from the inadequacies of his adult relationships including mature sexuality and from the strain of negotiating with the present and the future. Alain's space is, of course, his mother's garden in Neuilly, in which he often regresses to genuinely childlike behavior (*La Chatte* 821). Frequent reference is made to the dead tree that stands in the center and to the laburnum, evocative of death. The servants are old and moribund. Chéri finds his ideal space in La Copine's apartment, a low-ceilinged room where everything is old, including the photographs of a young Léa that transport him into the past. La Copine, a substitute for Léa, who was the maternal presence, recounts the past and ministers to his needs. It is here that he commits suicide with a drug overdose. Phil's space, the villa of Madame Dalleray, is enclosed by a wall; once inside, he undergoes a physical trauma, ostensibly caused by the cold, dark, cavelike interior, that will in fact worsen until the end of the novel. In this nocturnal abyss, images of fire and ice transcode the intensity of Phil's sexual initiation. On the road to this place inhabited by the mother figure, he notices that the Breton fog appears to have mixed milk into the sea (*Ripening Seed* 1216). When his mistress leaves, Phil is stricken with nostalgia. The entire experience has the effect of orienting him towards the past, though he is only sixteen.

Only in the case of Alain is this space actually figured as a garden, but I believe that in all three novels his space is in fact a negative variant of Sido's garden as it appears in Colette's works. Even the casual reader of Colette must be surprised by this statement, but I do not think it inconsistent nor do I mean in any way to challenge the significance of the refuge and return to the garden in other works. Typically, a young *female* character returns to the garden, her place of origin, after a disappointing experience with heterosexual love. She seeks legitimately to prepare the "rebirth" that Sido accomplished all her life at the break of day. From Claudine to *Julie de Carneilhan,* the "sentimental retreat" is a valid refuge, either in the short run as in *Claudine at Home* [Claudine en ménage] or in the long run as in *Julie de Carneilhan,* or in the nonfictional eulogy to the values of the garden in "Flora and Pomona" [Flore et Pomone].

But in *The Cat, The End of Chéri,* and *The Ripening Seed,* the claustral space and the entire symbolic system point instead to the need for the character to move beyond the garden. If the itinerary that leads back to Sido is a circle, it must in its first move depart from the space inhabited by her. The female self must be constituted with reference to the mother, but she also requires a broader experience, and there is a dangerous threat involved in remaining behind. The young women here are realistic and adaptive, as was Sido. They paradoxically represent the counterweight Colette found to be the need to return to the origin: the ability to adapt to change and to the present, both also guarantors of successful aging, as we know. It is especially striking that in these novels the familiar Colettian binary pair associated with Sido, abstention versus consummation, receives a somewhat different treatment. Camille, Edmée, and Vinca embrace life eagerly and sensually, while the excessive idealism and exacerbated sensitivity of Alain, Chéri, and Phil create varying degrees of difficulty in relating sensually to the young women and to reality. Strength is derived not from abstention as an approach to life, as "Sido" teaches "Colette" in *Break of Day*, but from a posture of attempted possession. Even if these young women sometimes offend by their aggressiveness—and we know from many autobiographical and journalistic references that Colette did find the new young women of the 1920s and afterwards to be aggressive and abrasive—it is clear that they nonetheless have a lot to teach these men about taking hold of life. The men's unwillingness to communicate or use language effectively suggests that they could not possess the world through writing either.

Colette may have chosen a male protagonist for these novels in order to emphasize the urgency of differentiating oneself from the world of the mother. These stories incorporate the traditional plot for women, but they consider it from a different angle that displaces its problematics, so they actually modify it according to the dynamic of the mother-daughter plot. The presentation of masculinity and femininity serves to describe the conflicts of the mother-daughter dynamic rather than genuine sexual difference. The mother figures themselves remain shadowy or absent, because it is really the "son's" way of relating to them that is in question.

Another text that reveals that the very condition of coming to writing was an act of separation from the mother is the short story "The Sick Child" [L'Enfant malade], written late in Colette's life, in 1944. Again the principal character, Jean, is male, a little boy of ten, and the story, a quasiclinical case study, is told from his point of view. He suffers from a potentially fatal illness and is cured, but only after a crisis. A moral is appended to the story, emphasizing its status as the embodiment of an abstract truth: "A time comes when one is forced to concentrate on living. A time comes when one has to renounce dying in full flight" [Un temps veut qu'on s'applique à vivre. Un temps vient de renoncer à mourir en plein vol] (130).

The child is bedridden and confined to his room, where his mother and a woman servant minister to his needs day and night. In this hermetic setting, it is not surprising that Jean's major symptom is paralysis of the legs, accompanied by a fever that allows him to live in an elaborately contrived fantasy world. Jean is an hysteric, exhibiting the very disorder that Freud believed originated in a girl's pre-Oedipal attachment to her mother (*SE* 21:222–23). Jean smiles "majestically" at his mother despite his helplessness ("L'Enfant malade" 335; White trans. 105). Freud refers to "his majesty the baby" and to "infantile omnipotence" arising from the experience of the mother as the "external ego" which protects the child from reality (*SE* 19:145). In "The Sick Child," this feeling is at once a symptom of illness (fever) and a source of infantile pleasure. Alone in his bed, Jean secretly and silently "takes flight" on fantastic voyages through walls and into a world of brilliant images:

> He mounted a cloud of fragrance that was passing within reach of his small, pinched white nostrils, and rode swiftly away. . . . Astride the scented cloud, he wandered through the air of the room; then he got bored and escaped . . . followed by a big silver clothes moth who sneezed in the trail of lavender behind him. To outdistance it, he pressed his knees into the sides of the cloud of fragrance, riding with an ease and vigor that his long, inert, half-paralyzed legs refused to display in the presence of human beings. When he escaped from his passive life, he knew how to ride, how to pass through walls; best of all, he knew how to fly. With his body inclined like a diver's plunging down through the waves, his forehead passed with careless ease through an element whose currents and resistances he understood. . . . Once he had rashly let himself come down too near the ground, over a meadow where cows were feeding. So close to the ground that he had seen, right opposite his own face, the beautiful, astonished face of a cream-colored cow with crescent-shaped horns, and eyes that mirrored the flying child like magnifying glasses while the dandelion flowers came up out of the grass to meet him, growing bigger and bigger like little suns. . . He had only just had time to catch tight hold of the tall horns with both hands and thrust himself backwards up into the air again; he could still remember the warmth of the smooth horns and their blunted, as it were friendly, points.

> [Il enfourcha un nuage de senteur qui passait à portée de ses petites narines blanches et pincées, et s'éloigna rapidement . . . A californchon sur la nue parfumée, il errait dans l'air de la chambre, puis il s'ennuya, s'évada . . . suivi dans son vol par celui d'une grosse mite d'argent qui éternuait dans le sillage de la lavande. Pour la distancer, il pressa de ses genoux les flancs de la nue de senteur,

avec une vigueur et une aisance de cavalier que lui refusaient, en présence des êtres humains, ses longues jambes inertes d'enfant à demi paralysé. Evadé de sa vie passive, il savait chevaucher, passer au travers des murailles; il savait surtout voler. Le corps incliné comme celui du plongeur qui descend à travers l'onde, il perçait nonchalamment . . . un élément dont il connaissait les ressources et les résistances. . . . Une fois, il s'était laissé imprudemment descendre, trop près de terre, au-dessus d'une prairie que paissaient des vaches. Si près de terre, qu'il avait eu contre son visage une belle face étonnée de vache blonde, ses cornes en croissant, ses yeux qui miraient l'enfant volant comme deux lentilles grossissantes, tandis que les pissenlits en fleurs, à même l'herbe, venaient à sa rencontre et s'élargissaient comme des petits astres. Il avait eu le temps de prendre appui a pleins doigts sur les hautes cornes pour se rejeter à reculons dans l'air et il se souvenait encore de la tiédeur des cornes lisses, de leur pointe émoussée et comme bienveillante.]

("The Sick Child" 328–29; White trans. 90–91)

The language of these passages, and the way they are inserted into the narrative describing the sick child's relationship with his mother, reveals much about the nature of his disorder. The long, fluid sentences combine a dense accumulation of sensory details, especially color and touch, with a freedom of movement that expresses Jean's own illusion of free flight.

These passages insist on Jean's use of words as a kind of material substance that is a direct source of sensory experience rather than an abstract or symbolic representation of it. Thus, at the end of a second ride on the cloud, he is thrown against an unyielding oak door, which is his concretization of the voices murmuring beside him: "But the inflexible barrier of a firmly chiseled voice . . . was whispering: 'See, he's fast asleep.' Numbed by the shock, anguished from head to foot, Jean was aware of the cruel harshness of the two words, 'See, he's, Seehees, Seeheeze.' They were sharper than a knife blade. Beside them lay three severed syllables, 'fa-sta-sleep.'" [L'inflexible barrage d'une voix fermement ciselée . . . chuchotait: 'Qu'il s'est endormi.' Suffoqué par le choc, navré du haut en bas, Jean perçut la cruelle consistance des deux mots 'qu'il s'est, Kilcé, Kilsé' plus tranchants qu'une lame. Auprès d'eux le mot 'en . . . dor . . . mi' gisait rompu en trois tronçons] (330; White trans. 94). On the same page, Jean sees the "Big Skating Rink" ["La Grande pati-noire] in the nickel paper knife as "immense," sometimes spelled with six *m*s, as he again reworks the malleable material of language to fit his individual perceptions. These are assimilated into his "illness," and there are many references to Jean as a disabled writer. He notes on an "invis-ible page" the secret wonders of his flights (334). An equivalence is sug-gested between the flights and his experience of the books he reads: "Protected and precocious, he had quickly mastered the hieroglyphs of print, dashing as wildly through books as he galloped astride clouds" [Protégé, précoce, il s'était emparé promptement des hiéroglyphes de la typographie, allait aussi follement au travers des livres qu'à chevaucher les nuées] (337; White trans. 109). Both are part of the same dysfunction: both provide sensual pleasure even as they isolate him sometimes, pain-fully, from reality and society.[10]

From the beginning, Jean's concern with language and the question of his ambiguous gender are associated in the text. One of the most persis-tent features of his selective misunderstanding of the words spoken by others is his tendency to transform common nouns into feminine proper names. This selective aphasia reveals a preoccupation with his gender identity; the ambiguity and ambivalence surrounding it seem to confirm that this drama is unfolding in the pre-Oedipal world of the mother-child dyad. This ten-year-old's persistent lack of *emotional* awareness of sepa-rateness, despite his *cognitive* awareness, can be seen as an exaggerat-edly prolonged pre-Oedipal bond, in which the boundaries between the self and the mother are still uncertain.[11] Sandra M. Gilbert and Susan Gubar in their book *No Man's Land* point out in their assessment of masculinist and feminist theories of language and its acquisition that the girl-child, if one subscribes to Nancy Chodorow's theory, may be at a disadvantage in terms of "linguistic privilege," because "if symbolic lan-guage acquisition is based on the separation from the mother's body and the resulting loss and anxiety, Chodorow's concept of the 'fluid bound-aries' between mother and daughter calls this acquisition into question since precisely the interidentification Chodorow posits could be said to deny girls the space language negotiates" (Gilbert and Gubar 265–66). In "The Sick Child," Jean's mother selects his books for him (337; 109). Jean communicates with her largely by means of a repertoire of very tiny, complex signs (328; 88). When he attempts to write for others to read, he is rudely censored by the doctor, who is offended by his handwriting (337).

The remedy clearly must come from someone outside the mother-child dyad; appropriately, it is the doctor. As Jean's fever rises to its highest, the boy is terrified, but "another person, whose decisions depended neither on helplessness nor on motherly kindness, made a haughty sign that imposed silence" [une autre âme, dont les décisions ne dépendaient ni de l'impotence ni des bienfaits maternels, fit un signe hautain qui imposait le silence](341; 118), and his mother remains on the other side of the wall as the decisive event occurs. He allows himself to be carried by a whirlwind of meteors and lightning, but this time, "just as he was on the very verge of being perfectly contented . . . he was aware that a sad little crystalline crash separated him from a bliss whose soft, airy name he had yet to learn: death." [tout près d'être parfaitement heureux . . . il perçut qu'un petit bris triste, cristallin, le séparait d'un bonheur dont il avait encore à apprendre le beau nom concave et doré: la mort] (341). Jean will not die because a crash, or in French "un bris," a necessary break or rupture, has occurred; it is in fact the separation from his mother, and the memory of it slows his flight. Significantly, he is suddenly able to understand a few words of the language spoken over his bed ["quelques mots d'une langue qu'il s'étonnait de comprendre"] and he wants to repeat them (342; White trans. 120).

Recovery is imminent, but it requires that Jean reexperience his mother's body as separate from his own, that his haughty ambivalence be left behind, and that his love for her emerge as something other than fusion. Breathing in the scent of his mother's hair, he remembers her and weeps from the intensity of his love. He falls asleep on the "nest" of her shoulder (343; 123). Sensation returns to his legs and he eats with pleasure. Finally, Jean sees himself in a mirror, which reveals to him that his magical powers and fantastic journeying are at an end (346; 129). But Colette's characters make constructive use of mirrors throughout her work, and Jean is no exception. He waves good-bye to his reflection, which also happens to be the window, an opening onto reality and life outside the family.

The appearance of symbolic language at the time of separation from the mother's body is not surprising, of course. What is new here is the feminine version of the appearance of the father object (the doctor), in which there is a shift of emphasis away from inscription into patriarchy per se, or the acquisition of heterosexuality, as Freud would have it, onto the father as facilitator of the more urgent project of the daughter's separation from the mother. Also specifically feminine are the intensity of the ambivalence and the prolonged difficulty as well as the paradox that creates a new form of union out of separation.

In fact, there is a loss as well as a gain in the imperfectly resolved ambiguity that closes "The Sick Child." The final words are: "children whom death lets go and who fall asleep, assenting, cured, and disappointed" [(les) enfants dont la mort s'est dessaisie et qui s'endorment consentantes, guéris et désappointés] (346; White trans. 130). In this very ambivalence Colette seems to have represented her own beginnings as a writer. The sick child has lost a source of inspiration based on a rich corporeal connection in favor of symbolic speech and writing, but the semiotic of the maternal connection will return in the materiality and sensuality of Colette's modernist language, and will play an ever greater role as she integrates her mother's life into her own and makes of this malleable language the basis of her late-life eroticism.

Resolution and Return

Sido appears for the first time as a character when Colette is already forty-nine, in *My Mother's House* (1922). This is a collection of short texts describing Colette's native village and her family. It is here, as in *Break of Day* (1928) and *Sido* (1929), that one finds the most lyrical and loving passages in all of Colette's work. The enclosed garden is the center of the fictional space as it is in *Sido*, where "Sido" almost assumes the stature of a divinity, receiving from within her garden the message of the four winds and pleading for respect for the independence and integrity of all living things, including oneself. She sometimes wishes to escape from the garden, to "soar to some high place where only her law held sway"[Il me semble qu'un besoin d'échapper à tout et à tous, un bond vers le haut, vers une loi écrite par elle seule, pour elle seule allumait (son visage)] (509); meanwhile, her four children have devised ways of leaving and returning. Here, the garden as a fictional and rhetorical space is not a claustral one.

In *Break of Day*, written when the author was fifty-five, a semifictional "Colette" is living alone in the south of France, meditating on the new life she will have now that the love of men is over for her. The book is punctuated by letters from her mother, which "Colette" tries to understand and apply, patterning herself after "Sido's" graceful renunciation and preparation for her death, as perceived by her daughter. "Colette" goes further: she seeks to merge with her mother, to assimilate her and be assimilated: "Now that little by little I am beginning to age, and taking on her likeness in the mirror" [Maintenant que je me défais peu à peu et que dans le miroir peu à peu je lui ressemble] (Colette 2; McLeod trans. III:278); "I felt stirring at the root of my being the one who now inhabits me, lighter on my heart than I once was in her womb" [Je sentis remuer au fond de moi celle qui maintenant m'habite, plus légère à mon coeur que je ne fus jadis à son flanc] (75; McLeod trans. 336). But I think this deliberate blurring of boundaries between the fictional "Colette" and "Sido" has to be understood as happening within a context of established differentiation between the real mother and daughter as achieved by Colette as a successful—and autonomous—writer. *Break of Day* epitomizes Colette's mature resolution of the problem of differentiation. It contains an often quoted passage: "Do you imagine, as you read me, that I'm portraying myself? Patience: it's only my model" [Imagine-t-on, à me lire, que je fais mon portrait? Patience: c'est seulement mon modèle] (29; McLeod trans. 297). The distinction between a portrait and a model is essential to understanding this re-creation of the self through the mother. A portrait is a replica, but in this text the character "Colette" had separated and even grown distant from her mother. No longer the same, she now seeks to establish sameness between herself and her "model."

In fact, the letters from the real Sido have been rewritten by Colette, who has thus imposed a limit on her loss of self, even as she seeks to reconstruct herself and her writing in the terms of a language inspired by Sido. The ambivalent feeling of a loss of authenticity and of a particular mode of expression connected with the mother's body (and hence with her space, the garden), like the one that appears at the end of "The Sick Child," returns now with the need to represent herself and the world as connected to the mother and as distinct from any patriarchal literary legacy. What is needed is nothing less than a new language that is somehow outside the symbolic order. In "The Anamesis of a Female 'I,'" Nancy Miller (170) points to one illegible letter written in "hieroglyphs" and described in *Break of Day* as a possible example. Like Jean's language, it consists of images and is "intransitive:" "strokes, swallowlike interweavings, plantlike convolutions—all messages from a hand that was trying to transmit to me a new alphabet or the sketch of some ground plan envisaged at dawn under rays that would never attain the sad zenith. So that instead of a confused delirium, I see in that letter one of those haunted landscapes where, to puzzle you, a face lies hidden among the leaves, an arm in the fork of a tree, a body under a cluster of rock." [des traits, des entrelacs d'hirondelle, des volutes végétales, parmi les messages d'une main qui tentait de me transmettre un alphabet nouveau, ou le croquis d'un site entrevu à l'aurore sous des rais qui n'attendraient jamais le morne zénith. De sorte que cette lettre, au lieu de la contempler comme un confus délire, j'y lis un de ces paysages hantés où par jeu l'on cacha un visage dans les feuilles, un bras entre deux branches, un torse sous des noeuds de rochers] (Colette 142; McLeod trans. III:371).

Renunciation . . . of All but Writing

Colette in *Break of Day* is not looking exclusively for reconnection with her mother, for, as Marianne Hirsch observes, "it is perhaps the most passionate story of mother/daughter attachment in literary history, yet that story is still inscribed in a conventional tale of heterosexual seduction"(107). Indeed, Colette is still negotiating her way between the inevitable sorrow of the traditional heterosexual plot and the possible opening onto another mode of existence offered by the maternal connection and connection to women. Nothing less than the nature of the woman's plot is at stake, as Colette realizes in a quotation reminiscent of *The Vagabond*:

How can men . . . still be so surprised when a woman so easily confides to the public her lover's secrets, her lies or half-lies about love? In divulging these, she saves from public scrutiny her greater, unclear secrets. . . . The big projector, the shameless eye which she manoeuvres so willingly, always lights up the same area of women's lives . . . around which the shadows thicken. It is not in this illuminated zone that the darkest plots are woven."

[Comment les hommes . . . s'étonnent-ils encore qu'une femme livre si aisément au public des confidences d'amour, des mensonges, des demi-mensonges amoureux? En les divulgant, elle sauve de la publicité des secrets confus et considérables. . . . Le gros projecteur, l'oeil sans vergogne qu'elle manoeuvre avec complaisance, fouille toujours le même secteur féminin . . . autour duquel l'ombre s'épaissit. Ce n'est pas dans la zone illuminée que se trame le pire.]

(McLeod trans. 315–16)

We have already seen Colette's departures from the strict definition of the traditional plot, in *The Vagabond,* and, to an extent, in the three novels of ambiguity as discussed before. From now on, Colette will begin to try to undermine the standard plot by introducing the "darker" story of what happens outside of love, which is in fact the buried story of passionate attachment between mother and daughter, and, by extension, among women.

But here as elsewhere, the two must still coexist in a sometimes uneasy tension. It would be impossible to say that Colette in *Break of Day* simply renounces her connection to men in favor of her connection to her mother; instead, the book is a description of a process, and she is in a state of becoming: she is looking for an identity that will enable her to refuse to be the object of a man's love yet will simultaneously enable her to resist the temptation to collapse into fusion of mother and daughter.

Renunciation is the primary lesson of "Sido's" letters to her daughter. In the first letter, which opens the book in a sort of epilogue, "Sido" responds to an invitation by refusing to go see her son-in-law and beloved daughter. If she did, she would miss the flowering of a pink cactus, which might not bloom again in her lifetime because she is already seventy-eight. In this letter I see a model for the renunciation "Colette" must learn with respect to men, as exemplified by her refusal of Vial's offer of love. Significantly, "Sido's" wish to remain with her plant and to abstain from indulging her love for her daughter sets up a necessary distance between mother and daughter as well, and places emphasis on the cultivation of the mother's *self,* rather than on her generous propensity to give of herself as illustrated elsewhere in the texts devoted to her.

In fact, this letter was entirely rewritten by Colette. Sido had accepted the invitation but was unable to visit because of ill health; she died very shortly thereafter, and it was Colette who in fact refused to go to the funeral and see her mother for the last time. Thus this most important model of renunciation was a construction of the daughter's, one in which she herself believed to the point of anxiously wondering whether she could live up to it (Hirsch 104). In coauthoring the letters she had received from Sido, Colette engaged in a deeply satisfying altering or mothering of her own mother. The image that she presents of her mother's middle and old age is thus in large part a creation of her imagination, which included distortions that may have made it more difficult for her to come to terms with her own aging. In *My Mother's House* and *Sido,* there are several telling examples precisely of Sido's *refusal* to renounce as she aged: she was troubled by passionate love for her son Achille, the doctor who cared for her as she died of cancer, and she attempted to move heavy furniture and do other difficult chores because of her refusal to acknowledge her dependence (Sarde, *Colette* 312). One can speculate that "Colette's" declared feelings of inferiority to her mother in *Break of Day* result in part from a failure to perceive that the mother, however youthful she may always have seemed (III:335), was in her seventies and very near a painful death, and thus that she was led to renounce sensual pleasure in a very different spirit from her daughter, who was at that time in healthy middle age.

The essential lesson of renunciation includes the paradoxical notion that true possession comes only with abstention. Far from new in the history of women's literature in France, this ascetic reaction to the dangers of being possessed by the male in *his* plot resonates with *The Princess of Cleves* of the seventeenth century. In "Colette's" view, "Sido" will always be superior in renunciation. She has spent her life in the garden, nurturing and observing the passing of the seasons. "Colette," though, like the real Colette at this stage in her life, has engaged in passionate physical love and has understood the impasse of sexual pleasure and possession, the failure of love between man and woman. And at this point, this love still seems inseparable to her from the domain of the senses in general. She is only beginning here to construct another sensual relationship to the world, a new extension of the sensual by the sensorial, which must pass, as I have suggested, through her relationship to writing. Here, her character still feels she must go on to renounce her sensuality itself, "[her] sensuality whose eyes, thank God, were always bigger than its belly" [(ma) sensualité qui eut toujours, Dieu merci, les yeux plus grands que le ventre] (28; III:292).

But the real Colette did not renounce her sensuality. Instead, she finally came to terms with it, a most significant psychological development of her old age. Colette was a hedonist in the original sense of the term, in that she continued to believe that sensuality and pleasure might provide a deeper understanding of the world. Although she concluded that sensual pleasure offered no real communication or understanding between men and women, where one person inevitably dominates and demolishes the other, her disappointment was finally with love, not with sensuality. Interestingly, even as she was writing about the renunciation of love in the personage of Vial, the author Colette was committing herself to her lifelong relationship with Maurice Goudeket. In *Break of Day*, there appears to have been exorcism of those aspects of a heterosexual love relationship that she feared most, those which had interfered with her sense of herself as an autonomous (writing) subject. Again, the text anticipates the life: years later, Colette was to let Goudeket know that their sexual relations had to end, but their relationship incorporated many aspects of the maternal and it endured. As Sarde says, "Sido had left, but Maurice remained. . . . Colette would 'renounce' Goudeket and she would keep him" (*Colette* 446).

Even in *Break of Day*, it is clear that "Colette" will not renounce writing any more than she will renounce her sensuality, and that they are in fact variants of one phenomenon. She takes the first steps towards redirecting her sensuality into writing when she derives inspiration from her mother's writing in order to transform the love object, newly named: "Fly, my favourite! Don't reappear until you have become unrecognizable. Jump through the window, and, as you touch the ground, change, blossom, fly, resound. . . . When you return to me I must be able to give you, as my mother did, your name of 'pink cactus' or some other flame-shaped flower that uncloses painfully, the name you will acquire when you have been exorcised" [Fuis, mon favori! Ne reparais que méconnaissable. Saute la fenêtre, et en touchant le sol change, fleuris, vole, résonne. . . . Lorsque tu me reviendras, il faut que je puisse te donner, à l'exemple de ma mère, ton nom de "cactus rose" ou de je ne sais quelle autre fleur en forme de flamme, à l'éclosion pénible, ton nom futur de créature exorcisée] (140; White trans. 369). What needs to be "exorcized" above all is the story of the heterosexual love affair, the plot to which she will nevertheless always refer and which still structures her late novel *Julie de Carneilhan* and some of her late stories. The heterosexual plot will always be there, as it is in *Break of Day,* even as aging female characters like Julie strain to define their subjectivity, or as the several semifictional "Colettes" act as observers of the effects of love and sexual involvement on other people. Colette is finally unable to free herself altogether from the traditional story and its pain. But she imagines an accurate representation of the bounds within which women were expected to live, and she makes a fully articulated protest. Her attempts to write her observations rather than her own or her characters' direct involvements place her and her reader at an ironic distance from the plot that is a kind of deconstruction. As she aged still further, this distance increased, indicating her mounting resistance to the fictional account and perhaps her frustration at not finding another that was totally outside the conventions of plot and ending. Finally, with *The Evening Star* and *The Blue Lantern,* she turned away from the fictional component altogether.

Stories of Late Life

At age sixty-four, Colette wrote an article entitled "My Ideas on the Novel," which appeared in the newspaper *Le Figaro* on October 30, 1937. She emphasized her difference from other authors as originating with her beginnings and her sources of inspiration, which were of course tied to her life story with Willy but also to her education as a girl in the 1880s. Although she does not say so, she may have been reacting to criticism from the literary and intellectual establishment, which lamented the lack of rigor in the composition of her works and the fact that she had practically no knowledge of the classics, not then included even in the secondary program for girls.[12] Her sexual tolerance appeared to these same critics as amoral, and her manner of taking the human body as the point of departure for psychological or moral descriptions was considered by many as aberrant and proof that she was not an artist in any recognizable way. But in her article for *Le Figaro,* Colette proudly affirms that she will never come to the end of her two sources of inspiration, nature and love, because: "There are not—what a blessing!—two identical loves, nor two leaves exactly alike . . . and I do not remember having endured two similar sufferings in love, nor having given, to a loved one, a name that was not his own" [Il n'y a pas—quel bonheur!—deux amours jumeaux, ni deux feuilles pareilles . . . et je ne me souviens pas d'avoir enduré de chagrins monotones, ni d'avoir donné, à un être aimé, un nom qui n'était pas le sien"] (qtd. in *Oeuvres* III:1831–32). Thus she assures us that if love remains her central focus, it is never the same twice, and it is wise to be wary of facile essentialisms.

Sexuality is always in question, and for those who believe this theme to be incompatible with literary virtuosity, she offers in the same year, 1937, the curious tale entitled "Bella Vista," in which the reader's capacity to foresee or accept the surprise ending reveals his/her sensitivity to the complex relationship between sexuality and textuality. "What being is not sometimes mistaken about where his/her real life is to be found?" [Mais quel être ne se trompe sur le lieu de sa vraie vie?] asks "Colette" as she spends several weeks at Bella Vista, more or less unwillingly, in the company of two strange innkeepers and a man who secretly derives pleasure from strangling birds (1128). The reality of what is usually considered without importance in a woman's life is thus called into question at the same time as is the sexuality of the characters, and this examination amounts to nothing less than an indictment of stories based exclusively on the classic plot for women. Older now, she will repair the error of simply repeating this story and gladly positions herself as an observer of others:

When love has gone, there comes a calm that revives friendships, passersby, as many episodes as in a crowded dream, normal feelings like fear, happiness, boredom, awareness of time and its flight. These 'blanks' that provided me with anecdotes . . . I didn't know, earlier in my life, that I should have considered them more romanesque than the drama of intimacy. I shall not finish my task as a writer until I have tried, as I will do here, to bring them out of the shadows where they were relegated by my shameless need to speak of my own personal experience of love."

[L'amour parti, vient une bonace qui ressuscite des amis, des passants, autant d'épisodes qu'en comporte un songe bien peuplé, des sentiments normaux comme la peur, la gaité, l'ennui, la conscience du temps et de sa fuite. Ces 'blancs' qui se chargèrent de me fournir l'anecdote . . . je ne savais pas, autrefois, que j'aurais dû justement les compter pour intermèdes plus romanesques que le drame intime. Je ne finirai pas ma tâche d'écrivain sans essayer, comme je le veux faire ici, de les tirer d'une ombre où les relégua l'impudique devoir de parler de l'amour en mon nom personnel.] (1097)

From the vantage point of her sixties, Colette returns one last time to the "sentimental retreat" as a solution with *Julie de Carneilhan* in 1941.[13] But the age of the heroine changes the terms: this time the retreat will be definitive because Julie is already forty-five at the time of her greatest disappointment. Her ex-husband, Herbert d'Espivant, left her for another woman whose enormous fortune enabled him to realize his political aspirations. Morally inferior to Julie, and indeed to his new wife, Herbert continues to torment Julie by asking to see her, but only to extort a receipt for a million francs from her so that he can use it to obtain another million from his wife. Still desperately in love with him, Julie remains in Paris just to be near him, in the vain hope that he will return to her.

But like Léa, Julie is lucid about her dilemma. Looking back over the choices she has made, she recognizes that she has been the victim of a particular prescribed destiny: "The things one might have done are the things that were impossible" [Les choses qu'on aurait pu faire, ce sont celles qui ont été impossibles] (92). Her lucidity extends to her foolish complicity in the present with Herbert and his ruses (149) and in the end, she accepts the need to renounce him and all love. Interestingly, in what must be one of the first literary references by a woman, she notes that she appears to be entering menopause and this influences her decision (127). On horseback, she and her brother return to Carneilhan, where, it is understood, she will spend the rest of her life. However, she is not serene when the novel closes, any more than Léa in *Chéri*. Her last words are of regret; about her brother, she says, "Ah! . . . he at least takes with him when he goes the thing he loves most in the world" [Ah! . . . lui du moins il emmène, en partant, ce qu'il aime le plus au monde] (186). We cannot follow her to Carneilhan, because it is unclear exactly how she will exist there. Unlike their creator, Léa and Julie cannot benefit from a subjectivity or a femininity created by work.

At age seventy, Colette gives us in "Le Képi" her own final "cure story" or "exorcism" with respect to anxiety about the aging female body and the necessary renunciation of men and sexual love. Marco, the central character, is about the same age as Julie, but her character and her story are very different. Marco writes fiction for "one sou per line" for a man who publishes it under his own name, a situation from which she will never definitively emerge; a very young "Colette," the narrator, is engaged in the same kind of work at this point. The parallels and differences with respect to Colette's real life are clear, but the most important difference is age. Marco had been married to an artist who abandoned her, and now, accustomed to poverty and abstinence, she is wisely learning to renounce all thoughts of love. When Marco suddenly becomes wealthy, she allows herself to experience and indulge her desire for a young army lieutenant, and the consequence is catastrophe. "Colette" comments with clinical detachment on her mottled complexion, the "secret" of her neck, her beautiful eyes, and her slender, youthful silhouette (40). As all Marco's appetites increase at once and she swells up with weight, she becomes grotesque, fat, "square," but above all *older* (63). "Colette's" gaze becomes cruelly judgmental, and highly reminiscent of the obsessive descriptions of Léa's obesity: " 'She's got a behind like a cobbler's, I thought . . . and, in addition, breasts like jellyfish, very broad and decidedly flabby.' For even if she is fond of her, a woman always judges another woman harshly" ['Elle a un derrière de cordonnier', pensai-je . . . et avec ça des seins en méduses, très larges et manquant de saillie.' Car la femme, même affectueuse, juge durement la femme] (61). "Willy" and a male friend are even harsher, however, saying, "A child of three could have told you that Marco's first, most urgent duty was to remain thin, charming, discreet, furtive, moist with rain, not to be bursting with health, not to frighten everyone by saying, 'I did it! I did it! I . . . ' " [Un enfant de trois ans vous dirait comme moi que le premier, l'urgent devoir de Marco était de rester maigre, charmante, crépusculaire, furtive, humide de pluie, de n'éclater point de santé, de ne pas faire peur aux foules en criant 'Ça y est! ça y est! je . . . '] (65–66).

When Marco finally puts on the lieutenant's hat (his képi) to amuse "Willy," he looks at her and suddenly sees her for the middle-aged woman that she is. "Colette" understands how she must have appeared under his gaze and fears that in addition Marco may lose her dignity, to which

Marco responds sarcastically that it has been lost, and "Colette" must agree. In the months that follow, Marco not only loses weight but indeed becomes too thin and sexless in a manner that (paradoxically) reminds us of the sexless, overweight Léa (80). Colette, as always, has used the woman's body as an infallible indicator of her moral state, and here the loss of control to one's appetite for pleasure, the failure to renounce, make the ending decidedly more tragic than Léa's. But Marco's real tragedy, the true paradox of her situation, is that from the beginning there was no longer any way for her to live her femininity. Her colorless existence, in which she appeared to be wisely abstaining, was not freely chosen, nor was it compensated by the rewards that Colette as a writer enjoyed, but the opportunity to resume a sexual relationship proved to be an unmanageable disaster greatly exacerbated by her age and the fragility of her beauty. That Colette realized how she herself had escaped Marco's fate by becoming an independent writer is evident in the ironic last lines, spoken by Masson: "There's been a great change in her existence. . . . Now Marco earns two sous per line" [Il y a un grand changement dans son existence! . . . A présent Marco touche deux sous la ligne] (81).

The Evening Star and The Blue Lantern

By the time she was seventy-three, in *The Evening Star* Colette has finally abandoned the fictional love plot in favor of the meditation begun in *Break of Day*. She is greatly relieved: "Now the impossibility of walking, and the years, make it impossible for me to commit the sin of inventing fiction, and banish any chance of a romanesque adventure" [Mais voici que l'empêchement de marcher, et les années, me mettent dans le cas de ne plus pécher par mensonge, et banissent de moi toutes chances d'évenements romanesques] (Colette 118; Le Vay trans. 149–50). Thus she makes explicit that ordinary narrative structures and novelistic conventions no longer work for her as she writes from and about a perspective of a woman's old age. In these late works, there is a culmination of thematic material first presented in *The Vagabond*. Here at last Colette enters into full possession of the riches of her own active contemplation of the world; that is, of the "gaze" that she sought to cultivate from her late thirties until the end of her life.

Colette wrote *The Evening Star* in the period immediately following World War II, confined most of the time to her room, which looked out on the gardens of the Palais Royal. She suffered from an arthritic lesion that had complicated a broken leg, and she was increasingly immobilized and in chronic pain until her death in 1954 at age eighty-one. Goudeket, who was Jewish, had been sent to a prison camp during the war, and although Colette's efforts resulted in his release, she remained haunted by the separation. The pain of her anxiety coincided with the deaths of a good many of her contemporaries. Thus she associates the postwar era with her own old age, proudly emphasizing her differences from a rapidly changing society and sometimes deliberately refusing to adapt. There is no nostalgia here for past lovers; she has burned her love letters, while carefully preserving other correspondence. Relationships with colleagues, many of them women, are now considered to comprise the real past.

She makes clear the platonic nature of her rapport with Goudeket, now that she is old and no longer feels herself to be a desiring or desirable woman (102; Le Vay trans. 128). While it is obvious that he is very dear to her, she feels the constant need to deceive him in new ways, by reassuring him that she is not suffering or by not revealing that she is often lost in her memories, which she secretly considers a valuable activity for this time in her life. She is in fact surrounded by loving friends, but she also often chooses solitude, for only when she is alone can she discover an authentic self and devise a way of writing that will prepare her for the end. She compares herself to a rose: "I've just heard fall on a nearby table the petals of a rose which also only waited to be alone before shedding its blossoms" [Je viens d'entendre choir sur la table voisine les pétales d'une rose qui n'attendait, elle aussi, que d'être seule pour défleurir] (30; Le Vay trans. 33). She is also the evening star, the planet Venus, often mistakenly thought to be rising at sunset when it is in fact setting: "With her third name, Vesper, I associate, I link that of my own decline" [A son troisième nom, Vesper, j'associe, je suspends celui de mon propre déclin] (17; Le Vay trans. 15). She is at once the planet of erotic love and of a certain idea of old age, of a leaving off or decline with respect to love.

In *The Evening Star*, Colette seems to have recognized the tension between renunciation, as first addressed in *Break of Day*, and writing as a form of possession, which had long been implicit in her work. The final resolution of this problem seems to be occurring here and to be more

complete in *The Blue Lantern*, three years later, in 1949. Having renounced sexual love, in *The Evening Star* she begins a further redefinition of possession, of having or owning, which involves separating
herself above all from earthly or material possession. This dissociation is
undoubtedly related to her sense of no longer fully possessing her own
body; when she cannot get off her bed to look at the stars and heavenly
bodies, for example, she imagines their presence, and thus considers
them to be her possessions, though she only sees them in her imagination (17; Le Vay trans. 15). She describes her experiments with both hold-
ing on to material relics of her past, which she had previously hoarded,
and letting go: "A superficial wisdom murmurs in my ear that these glass
marbles would be more appropriate for children. . . . Shall I give them?
I'll give, I'll do it while I am still attached to what I want to give. . . . It
wasn't until I'd become old that I understood that my acquisitiveness was
a falsehood. . . . If I open my fingers, if I turn over and empty out the
chest, the drawer, I discover that I'm on longer really attached to anything." [Une superficielle sagesse me murmure à l'oreille que les billes de
verre conviendraient à des enfants. . . . Donnerai-je? Donnons, profitons
du moment où je chéris encore ce que je veux donner. . . . J'ai mis, à
comprendre que mon âpreté était un mensonge, autant de temps qu'à
devenir vieille . . . si je desserre les doigts, si je retourne et vide le coffret,
le tiroir, je découvre que je ne tiens plus à rien.] (64; Le Vay trans. 77–78).
The discovery that material, earthly attachments are illusions is even
more radical than her supposed triumph over herself in giving away what
she still cared for. Aging brings to the fore truths about oneself that have
long been obscured by certain appetites, or by the "burning fire of passion" described in *The Vagabond* that glow so brightly that at first one can
see nothing else.

At the same time, this writing expresses more clearly than ever before
a hunger to possess the world, inexhaustible in its riches, and this sensual desire to possess the aesthetic dimension of things remains her
fundamental attitude toward life: "We do not look, we shall never look
enough, never carefully enough, never passionately enough" (*Paris from
My Window* 109). Again, she asserts that she will possess the world
through writing, through transcribing the world as revealed to her by her
gaze. There is also an immediate physical connection between writing
and the world: throughout *The Evening Star*, writing is depicted as an

intensely physical activity that reveals, through graphological analysis, a writer's true sexuality, his/her photographic image, or his/her portrait (57; Le Vay trans. 68–69). In a nostalgia for a concrete language of images reminiscent of "The Sick Child," she recalls that at a younger age, when she could not find the right word, she would put a drawing in its place, and she regrets losing these manuscripts: "Decorated with insects and butterflies, these manuscripts didn't seem "serious" to me. Now I miss them. Those that remain are less valuable than they were" [Agrémentés d'insectes et de papillons, je trouvais que mes manuscrits ne 'faisaient pas sérieux'. Je les regrette. Ceux qui survivent ne les valent pas] (119; Le Vay trans. 150–51).

Continuing her determination to reinvent the language, or an alternative alphabet for her writing in a tradition faithful to her mother Sido, she invents a sign system in the form of her embroidery (143; Le Vay trans. 180), which she now claims is of equal importance as the letters of the written alphabet. This assertion also reflects Colette's uneasy relationship to the masculine profession of writing as sacralized by the intellectual establishment and the scholarly canon, and her lifelong refusal to see writing as anything but a form of work like the music hall, the cosmetics business in which she was briefly involved, or the everyday tasks ordinarily accomplished by women. Her need to reserve for herself the pleasure of sensual possession through writing, and the imperfectly resolved conflict between this pleasure and the need to renounce, are expressed in the closing lines of the book: "On a resonant road the trotting of two horses harnessed as a pair harmonizes, then falls out of rhythm to harmonize anew. Guided by the same hand, pen and needle, the habit of work and the commonsense desire to bring it to an end become friends, separate, come together again . . . Try to travel as a team, slow chargers of mine: I can see from here the end of the road" [Sur une route sonore s'accorde, puis se désaccorde pour s'accorder encore, le trot de deux chevaux attelés en paire. Guidées par la même main, plume et aiguille, habitude de travail et sage envie d'y mettre fin lient amitié, se séparent, se réconcilient . . . Mes lents coursiers, tâchez à aller de compagnie: je vois d'ici le bout de la route] (143–44; Le Vay trans. 181).

But for the moment she allows herself to continue to write. *The Blue Lantern* will end with a final acceptance of her writing as a necessary part of her identity, "for I can feel stirring within me . . . an insurrection of the spirit which in the course of my long life I have often rejected, later outwitted, only to accept it in the end, for writing leads only to writing . . . To be continued . . . " [en moi bouge . . . une insurrection qu'au cours de ma longue vie j'ai plusieurs fois niée, puis déjouée, finalement accep-tée, car écrire ne conduit qu'à écrire . . . A suivre . . .] (Colette 161; Senhouse trans. 156). She no longer seems to feel a need to impose an end to writing or to the enjoyment of the world which it allows. Now that in *The Evening Star* she is free of the arbitrary conventions of fiction, she seeks above all to record the immediate sensation, the fleeting impres-sion. Her attention to the sensory impression of the moment reveals the importance of the present in her work, which is an essential element in successful aging: "Everything alters the moment I take my eyes off of it. . . . The life of a virtually immobilized being is a vortex of hurry and variety" [Tout change si je détourne un moment les yeux. . . . La vie d'un étre à peu près immobile est un tourbillon de hâte et de variété] (141; Le Vay trans. 178). Thus, despite her new preoccupation with the past, and although her life in the present is a highly personal one with little con-nection to the public world, a balance and a harmony subsist; it is only in these conditions in which the present is also an unending source of sen-sory pleasure that the past can truly be a source of joy to the aged.

In these last two works, *The Blue Lantern* and *The Evening Star,* the vast reserve of Colette's memories is called up by an association in the present. To remember is to reexperience, with all the immediacy of the present. Her memories pierce her: "The husk is beginning to split and through this cleavage can be seen the gleam of the three light mahogany fruits. By a trick of my particularly tenacious memory . . . all I have to do is clamber up as far as the solid wall of leaves to reach the neighboring pines. . . . Just let me go there, I shall not lose myself. Shut the door of my bedroom. I need nobody to guide me on my walk. All that I needed were these three chestnuts. . . . Au revoir, au revoir. I may be a little late for dinner" [La bogue s'entrebaille, les trois fruits d'acajou clair luisent dans la fente. J'empoigne, de ma mémoire crochue . . . je n'ai plus qu'à re-monter jusqu'au feuillage solide, gagner le voisinage de pins. . . . Laissez-moi aller, je ne me perdrai pas. Fermez la porte de ma chambre. Je n'ai besoin de personne pour guider ma promenade. Je n'avais besoin que de ces trois châtaignes. . . . Au revoir, au revoir. Je serai peut-être un peu en retard pour le dîner] (*Blue Lantern* 81; Senhouse trans. 79–80).

The meandering, free-associating style of these works is also explained by Colette's relief at being freed from the exigencies of deadlines and hurry. In *The Blue Lantern,* she says: "On my outings I drive along at the leisurely pace of a lady of the Second Empire. . . . There is always so much to look at when one travels slowly" [En voiture, je vais d'un petit train de dame du second Empire. . . . C'est qu'il y a tant à regarder, quand on chemine lentement] (29; Senhouse trans. 30). The project of capturing the moment, of giving duration to the instant, reveals the corollary project of mastering time, of creating a leisurely pace in both her and the reader's experience of her text. She expands the moment of observation, amusing herself by saturating her text with concrete details and metaphors that call attention to themselves and finally lend to her descriptions of ordinary things an air of discovery: "The moon enters my room at will, advances at a cat's pace, extends a white claw to attack my bed . . . she at once loses heart and climbs down again. At the time when she is full I rediscover her at dawn, all pale and bare, straying in a chill region of the sky. Returning to its slumbers, the last bat slashes her with a zigzag stroke" [La lune entre chez moi comme elle veut, avance à pas de chat, étire une griffe blanche à l'assaut de mon lit . . . elle se décourage tout de suite et redescend. Vers le moment de son plein, je la retrouve, à l'aube, toute nue et pâle, fourvoyée dans une froide région du ciel. En rentrant se coucher, la dernière chauve-souris, d'un trait zigzagant, la biffe] (69; Senhouse 84).

Because it made possible—even necessary—her leisurely contemplation of the world, Colette can say that her enforced immobility actually served her insatiable need for active contemplation. Although she suffers and resents the pain, and on occasion complains, she can also say: "We do well to adapt misfortune to our requirements and even to our convenience. This is a mode of exploitation to which the young and robust are ill-suited, and I can well appreciate, for example, that . . . near-immobility is a gift" [Mieux est de façonner le mal à notre usage, et même à notre commodité. C'est une manière d'exploitation à laquelle les jeunes, les robustes sont malhabiles, et je conçois bien que . . . la quasi-immobilité est un cadeau] (11; Senhouse trans. 7–8). One is reminded here of Betty Friedan's comment that research on aging has rarely looked at the question of coping with extreme stress in old age from the point of view of the positive characteristics that may emerge from the struggle (126). At the same time, Colette also provides an example of strong aging in that she "realistically monitored [her] own aging. [She] became aware of other changes in (herself) that could override decline" (Friedan 83). Always a lover of paradox, Colette seems to have appreciated the fact that as a bedridden, aged woman, once a great traveler and physically active, she is not to be pitied. Her bed is metaphorically figured as a boat or a raft throughout *The Evening Star,* and she travels when other people travel to see her. It is interesting to contrast this continuing engagement with the world despite her illness with her fictional portraits of ailing characters, almost all of whom are male.

She takes this spirit of contradiction even further, engaging in a sort of constructive denial of certain aspects of her existence. Rather than thinking about her friends' deaths, she remembers the way they were when they were with her (*Blue Lantern* 9; Senhouse trans. 11). She refuses to dwell on her leg and its misery. Another defensive process of the same kind is her acceptance and even enjoyment of her illusions, or her failure to understand the rapidly changing modern world: "For anyone not able to dawdle along a pavement and indulge the fortuitous whims and luck of the stroller, there remain only the superficial sights. . . . Illusions crowd thick upon me. What I take to be a hedging implement, can it really be the latest implement for making coffee" [A qui ne peut flâner sur un trottoir, se fier à des chances et des caprices de piéton, il n'est que des vues superficielles. . . . Les illusions accourent. Mais non, ceci n'est pas une tondeuse à haies, c'est le nouvel ustensile qui fait le café tout seul] (15–16; Senhouse trans. 17–18). Again, she turns her infirmity to advantage in a paradoxical reversal.

Her willed evasion into her past, as in the "journey" described above, is another such mechanism, but Colette will not escape into madness, as the poet Hélène Picard did at the end of her life. *The Evening Star* contains a series of portraits of women artists, mostly writers, who have aged. Some have suffered physical and/or mental infirmity; some have died. The portrait of Hélène Picard is also a lesson, or an exercise in preparing for the end, much in the way that "Sido's" letters were meant to prepare her for the end in *Break of Day.* It is also a meditation, which Colette applies to her own life, on the multiple connections between love and art in a woman artist's life. Picard too had separated from her husband, and like Colette had the earthy knowledge and skills of provincial women. Picard is described as physically still beautiful at fifty and child-like until her death. But mental and physical illness overtake and destroy her, causing a flight into paranoia and immobilizing her towards the end. Picard's best work, according to Colette, was her piece "For a Naughty Boy"("Pour un mauvais garçon"), supposedly about the delights and pain of somewhat illicit love and desire. But Colette makes it very clear that the essential pleasure for Picard was of the imagination: her superiority consisted in having avoided the lived reality or, unlike most women, in having salvaged something from the experience of love: "Poetry alone possesses, seizes, lets fall, distributes to its eternal champions that which human love scatters so parsimoniously among its creatures" [La Poésie seule possède, prend, laisse, distribue, à ses tenants éternels, ce que par-cimonieux l'amour humain émiette entre ses créatures] (*Evening Star* 79; Le Vay trans. 97–98). As for her immobilization and the sad lesson to be derived from it, Picard bit by bit went mad as she was deprived of the sensory contact with the world that she had loved. It is impossible not to see Colette herself in this description of an immobilized woman in search of colorful objects to describe, and Colette did practice a form of willed evasion into her imagination, but she knows the limits, and her escape remains within the bounds of her art.

At the end of her life, Colette not only accepts her sensuality but actually cultivates and exploits it to distract her from her pain. In the late afternoon, a jeweler comes to her by appointment so that she may delight in the display of his creations and treasures. There are pages of descrip-tions in *The Blue Lantern* of dazzling colors. The effect of this visual pleasure on her is complex and essential to her well-being: "My friend and neighbor, the jeweler, assures me that the contemplation of precious stones brings relief to arthritic pains, that the majority of the gems snatched from the bowels of the earth are of beneficent effect" [Mon voisin et ami l'orfèvre assure que la contemplation des joyaux constitue un traitement de la douleur arthritique, que la plupart des gemmes arrachées aux abîmes demeurent bénéfiques] (152; Le Vay trans. 147). But the jeweler insists that few stones are truly beautiful. It is a mistake, he declares, to try to include the semiprecious. They aren't genuine and can only disappoint us (154; Le Vay 149). Similarly, when enumerating the cats, dogs, and birds that come to visit her, she acknowledges that they are few: "It is a short list, the list of my evening visitors. The Eden permitted us has nothing of a Noah's Ark about it" [Elle est vite close, la liste de mes visiteurs du soir. L'Eden qui nous est permis n'a rien d'une arche de Noé] (159; Le Vay 153).

The list is short, even in Eden, but it is enough. We have only the earthly splendors that we have been given, and Colette counsels herself not to make the mistake of wanting others or of wanting more. Within these limits, she practices the innocent possession of the world that writing paradoxically makes possible even in renunciation. Her example recalls Erik Erikson's hypothesis in *The Life Cycle Completed* on sensuality in old age: "And what final psychosexual state can we suggest for . . . old age? I think it is a generalization of sensual modes that can foster and enrich bodily and mental experience even as part functions weaken and genital energy diminishes" (64). Colette seems to have known such a "generalization" at the end of her life. But even before, her kind of writing had saved her from the fate of Léa or Marco by rescuing her from conventional plot and gender, while opening the way in her old age to a new feminine identity, secure in intimacy and autonomy and rich in sensual enjoyment.

SIMONE DE BEAUVOIR: ON BECOMING A WOMAN

Simone de Beauvoir is perhaps the most interesting example of the women writers who were heirs to a literary and philosophical tradition without women representatives. Women appeared to her as intellectually inferior to men because of the enormous difference in their situations under patriarchy, but this imbalance could and—she hoped—would change when equal opportunities to exercise women's freedom became available to them. In *The Second Sex,* she goes so far as to say that there have been no great women thinkers, writers, or other artists (Beauvoir 663–70; Parshley trans. 306–14). Beauvoir's insistence on the historical absence of women writers is especially puzzling, since her knowledge of English and the ready availability of translations into French would have made the works of George Eliot, Virginia Woolf, Jane Austen, the Brontës, Madame de Staël, and Madame de Lafayette accessible to her. Indeed, *The Mill on the Floss* is invoked in her memoirs as her model of female literary accomplishment from her girlhood on.

Toril Moi's reasoning on this point about Beauvoir's position supports my arguments about the defining power of the canon in French culture and the tacit acceptance of these judgments even by women writers, including Beauvoir: "Where *The Second Sex* in general provides an exhaustive catalogue of patriarchal crimes against women, there is not a single reference to the fact that, more often than not, the reception of women's works has been cruelly sexist and unjustly dismissive. Ironically, this has proved to be no less true for *The Second Sex* itself than for other books by women" (195).

In other words, Beauvoir does not go so far as to challenge the masculine criteria for great works of literature as they were and are still imposed in France. In this respect she is not different from the very few other women of her generation educated beyond the secondary level, even if we cannot help feeling a twinge of disappointment from our vantage point in time and space. Yet we must guard against falling into the same trap of "disregarding the historicity of value judgments" (Moi 195). No one else in France imagined criticizing the works included in the official canon in 1949. And in fact, Beauvoir might not have been a likely candidate for such an enterprise, despite her belief that women would achieve new creative heights as yet impossible even to imagine. Her own identification with the masculine intellectual establishment was even more complete than her unusual status as an *agrégée de philosophie* implied. As a young girl, she was proud when her father said, "Simone has a man's brain; she thinks like a man." (*Memoirs* 121). She did not regret being a woman, but as her biographer Deirdre Bair points out, from an early age "she identified herself with her father, not as a man . . . but as a superior woman, and more deserving to be her father's partner than her mother." (60). This was all the more true when her father withdrew his affection from her as she ceased to be a pretty child and became an ungainly adolescent. It was only intellectually that she could still hope to please him. Later, she would of course learn that to be appealing to a man required more than a simple display of intelligence, but for this young woman destined to become an intellectual, this early refusal of a large part of the conventional feminine role was of paramount importance. As a young, independent woman she was more at home in the company of Sartre and his male friends while the wives and female companions conversed elsewhere. And before conceiving the project of *The Second Sex,* it had apparently never occurred to her to consider the category of gender when assessing her own almost unique experience as a female intellectual and writer.

Yet this contradiction—that a woman who had sought to identify in fundamentally important ways with men and to reject her conventional feminine role was the one to write the essay on women that revealed the absolute contingency of their inferiority under patriarchy—reveals the fact that femininity, or rather a certain idea or construction of femininity, was a central *problem* for Beauvoir. I believe that the working out of this problem in both her texts and her life *also* constituted much of the psychic work of accepting her aging. Torn by conflict over a conventional feminine role complicated by the painful compromises she had to make in her relationship with Sartre, she produced works of fiction throughout her life that suggest that the marriage and motherhood plot for women are unacceptable and even unbearable. It was much harder for her to go beyond this critical stance to imagine alternatives, but I think that as she aged she began to portray at least the possibility of another kind of life.

In this chapter, I will examine *The Mandarins* as a story of arriving at middle age; *The Coming of Age, The Woman Destroyed,* and certain parts of *Memoirs of a Dutiful Daughter, The Prime of Life,* and *The Force of Circumstance* as essentially serving to stave off, but also to work out, the problem of age that she felt was upon her; and finally the text "Misunderstanding in Moscow" [Malentendu à Moscou], published in 1992, *A Very Easy Death* [Une Mort très douce], and the first part of *All Said and Done* [Tout comte fait] as examples of a late style that reflected another way of being a woman. In the writings of her forties and fifties, there are "cure stories," in the form of passages of personal confession that erupt in the midst of her otherwise impersonal memoirs or essays, or the obsessive repetition of certain kinds of female characters and devastating plots. But eventually there is change as well, in her writing as in her life.[1]

In the Beginning and in the End, We Are All Women

Several other critics who have rightly noted the presence of certain problems or themes that are more explicit than femininity per se have associated them with Beauvoir's recurrent fits of depression, which were sometimes almost suicidal. Moi identifies these as the "cluster of Beauvoirian depressive themes: death, anxiety, emotional loneliness, loss of love" (245). Woodward too notes the "terror of death, a preoccupation dating from early childhood," which later became associated in Beauvoir's mind with aging and which explains the revulsion she so obviously felt for a long time towards her own and others' aging (Woodward 92). Woodward intuits that even at an early age, and certainly when she wrote *The Coming of Age* at age sixty-two, old age was in fact a metaphor for other things that obsessed Beauvoir, especially the fear of abandonment by Sartre. Woodward also notes the disgust and exaggerated fear and danger in Beauvoir's accounts of women's experiences of menstruation and childbearing. In *Memoirs of a Dutiful Daughter*, Beauvoir records how disgusted she felt by a number of things: soft, "clammy" foods; the decrepit body of an aged person which also appeared to her to lack "firmness, solidity, and (by a curious extension) identity" (95). Becoming a woman at puberty horrified her, according to these *Memoirs*, because of the instability or changeability in the human body that it implied, and of course menstruation and childbearing also give evidence of bodily changes: "She asserts that this is the condition of women and concludes that relative to the bodies of men, the bodies of women are characterized by weakness, instability, lack of control, and fragility" (196) Sexuality in general was problematic and in particular any bodily change, which carries within it the implication that we shall die; this is of course an easy association to make with aging, especially for a woman, for whom aging might lead to abandonment by a man, a form of death-in-life for Beauvoir.

My own interpretation is that Beauvoir's aversion to change is indeed one of the "cluster" of obsessive themes that haunt her memoirs and fiction, but I would propose a more gender-specific reading of this sampling of Beauvoirian horrors. She inevitably associates change, aging, loss of love, and fear of abandonment with a particular notion of femininity, and it is her extreme discomfort with this idea of womanhood that inspires her fear of change and aging, rather than the other way around. In *The Second Sex*, Beauvoir makes the following surprising statement about all people's feelings about their own bodies: "men and women all feel the shame of their flesh; in its pure *inactive* presence, its *unjustified immanence*, the flesh exists, *under the gaze of the other*, in its absurd contingence" [hommes et femmes connaissent tous la honte de leur chair; dans sa pure présence immobile, son immanence injustifiée, la chair existe sous le regard d'autrui comme l'absurde contingence] (I:425; Parshley trans. 447–48, emphasis mine). The passivity of this flesh, object of another unidentified but more active gaze, seems to be marked as feminine. This, then, is the bodily condition that is a given of human existence. At some deep level we are all women. Yet the male knows salvation from this state: a bit further on, with reference to the phallus, Beauvoir presents the apparent ideal state for the human body in a description antithetical to the former one: "and indeed through erection the flesh becomes activity, potency, the sex organ is no longer an inert object, but, like the hand or face, the imperious expression of a subjectivity" [par l'érection en effet la chair devient activité, puissance, le sexe n'est plus objet inerte mais comme la main ou le visage l'expression impérieuse d'une subjectivité] (I:448; Parshley trans. 425). At this point in her life (Beauvoir was forty-one), as many critics have observed, she obviously valorized a very conventional masculinity and simultaneously revealed the impossibility of accepting even her own concept of femininity for herself. However, by the time of her late work in her sixties and seventies, the notion that somehow a universal human femininity underlies our conventions of gender began to surface more or less consciously in her work, and in this new context free of dichotomization, and consequently of her subservience to Sartre, Beauvoir was better able to accept herself as an aged woman.

In a brilliant article by Elaine Marks entitled "Transgressing the (In)-cont(in)ent Boundaries: The Body in Decline," Marks revises her own earlier work on Beauvoir and her writing about or denial of death. In the light of hostile critical reception by feminists and nonfeminists alike to *Adieu: A Farewell to Sartre*, Marks concludes that *Adieux*, like *A Very Easy Death*, *The Coming of Age*, and certain passages of *All Said and Done*, is a text that "transgresses the (in)cont(in)ent boundaries . . . [and] goes beyond the limits of what is considered legitimate for a woman or a man to write" (187). This transgression involves the concrete, detailed representation of aging and dying, which have traditionally been obliterated in Western literature, including French literature, as femininity has been. Certain feminist readers have missed other truly transgressive aspects of these texts, which are their insistence that a certain aspect of the Real, of "material life and its structuring influences on social life," is *representable* (189). These critics have tended instead to subsume these representations under psychoanalytic interpretations of fear of the pre-Oedipal mother, fear of the female body and the irrational, and as further challenges to marriage and maternity. While such readings are reasonable, they ought not to blind us to the fact that Beauvoir, in openly discussing the incontinent bodies of her mother or of Sartre, is simultaneously making a political move by opening up new territory to literature, in violation of the heretofore tacit agreement, supported by the canonical texts of French literature, that neither mothers nor fathers should be discussed in this way.

Aging and femininity are in fact inextricably intertwined in the Beauvoirian corpus, and what appeared shocking and distasteful in certain depictions of aged bodies (including but not limited to Sartre's incontinence in *Adieu: A Farewell to Sartre*) was in fact the persistent metaphor of *femininity* for *aging*: "The disgust and fear provoked by the female body in Western discourses are related to similar effects provoked by old bodies. . . . Old bodies, in texts by Simone de Beauvoir, are always feminine or feminized bodies" (194). In other words, aging in Beauvoir's works was perceived as scandalous in part because it blurs conventional gender definitions and, in the process, suggests one possible and potentially disturbing redefinition of femininity: "What her writing is up to, and this must be the source of the critics' malaise, is the affirmation that incontinence, like death, is a great equalizer. 'Jean-Paul Sartre' with bed sores and incontinent is not very different from 'Françoise de Beauvoir' with bed sores and incontinent. Between the old man who wets his chair and the old woman who wets her bed, the readers of both sexes who wait their turn . . . must read that, at the end, sexual difference fades and that the body that remains is the unrestrained, uncontrollable body of the old woman" (199).

If I have shocked my readers by plunging into this aspect of Beauvoir's writing about old age without much warning or preparation, perhaps it is all to the good. Those unfamiliar with her work will feel the discomfort that some of these texts produced when they were published, especially the descriptions of Sartre's incontinence in *Adieu,* which were greeted with vociferous outrage by many readers and some critics. Yet, the truly extravagant and more numerous descriptions of decrepitude and loss of function among several aged women friends in *All Said and Done,* published eleven years earlier, had not evoked this response. It seems clear that such discourse became shocking when a man was described, not just because he was a famous figure, but also because it was only then that the equivalence between aging and a certain idea of femininity could become apparent. It is striking that Beauvoir was unable to represent the aging body in this way until she herself aged. The texts Marks cites, which overlap with several I have chosen to examine, are all late works that confront the aging and aged body quite differently from the more anxious works of middle age (*The Mandarins,* for example).

I do not believe that the late treatments of aging—of her mother, her friends, or Sartre—were symptoms of the same anguish as we find even in *The Coming of Age.* I do not think that Beauvoir herself was horrified by her descriptions in the same way as certain readers, but rather that her transgression of what was permissible to write was natural to her and constituted the last phase of a working through of, and coming to terms with, the question of femininity. Simone de Beauvoir had always written in ways that others found excessive, out of control, and transgressive. The uproar that greeted *The Second Sex* as a sexually transgressive work was even greater than the outrage expressed by readers of Sartre's incontinence, and even her English translator complained that she seemed to suffer from "verbal diarrhea."[2] Understanding and accepting her own femininity was an original enterprise for Beauvoir that elicited scandal at every step of the way. Furthermore, I do not think that the dependent, uncontrolled body (which is therefore a body expressing its feminine sexuality) was repugnant to her by the end of her life. Coming to terms with femininity meant understanding it differently in old age, and a good deal of acceptance and compassion finally came to replace the dread and anxiety that dependence, the past as part of the present, and certain other aspects of her earlier concept of femininity had always evoked in her. But it is wise in reading her work to remember that the feminine sexuality that erupts in the form of passive and dependent aged bodies also constitutes a transgression of literary norms, a stepping out of bounds.

A First Notion of Femininity

When a child, as we have seen, Simone identified intellectually with her father. This fact is important to understanding not only the young

Simone's sometimes desperate attempts to differentiate herself from her mother but also what Deirdre Bair characterizes as "a pattern of emotional deprivation so severe that even such a spirited child as she needed the refuge offered by books in order to cope with it" (70). For in addition to the joy she felt when her father praised her intellect, she had this to say about other aspects of their relationship: "I don't remember ever sitting on my father's knee. . . . I don't think he ever embraced me. He never, as far as I can remember, had any physical contact with us at all. . . . He took care of our education, but that was all. . . . One could say there was no human rapport with him. All this was entirely the responsibility of my mother" (Bair 59–60). Beauvoir always recalled the intrusive behavior of her mother in her life and her sister's; as she confided to Bair, "She said she wanted to be my friend, but she treated me like a specimen under a microscope. She probed into everything I did, from reading my books to reading my letters" (95). The young Simone experienced this as oppression. She also had to contend with the atmosphere of mounting tension and hostility that reigned in the Beauvoir apartment after 1919, when her father's poor health and financial impoverishment made it necessary to move to a dreary little dwelling where she had no privacy at all. By the time she entered adolescence she began to plan for a different kind of womanhood from that of her mother and other women relatives. The changes in the family situation and the changes in her pubescent body coincided and convinced her that her life would be a constant struggle to impose her own standards of perfection and permanence when she became a woman.

Yet the fear of physical change, like her fear of aging and death, was actually even more archaic, dating from early childhood, and both can be seen to relate to her mother. She was only three, she recalls at age fifty, when she first feared growing up because it would mean she could no longer be so close to her mother: "'I won't be able to sit on her knee anymore if I go on growing up.' Suddenly the future existed; it would turn me into another being, someone who would still be, and yet no longer seem myself" ["Je ne pourrai plus m'asseoir sur ses genoux." Soudain l'avenir existait; il me changerait en une autre qui dirait moi et ne serait plus moi] (*Memoirs* 7; Kirkup trans. 13). But the desire to merge with her mother, to be like her mother, is not her only feeling; paradoxically, she also fears that physical changes will make her more like her mother.

Hence she is especially fascinated by a fairy tale about "Charlotte," with whom the little Simone identifies, whose body alternately shrinks and swells, not unlike Alice in Wonderland. Again, Beauvoir associates her fear with her mother and with maternity: "I came out of the adventure safe and sound after having been reduced to a *fetus* and then blown up to *matronly* dimensions." [j'émergeais saine et sauve de l'aventure qui m'avait tour à tour réduite en foetus et changée en matrone] (8, emphasis mine; 13). I have long wondered whether such a sense of oppression and terror with respect to her mother and her mother's body is not at the heart of her sometimes questionable generalizations about men's view of women's bodies and death in *The Second Sex:* "From the day of his birth man begins to die: this is the truth incarnated in the mother" [Du jour où il naît, l'homme commence à mourir: c'est la vérité qu'incarne la Mère] (*The Second Sex* 187; Parshley trans. 228).

It is certainly the case that we begin to age as soon as we are born, if not before. But this is not necessarily a frightening thought if we allow that "all modifications in the organism during the course of its existence that are constant and irreversible are not necessarily negative" (Pequinot 104; translation mine). The point is that Beauvoir does not distinguish between maturation and morbid aging, because she is in fact projecting onto the masculine psyche in *The Second Sex* her own metaphor of change and death as femininity, exemplified by the mother. This is even clearer when she claims that man actually sees in woman's body a "reflection" of something else, namely his own mortality, and feels *himself* threatened by the deterioration of *her* flesh [C'est sur le corps de la femme . . . que l'homme éprouve sensiblement la déchéance de la chair] (180–81).

At the end of *She Came to Stay* [L'Invitée], Beauvoir's first novel published in 1941 when she was thirty-three, the female protagonist, Françoise, kills a young woman who has formed a triangular relationship with her and her male companion. This murder has often puzzled Beauvoir's readers because it seems insufficiently motivated by the plot, which is not primarily a story of sexual or Oedipal jealousy but rather one of symbiotic, virtually asexual relations. And there is no precipitating event that would seem to warrant such a violent act. A close reading of the paragraph preceding the actual murder enables Toril Moi to conclude: "Killing Xavière, Françoise attempts to kill a devouring and destructive monster, one that has weighed upon her from the earliest times, a monster that exists outside time and space, dimensionless, endless, omnipresent and forever resting in itself" (117). This language refers to a phantasm of an evil mother, whose immobility and "immanence" ("forever resting in itself") again recall the troubled descriptions of woman's condition in *The Second Sex*. Moi concludes that if the mother figure is thus represented even as the father and his phallic virtues are idealized, it is because the underlying structure is "a curiously ambivalent position, one in which the daughter casts her mother as her evil enemy precisely because she has *not* completed the process of separation from her" (120). This fundamental ambivalence refers back to the three-year-old Simone, who feared she would grow too old to sit in her mother's lap but was at the same time relieved not to be like Charlotte, that is, like her mother.

This was the original "problem" posed by identification with both parents and her ambivalent sense of herself as a girl or a woman. Most readers are familiar with the symbiosis, or "dual unity," in many of Beauvoir's attachments. Her fiction is similarly peopled with female protagonists who have "doubles." After her mother, there were also her nurse, Louise, her younger sister, Hélène, and her best school friend, "Zaza" Mabille. Zaza dies of grief at a young age because of her own mother's tyranny in imposing a prescribed feminine role, including an arranged marriage, and refusing to let Zaza marry the man she loves. Although *Memoirs of a Dutiful Daughter* draws to a triumphant close in other respects as Beauvoir meets Sartre at age twenty, the tragedy of Zaza's death is strategically placed in the final paragraph. The choice of such a dysphoric ending seems to suggest that one member of this pair of doubles had to be somehow portrayed as in error, frightening, or threatening to the other. Simone's reluctance to yield to social pressure to marry is illustrated and reinforced by the account of Zaza's death, which thus becomes a cautionary tale. The same pattern of a "warning" in the form of a "double" occurs in other works: *She Came to Stay, The Mandarins, The Woman Destroyed,* and in her relationship with her mother, with Violette Leduc, and with several of her female students. After her mother's death, in the lasting relationship she formed with Sylvie Le Bon, this profound ambivalence was apparently finally dissipated.

The symbiotic relationship with Sartre was of course different in certain essential ways. Until his death, Beauvoir never stopped believing that they were united as one person. In fact, this had been a decision she made at age twenty-one and then required a lifetime of endeavor to maintain. At the end of *Memoirs of a Dutiful Daughter*, she announces: "When I left him at the beginning of August, I knew he would never go out of my life again" [Quand je le quittais au début d'août, je savais que plus jamais il ne sortirait de ma vie] (345; 482). In the next volume of her memoirs, *The Prime of Life*, further statements about the perfection of their symbiotic union abound: "We were two of a kind, our understanding would endure as long as we did" [Nous étions d'une même espèce et notre entente durerait autant que nous] (28); there was "an identical sign on both our brows" [ces signes jumeaux sur nos fronts] (31–32); "I knew that no harm could ever come to me from him—unless he were to die before I died" [je savais qu'aucun malheur ne me viendrait jamais de lui, à moins qu'il mourût avant moi] (29); she also makes explicit comparisons between her relationships with Sartre and with Zaza (33).

But Sartre was a man who "was not cut out for monogamy" [Sartre n'avait pas la vocation de la monogamie] (28). Beauvoir had to deny much pain and anxiety caused by his sexual and emotional relationships with other women. Her massive psychic work of denial, which lasted most of her life, sought to protect her tremendous investment in Sartre as the "good" half of the split mother object. In order to shelter this mythic relationship from the shattering effects of certain realizations, she was forced to situate it on a primarily intellectual plane, as she had learned to do with her father. She could thus receive his confidences about other women and still believe their couple to be indestructible. She told herself that they existed together somewhere outside the ordinary domain of male-female relations, and although this legend never entirely fit the truth of the situation, it enabled her to construct her existence around the relationship despite fairly frequent bouts of depression. It is difficult not to see in this determination to occupy a special place in Sartre's life from which she could exert influence over him, if only indirectly, a continuation of the long French tradition according to which a woman accepts to be in second place in exchange for certain privileges.

But her own role in this had nevertheless to be most unconventional as a woman. Most of all, she strove to maintain her autonomy, eschewing any form of behavior that could be construed as dependent. After two years of happiness during their initial "pact," she accepted a teaching assignment in Marseilles, rejecting Sartre's offer of marriage. She asserts in *The Prime of Life* that Sartre had no tendency or desire to dominate her, but Moi astutely observes that by this denial, "Beauvoir in fact hopes to dispel any lingering suspicions about *her own* tendencies to alienation, merger, and dependence" (219). It was also essential to her to avoid change, or any of the effects of time in the situation with Sartre and in her life generally, thereby minimizing occasions for loss or abandonment, all of which were regarded by Beauvoir as the "undesirable" aspects of her mother's femininity and of femininity as almost all women knew it. This must have been part of the reason she arranged to live all her life in the Montparnasse district of Paris, where she had been born and where Sartre also lived much of his life. Refusing marriage and/or maternity allowed her to avoid the brutal evidence of the passing of time that children invariably bring. For a long time, she lived in hotels, spending her time with Sartre and friends who were similarly unattached and, as the years went by, increasingly younger than they were. Beauvoir thus made choices about the way she would age and the way she would live as a woman that were inextricably linked. Most striking about all these arrangements during this period is the degree to which she attempted to control her life in every aspect, denying even the minimum, universal need for some dependence and the right to evolve and change.

The Second Sex: An Awakening

Beauvoir quickly and unswervingly adopted Sartre's basic existentialist philosophy as set out in *Being and Nothingness* in 1943. Hence a paradox in her deeply felt intellectual beliefs and the way she lived must have been apparent in some unsettling way: her difficulty in accepting change, which in fact hides an attachment to the past, was in contradiction to the perpetual self-definition and self-renewal required by existentialism. The "transcendence" required of the subject in order to give meaning to his/her life is a permanent state of striving towards a goal, a constant projection of him/herself into the future. Characterized more or less explicitly as masculine and phallic in both *Being and Nothingness* and in Beauvoir's faithful transposition in *The Second Sex*, it is "immanence," or "being in itself," that is simultaneously connotated as feminine and negative in these works. The latter includes absence of a project, passivity, fixation on maintaining the status quo, unwillingness to accept the past as past, and hence refusal to acknowledge change.

It is not my intention to review here the sexist blind spots in Sartre's philosophy.[3] Nor do I have room to examine all the ways in which *The Second Sex* incorporates Beauvoir's remaining ambivalence towards femininity and her well-documented valorization, usually expressed on the level of metaphor, of masculinity. But I believe that writing *The Second Sex* was a decisive moment in both her personal and literary development with respect to *aging,* in that by writing about femininity as a human condition to be constructed and reconstructed throughout a woman's life, she opened herself up for the first time to the possibility of accepting change. And with change came the possibility of accepting aging and other kinds of relationships from the one she had with Sartre, which was sometimes stultifying for her because it not only caused her anxiety and pain but also kept her in second place. What Beauvoir perceived as impending old age—which she described as horrifying, reiterating that "in the old woman re-emerges the disquieting figure of the mother" [En elles se retrouve la figure inquiétante de la Mère] (181; Parshley trans. 220)— nevertheless now became, like other bodily states, "a field of interpretive possibilities" (Butler 45). These realizations served to fix the thematics of most of the rest of the fiction she would write.

When she wrote *The Second Sex* in 1949, Beauvoir was forty-one and had already had a passionate love affair with the American writer Nelson Algren. Although she does not say so in her memoirs, this relationship, quite different from what she had known with Sartre or other men, must have had a profound impact on her understanding of feminine sexuality. There is much evidence for this conclusion in the character Anne of *The Mandarins,* as we shall see. In any case, Beauvoir had reached what was for her the crucial age of forty, and aging became a primary theme in both her autobiographical and fictional works. From this point forward, certain women who revealed themselves to be inflexible, resistant to change, or unwilling to accept that time passes are characterized (and sometimes caricatured) as old. Thus Beauvoir engaged at this point with a personal problem that had its origin in her particular fears about femininity and that would have precluded the emergence of her late style if it had not been addressed. At the same time, however, the issue of dependence remained to be dealt with later, and she was only as yet able to set the stage in *The Second Sex* for the resolution of her feelings about the aging body.

The Second Sex also marked a first move in the direction of an identity separate from Sartre's, for although she unfailingly subscribes to his existentialist ideas, in writing about women she appropriated a totally unexplored territory in 1949, and by transposing Sartre's ontological concerns into a sociological domain, she effected a subtle shift with respect to his meaning and intention. She simultaneously broke with the traditional French understanding of femininity by denying that the "eternal feminine" or any other fixed essence of femininity exists. She is above all concerned with placing women on an equal footing and in the same social space as men, arguing that in terms of economic, political, and social rights there should be absolute equality between the sexes, rather than any notion of privilege accorded to women. In this way, and only under these circumstances, can the unfair oppression of women by masculine power be ended. We have seen in chapter 1 to what extent this position was a radical one in France, and this view is true even today in certain ways, for if the scandal provoked by *The Second Sex* and various other works has long ago subsided, Simone de Beauvoir is very seldom read or appreciated by the French intellectual establishment.

In a world of more rights and freedom, it may eventually be possible for women to define themselves through their actions in the way that men do, but Beauvoir doesn't claim to know exactly how they will do this. There will be as many feminine identities as there are free consciousnesses. The female body alone cannot determine identity, because while transcendence must be understood as embodied, the female body, like the male, is merely "a field of interpretive possibilities," and "in as much as gender ambiguity can take many forms, gender itself thus promises to proliferate into a multiple phenomenon for which new terms must be found" (Butler 45,47). Beauvoir claims there are no inherently masculine or feminine virtues, only human qualities that different situations have brought to the fore in the two sexes.

For the moment, while calling into question certain aspects of her way of living, she justified others, notably her refusal of marriage and maternity as forms of enslavement. Michèle Sarde points out that here Beauvoir is re-evoking the values and desires expressed by French women under *courtoisie*, for whom love was also ideally dissociated from marriage and for the same reason: erotic love presupposes two autonomous beings joined only by their love (*Regard sur les Françaises* 507). We have seen that Madeleine de Scudéry and Germaine de Staël were also predecessors in this regard. Sarde also reminds us that despite the moralizing, pro-family rhetoric of the nineteenth and twentieth centuries, there is a long tradition in France and French literature, especially in the literature of women, of practicing contraception, employing wet nurses, or simply refusing to participate actively in child rearing. Thus these ideas were not new in France, and one may wonder to what extent Beauvoir had happened upon the same reactions to patriarchal oppression as her predecessors, or to what extent she was influenced by this countertradition, despite the obviously original scope of her thought.

The Mandarins: The Changed World of Middle Age

At the end of World War II, Beauvoir, Sartre, and other French intellectuals had to face the fact that the world and the situation of France would never be the same as in their youth. Their dreams of a return to familiar, prewar conditions quickly proved to be illusory, and Sartre's attempts to form a noncommunist leftist coalition that would simultaneously shelter France from domination by either the United States or the Soviet Union and prevent the Gaullist party from coming to power ended in failure.

The role of the writer and intellectual as socially and political committed, or as socially valuable at all, was seriously debated. Whether or not we read *The Mandarins* (1954) as a roman à clef or, following Beauvoir's warning in *The Force of Circumstances* [La Force des choses] (I:364), refrain from doing so, what seems important and unique about the writing of the postwar period in France is that even more than in other eras following upheavals, it demanded a focus on the *present* and a radical severing with the past.

For Beauvoir, who had played little or no active role in the Resistance, and whose journal and letters to Sartre during the war seem full of strictly personal gossip, this sobering climate provoked a real intellectual coming of age. By 1954, she was forty-six and her experience with Nelson Algren had already brought her sexual fulfillment, pain, and disappointment. Despite the fact that she was engaged in another love affair with

Claude Lanzmann, seventeen years her junior, which again allowed her to experience desire and what she thought of as a physical rejuvenation, the affair with Algren seems to have impressed her deeply with the fear of impending decline. In the milieu in which Beauvoir had been raised, the age of forty was a point of no return for a woman, a beginning of old age (*La Force des choses* II:9). Losing Algren seemed to her then the loss of all erotic possibility; it was a living death:

> I had for the second time buried my memories of Chicago, they no longer wounded me: but what sadness there was in that tranquillity! "That's all, it's over," I said to myself; and I wasn't thinking only of my happiness with Algren. But something inside myself refused to submit to that indifference. "Never again will I sleep in the warmth of another body." Never! What a death knell! When that thought came over me, I felt the approach of death. Nothingness had always terrified me, but until now I had been dying a little day by day without noticing: suddenly, in one blow, a whole piece of myself was disappearing; it was as brutal as a mutilation and inexplicable."

> [J'avais une seconde fois enterré mes souvenirs de Chicago, je ne m'y blessais plus: mais quelle tristesse dans cet apaisement! "Voilà, c'est fini," me disais-je; et je ne pensais pas seulement à mon bonheur avec Algren. Mais quelque chose en moi ne se soumettait pas à cette indifférence. "Plus jamais je ne dormirai dans la chaleur d'un corps." Jamais: quel glas! Quand cette évidence me saisissait, je basculais dans la mort. Le néant m'avait toujours épouvantée; mais jusqu'ici je mourais au jour le jour sans y prendre garde: soudain, d'un coup, tout un grand morceau de moi-même s'engloutissait; c'était brutal comme une mutilation et inexplicable.]

> (*La Force des choses* I:347)

In other words, the political climate of disillusionment and disappointment resonated with Beauvoir's feelings of loss and disappointment in love, and both seemed to be related to the passing of time and advancing age and thus with the loss of her body.[4] *The Mandarins* is a kind of bildungsroman of middle age, which is not exactly a "progress novel" in Gullette's sense or a "decline narrative" either. It was Beauvoir's attempt to come to terms with the chaotic disarray that she and the members of her cohort were feeling, "the multiple and unstable meanings of this changed world in which I awakened in August 1944" [les multiples et tournoyantes significations de ce monde changé dans lequel je m'étais réveillée en août 1944] (*La Force des choses* I:358–59). It is a dialogic novel in which the reader is tempted to take sides among the positions represented by the male characters, who are for the most part journalists and writers. Yet the positions are very complex, and the disarray and uncertainty are honestly presented. On many points, no final position is taken by the text, and to a great extent the "apprenticeship" or *Bildung* is experienced through this disarray, the "multiple and unstable meanings in this changed world."

But apart from the dialogism in the chapters devoted to Henri, Robert, and the other male characters, *The Mandarins* is deeply divided, or double, in another way as well. In between the third-person accounts of Henri, the writer and journalist protagonist, there are an almost equal number of pages devoted to a plot featuring Anne, a woman of Henri's age who is Robert's wife and a psychoanalyst and who writes a journal in the first person. And if the novel leaves certain subjects of debate unsettled among Henri, Robert, and their friends, the plot involving Anne fills the final pages and also remains open-ended as Anne decides, just in time, not to commit suicide. Her existence seems empty, and we watch her leave the room on the last page to begin the as yet unimaginable story of the rest of her life. Through Anne, Beauvoir begins in *The Mandarins* her explicit treatment of the theme of aging in her fiction.

Beauvoir's own perception of Anne's place in the novel is to give her an opportunity to express "a great many things that I wanted to say and that were linked to my condition as a woman" [j'attribuai un des rôles privilégiés à une femme, car un grand nombre des choses que je voulais dire étaient liées à ma condition féminine] (*La Force des choses* I:360). Beauvoir claims that Anne is not herself but resembles her: "It is mostly the negative aspects of my experience that I express through her: the fear of dying and vertigo in the face of nothingness, the vanity of earthly pleasure, feelings of guilt about forgetting, the scandal of living" [Ce sont surtout les aspects négatifs de mon expérience que j'ai exprimés à travers elle: la peur de mourir et le vertige du néant, la vanité du divertissement terrestre, la honte d'oublier, le scandale de vivre] (365). This is the period in which Beauvoir was still denying all identification with what she considered to be certain feminine fates, and Anne is in fact abandoned by her American lover Lewis. Her work as a psychoanalyst also gives her the responsibility to help victims of the war not to forget or repress their memories, but to learn to understand and accept that the past was real and that the present is also real and different. This deliberate remembering of the past *as past* is a first step away from Beauvoir's original existentialist philosophical position of devaluing the past in favor of the future.

It is also possible to read Anne's story with Lewis as in fact not secondary to the main story, that is, the story of Henri, Robert, and their male friends and female lovers. It is true that it is quite different, but I think there is considerable evidence that Anne and Henri, who share the role of narrator, are in fact doubles in many ways. Of Henri as character, Beauvoir says: "The joy of existing, the joy of trying out new ideas, the pleasure of writing, I gave these to Henri. He resembles me at least as much as Anne, and maybe more" [La joie d'exister, la gaité d'entreprendre, le plaisir d'écrire, j'en ai doté à Henri. Il me ressemble autant qu'Anne au moins, et peut-être davantage] (*La Force des choses* I:365). Yet the heights of joy experienced in the novel are certainly Anne's, and—more important—it is Anne's first-person journal that we are actually given to read. Even if she is not interested in publication, she is an authoritative voice to us as readers. The two narrators together give us the perspectives of the public world of action and the private world of reflection and passion. Anne and Henri give us a male and a female experience of aging, as Beauvoir believed these to be at this point in her life.[5] Later, in "Misunderstanding in Moscow," she will again use the technique of interspersing female and male accounts, but without the rigid demarcation of chapter divisions, so that the characters seem to merge at certain moments. Still later, in *All Said and Done*, she will incorporate fragments of both this man's and this woman's accounts into a single narrative, which she will claim as her own. In *The Mandarins*, this process of experimenting with a position beyond fixed gender begins (the narrator is both Henri and Anne and yet neither one exactly), although the characters remain separate and, according to literary convention, Henri's plot remains the official one.

The thousand-page novel opens with a New Year's party to celebrate the arrival of 1944 and the anticipated end of the war. Henri sees only the future and the promise of a new freedom and identity. Paule, with whom he has lived for ten years, wants only to cling to the relationship they have had although it is clearly over. In fact, Paule is literally defined by three characteristics of the feminine and the old as we have seen them in Beauvoir's early works: she is totally dependent on Henri, totally unable to accept change and the past *as past,* and completely unwilling to project herself into the future by resuming her abandoned career as a singer. The alienated portrait of Paule as mired in immanence and aging physically as the novel unfolds is a cruel one, as rendered by Anne's terrified gaze. Paule's physical demise translates her loss of all reality when Henri finally leaves her, but in fact she has been pretending for so long that the line between her normal state and her insanity is difficult to trace. (In French, the term *aliéné* can denote either a state of alienation from oneself in the philosophical sense often used by existentialists, or else a state of insanity.)

At the same point early in the novel, both Henri and Anne come to the realization that they have arrived at middle age. On vacation in Portugal with Anne and Robert's daughter Nadine, Henri wonders why he can no longer find the simple happiness and pleasure in his private life that he had known before the war (*Mandarins* I:154). A bit later, wrestling with a novel that he had mistakenly attempted to set in the prewar period, he notices how he has changed: "But now, he had to admit to himself that he was a mature man whose career was made: young people treated him as older, adults as one of their own, and some of them even held him in high esteem. Arrived, limited, finished, himself and no one else: who?" [Mais maintenant, il lui fallait s'avouer qu'il était un homme fait: les jeunes gens le traitaient en aîné, les adultes comme un des leurs, et certains lui témoignaient même de la considération. Fait, limité, fini, lui et pas un autre: qui?] (I:226).

Anne's first awareness takes a different form; predictably, it comes to her through her body. She has been to bed with the Russian dissident Scriassine, who approached her as she sat considering her own leg at the New Year's party, thinking that "soon it would be buried without ever having lived" [un jour elle serait enterrée sans avoir jamais existé] (I:49). Their sexual experience has turned out badly. Looking at herself in the mirror afterwards, she considers that now, at age thirty-nine, it is already too late for her to have certain experiences of sensory pleasure: "It was too late. And suddenly, I understood why my own past sometimes seemed to belong to someone else, it was because now *I* was someone else: a woman of thirty-nine, a woman of a certain age!" [C'était trop tard. Et soudain j'ai compris pourquoi mon passé me semble parfois celui d'une autre; c'est à présent que je suis une autre: une femme de trente-neuf ans, une femme qui a un âge!] (I:126). In the paragraph that closes this chapter, Anne already imagines herself as old, her hair turned white, decrepit. Like Henri, she does not know how to proceed, how to live, but unlike him, she feels that her life is or will soon be over.

Yet Anne in many respects has lived an exemplary life from the point of view of Beauvoir's ideology as expressed in *The Second Sex* and elsewhere. She has a demanding career, although she doesn't talk very much about it, and her intellectual independence is important in her relations with her husband and other men. When she feels "already dead," as though she already belonged to the past, she is wrenched from this ironically comfortable position by the needs of her patients in the present. Her lucidity about the past and the present also enables her to help Paule and later to recover from the searing pain of her own loss of love. Anne is married to Robert Dubreuil, who is twenty years older and had been her professor. He remains a mentor figure to her after all their years of marriage. Indeed, there is something almost Godlike about him in the novel as a whole: "Thanks to Robert," says Anne in recounting her personal history, "ideas came back down to earth and the earth became as coherent as a book" [Grâce à Robert, les idées sont descendues sur terre et la terre est devenue cohérente comme un livre] (*Mandarins* I:72). There is no more physical desire between them, but they are welded together by a symbiotic union that is worth even more in her eyes.

Despite the originality and solidity of this plot for her life, Anne cannot rid herself of a malaise that settles in after the war. Robert, always surrounded by young people, is resolutely turned towards the future, reminding us that age, like gender, is not a simple function of the body, but rather of the body as a *situation* from which certain choices are made. And this situation is easier for men than for women, at least in postwar Paris. By the end of the novel, however, Anne's subversive pessimism and subplot seem to gain credibility after Robert is disillusioned by the revelation of the Goulag and the discrediting of the idealized Soviet state. Nadine is incapable of showing affection to her mother, and the problem is reciprocal. Finally, we are forced to realize that, despite the network of friendships that surround her and the dependence of her patients upon her, Anne is lonely, and this feeling is in large part what causes her terror of aging. Robert will surely die before her, and even Nadine had lost her young lover to death. Anne experiences this pain through the body, in her growing awareness of its aging, just as Nadine attempted to console herself by means of her body by sleeping with many men after her loss.

Henri's capacity to realize his erotic potential and even to start a new family at the end of the novel stands in contrast to Anne's sense that all is over for her. Henri is hardly even conscious of his physical aging. On the only occasion when he does feel that he has gotten somewhat rusty or out of shape he is on a bike trip with Robert and Anne. But he quickly overcomes his problem: "but once the first stiffness had gone, Henri was thoroughly glad to have recovered his excellent body; he had forgotten how efficient a body can be" [mais passé les premières courbatures, Henri se sentit tout heureux d'avoir récupéré un si bon instrument; il avait oublié combien ça peut être efficace, un corps] (I:363). His coming to terms with the past and the present occurs through the medium of his writing. Like a number of the other characters, he is tormented by the question of the value of literature in a world requiring collective action. After rejecting his initial project to write a novel set in prewar France, he writes a play focusing on the importance of *remembering* the horrors of the war, but as *past* events within the present. He then goes on to the novel on postwar France, which we never actually see but which appears to be a *mise-en-abyme* of *The Mandarins* itself, and Beauvoir's commentary on her own move in writing about the harsh necessity of existing in the present in this changed and changing world (I:426).

Henri's novel is also about his rancor towards Paule, who represents the dangers of stagnation and the inability to accept change. Anne's loneliness is punctuated by disturbing visits to Paule's apartment. These two are also doubles, though this only becomes apparent after Anne has been to America, fallen passionately in love, and returned for a while to France. By this time, Henri has moved out of Paule's apartment. In fact, the text is clear on the point that all men inevitably cease to desire a woman after a certain time: it is simply their nature. This happens first to Paule, then to Anne; it has already happened to the young Nadine through death, and Anne expects it to happen to her again with Robert's death. But

Paule is the dark fate of the aging woman who lacks Anne's lucidity, her ability to narrate her own story and hence to participate in an aspect of masculinity (Paule's attempts to write all end in failure), and her ability to face the harshest truths without "dying" (Paule is no longer the same person after her cure, which is effected at the cost of *obliterating* her memories of Henri and lying to herself about him).

Our perception of Paule's breakdown is entirely filtered through Anne, who is a reliable witness in that she is a psychoanalyst but whose descriptions change dramatically in the second volume. By this time, Anne has been to America after long hesitation about disturbing "her quiet little existence of a woman already dead" [ma sage petite vie de morte] (I:288), and there she has met and fallen in love with the writer Lewis Brogan. With Lewis she knows real passion and her body is returned to her, reborn, transfigured by Lewis's desire (II:37–39). She catches sight of herself and Lewis in a mirror and has to remind herself, with a foretaste of the anguish to come, that they will never be able to live as a couple. She is a mature woman, with work and important allegiances in France. Upon her return to Paris, she suffers from the separation, using the same phrase that Beauvoir will use in the dedication to *Adieu: A Farewell to Sartre:* "From him to me, no communication existed." [Non, de lui à moi il n'existait aucun passage] (II:76).

Paule's psychic decompensation, which ends with her hospitalization and cure, is strategically placed at this point in the narrative. Beauvoir offers one of her most obsessive, cruelly detailed descriptions of a suffering and aging woman; nowhere is the equivalence between a certain kind of femininity and aging made more explicit. True to her commitment to describe aging "without indulgence" (*Coming of Age* 172), even if her readers find her shocking, Beauvoir here maintains the same rigorous (some would say pitiless) gaze on the phenomenon of aging that she so admires in the work of Montaigne. In a rare moment of personal confession in *The Coming of Age,* she identifies strongly with Montaigne, saying that he is one of the few writers to have escaped the destructive effects of senescence: "On the basis of his own experience, he questioned himself about old age as though no one before him had ever spoken about it; this is the secret of his profundity: the direct and exacting gaze that he brought to bear on a reality that others generally seek to mask" [D'après sa propre expérience, il s'est interrogé sur la vieillesse comme si personne avant lui n'en avait parlé; c'est là le secret de sa profondeur: le regard direct et exigeant qu'il dirige sur une réalité qu'on s'efforce généralement de masquer] (170).

I emphasize these kinds of descriptions in *The Mandarins* because they are as painful for many women readers as the much discussed descriptions of incontinence in Beauvoir's work. Thus Anne's first new view of Paule, who has begun her flight from reality, includes and even depends on her perception of Paule's loss of beauty:

> She was looking at herself in a hostile way and suddenly, for the first time in many years, I too saw her with new eyes; she looked tired, her cheeks were purplish, and her chin looked more solid; the two deep lines that surrounded her mouth showed up the virility of her features. Formerly, Paule's creamy complexion, her velvety eyes, her shining black hair all softened her beauty: without this ordinary attractiveness, her face became bizarre. Instead of inscribing itself imperceptibly, time had dealt a brutal blow to this noble and baroque mask, which still deserved to be admired but which belonged rather in a museum than in a drawing room.

> [Elle se regardait d'un air hostile et soudain, pour la première fois depuis bien des années, je la vis moi aussi avec des yeux étrangers; elle avait l'air fatiguée; ses pommettes avaient pris une nuance violacée, et le menton s'empâtait; les deux entailles profondes qui cernaient sa bouche accusaient la virilité de ses traits. Naguère, le teint crémeux de Paule, son regard voulouté, le noir éclat de ses cheveux adoucissaient sa beauté: privé de ce banal attrait, son visage devenait insolite. Au lieu de s'y inscrire sournoisement, le temps marquait d'un signe brutal ce masque noble et baroque qui méritait encore l'admiration, mais qui aurait été à sa place dans un musée plutôt que dans un salon.] (*Mandarins* II:78–79)

A few pages further on, Anne accompanies Paule to a reception where Henri's new young lover makes a dramatic entrance in her almost unearthly beauty. Anne is herself moved by the injustice of life towards women, despite her lucidity about Paule's errors.

Paule's chimeric view of reality disintegrates into paranoia. The second time Anne goes to visit, and during her succeeding visits, the long description of Paule's physical decline proceeds rapidly: she gains weight, her face turns blotchy and red; later her nose will swell (II:193), and finally she will destroy all her clothing, saying, "Now I am even imitating myself!" [Maintenant je me singe moi-même!] (II:218). The page preceding Anne's second visit is filled with a journal entry about the effects of her own aging on the long-distance love affair she is still having with Lewis. She is suffering above all because her awareness of her aging is acute and growing, largely because of Paule. When Paule finally allows Anne to arrange for her hospitalization, she has begun to see that Paule is not alone in her decline, which is simply more rapid and dramatic than other people's. As Paule leaves for the clinic, Anne takes a bottle of poison from Paule's bathroom and puts it in her own purse. Her recognition of her double is complete, though in fact there are differences, as she will discover.

Later in the novel, Anne presciently realizes that the end of her affair with Lewis, overdetermined by the text, is at hand. After yielding after all to a temptation to buy new clothes and perfume so as to appear younger and more desirable, she flies again to Chicago, where she is to spend the summer with Lewis. What follows in chapter 10 is the description of a summer spent in the company of a man who no longer loves her—and whom she still loves. Nowhere else in Beauvoir's corpus is there such a thorough and moving exploration of what was after all one of her principal themes, her fear of abandonment. The terms of Anne's suffering are set by her gender and her age, as we understand by now. With all her frankness and lucidity, she struggles against the engulfing depression and sense of unreality that threaten to destroy her. There is something primal in her inability even to comprehend that Lewis has withdrawn his love from her, perhaps because it had given her back the feminine identity usually conferred by life's earliest relationships and that she had felt she was losing. Anne suffers as Paule did, but Anne is not Paule. She fights valiantly, attempting to enlist all her other loves, especially that of the world itself, saying: "We always imagine it is love that gives to the world all its brilliance, but it is also true that the world fills love with its riches. Love was dead and the earth was still here, intact, with its secret songs, its odors, its love. I felt moved as a convalescent who discovers that during his delirium the sun hadn't been extinguished" [On croit que c'est l'amour qui donne au monde tout son éclat: mais aussi le monde gonfle l'amour de toutes ses richesses. L'amour était mort et voilà que la terre était encore là, intacte, avec ses chants secrets, ses odeurs, sa tendresse. Je me sentais émue comme le convalescent qui découvre que pendant ses fièvres le soleil ne s'est pas éteint] (II:419).

Anne has in fact not committed the "errors of femininity" of dependency and rigidity that Paule committed. She has lived her own life and projected herself into useful activity in the world. But when she returns to Paris this time, Henri notices that she looks much older (II:447). Unlike Paule, she refuses to forget Lewis, though she accepts the past *as past*. There is unquestionably a great deal of ambiguity in this portrait of an aging woman. It is as though Beauvoir were for the first time questioning the validity of her own interpretation of gender roles in relation to aging. Most important to the novel as a whole is the question of the role of the past in one's life and the ability to change. The characters here do not actually succeed in integrating the past into the present—that remains for later works—but the process begins with the harsh though necessary coming to terms with one's personal past imposed by the events of the war on some, by disappointment in love on others.

Also important to a reconsideration of gender roles is that Anne comes to the perfectly realistic realization that Robert doesn't really need her; Nadine, who has now married Henri and has a baby daughter, similarly has no need of her: her solitude is real and it weighs depressingly on her as she ages. There is a way in which her longing for connection, even for a degree of dependence, seems to have been justified by the narrative, and these are Anne's own conscious discoveries about herself as she ages. Is Beauvoir glimpsing for the first time a legitimate need for greater dependence? In any event, Anne neglects her infant granddaughter long enough to find Paule's vial of poison and very nearly swallows it. She is prevented from doing so by Nadine's angry remonstrances, but I think that in any case this highly unconventional plot could hardly have been closed in such a conventional, canonical way. Several aging Beavoirian heroines who are less lucid than Anne also desire suicide, but not one of them commits it. Instead, their stories have open endings as does *The Mandarins:* Anne gets up and walks through the door into the life of a woman in her forties. It appears that she, like the intellectuals who give the novel its name, will be able to master the greater and more numerous adaptations required by the "changed world" of the second half of the twentieth century.

As Anne comes to the end of the traditional plot for a woman's life, in lived reality or as defined by French literary history, it would be a mistake to underestimate the importance Beauvoir grants to eroticism in this passage from youth to age. It is not that she adopts the position that older women are sexless or that they are sexually voracious or any of the other familiar stereotypes. In *The Coming of Age* she notes that there appears to be no disappearance of libido in the aging female, as there is in the male, but that the cessation of sexual activity is due rather to masculine perception of her as no longer desirable, or to the effects of her own wounded narcissism (371). Even more important than these notations of woman's thwarted sexual destiny in the narrow sense is the penetrating observation in *The Coming of Age* of the true role of eroticism in all human life. Because it conditioned much of Beauvoir's late writing about women and her attempt to forge a new story for them, I quote it in full:

"Only after a long and complex evolution in the child does the sexual drive become organized genitally. At that point it seems to assume the fixedness and permanence of an instinct" (J. Laplanche and J.-B. Pontalis, *Vocabulaire de la Psychanalyse*). It immediately follows that an individual whose genital functioning has diminished or disappeared is not for this reason "unsexed": he or she remains a sexual being—even the eunuch or the impotent man remain sexual—who simply has to live out his/her sexuality despite certain physical changes. [Sexuality] only disappears with death. Sexuality is much more than simply a group of reflexes that give rise to a configuration of sensations and images. It is an *intentionality* experienced by the body, directed at other bodies that espouses the general flow of a person's existence. It is invested in the world, to which it lends an erotic dimension.

["Ce n'est qu'au terme d'une évolution complexe et aléatoire que la pulsation sexuelle s'organise sous le primat de la génitalité et retrouve alors la fixité et la finalités apparentes de l'instinct" (J. Laplanche and J.-B. Pontalis, *Vocabulaire de la Psychanalyse*). On peut immédiatement en conclure qu'un individu dont les fonctions génitales sont diminuées ou disparues n'est pas pour autant asexué: c'est un individu sexué—même l'eunuque et l'impuissant le demeurent—qui a à réaliser sa sexualité en dépit d'une certaine mutilation. [La sexualité] ne disparaît qu'avec la mort. C'est qu'elle est tout autre chose qu'un ensemble de réflexes engendrant une mosaïque de sensations et d'images. C'est une intentionnalité vécue par le corps, visant d'autres corps et qui épouse le mouvement général de l'existence. Elle s'investit dans le monde auquel elle confère une dimension érotique.] (*The Coming of Age* 337)

Thus we live our sexuality to the end of our lives. We also need to maintain physical contact with others if at all possible. Anne's demoralization at the end of *The Mandarins* stems from her simultaneous recognition of this need and the apparent impossibility of satisfying it, perhaps because of her wounded narcissism. But it is not only her body that suffers; the quotation above shows precisely that there is no possible separation between the moral and the sexual domains.

In fact, Beauvoir's autobiographical discourse in the epilogue to *The Force of Circumstances,* though written nine years later, when she was fifty-five, echoes many of the feelings expressed by Anne in the last chapter of *The Mandarins*. Beauvoir begins this text, which she believes will be the closing sequence in the series of autobiographical works begun five years earlier with *Memoirs of a Dutiful Daughter,* with a tribute to the one incontestable success of her life: her relationship with Sartre (*La Force des chose* II:489) On that page alone, the word *twinship* appears, *same* appears four times, *identical* once, and so forth. She quickly defends herself against possible accusations that she did nothing but follow Sartre: he led the way, but she followed because she was genuinely interested in doing so (491). She also confidently defends herself against the various grotesque images of herself that are in circulation. She has written her *Memoirs* in order to correct these and—she does not balk at the word—to make herself loved (496).

But after this strong, even euphoric beginning, she sinks into uncertainty and despair about the future, and it is on this note that she closes the book. We cannot help thinking of *The Mandarins* when we read: "The most important, irreparable thing that has happened to me since 1944 is that . . . I have aged" [Ce qui m'est arrivé de plus important, de plus irréparable depuis 1944, c'est que . . . j'ai vieilli] (*La Force des choses* II: 501) It seems to be the *world* that has changed, dwindled, grown smaller, lost its capacity to astonish, console. "To grow old is to be defined and reduced" [Vieillir c'est se définir et se réduire] (503). Memories have no real capacity to evoke the past and, besides, they are fading. Most of all, her body is old and strange to her. She describes her face in the mirror in the same cold terms she used for Paule and for others: "I loathe my appearance now: the eyebrows slipping down towards the eyes, the bags underneath, the excessive fullness of the cheeks, and that air of sadness around the mouth that wrinkles always bring" [Je déteste mon image: au-dessus des yeux, la casquette, les poches en-dessous, la face trop pleine, et cet air de tristesse autour de la bouche que donnent les rides] (506). A paroxysm of regret brings the essay to an end: "The moment has come to say: 'never again!' . . . never again a man. Now, my imagination as well as my body has come to terms with this. Yet it's strange not to be a body any more . . . what breaks my heart, much more than these deprivations, is to find within myself no new desires . . . if this silence is to last, how long my brief future will seem!" [Oui, le moment est venu de dire: jamais plus! . . . jamais plus un homme. Maintenant, autant que mon corps mon imagination en a pris son parti. Malgré tout, c'est étrange de n'être plus un corps . . . ce qui me navre, bien plus que ces privations, c'est de ne plus rencontrer en moi de désirs neufs . . . si ce silence doit durer, qu'il semble long, mon bref avenir!] (657).

Whether because all women in France had lived with the unspoken assumption that their eroticism and hence their life ended well before they died, and/or because, as Beauvoir perceives, sexuality and the possibility of deriving pleasure from any aspect of one's existence are inseparable, she is like Anne in these pages, in that the future has yet to be imagined. For the moment, she has the impression of having been "swindled," and of course this closing word elicited a great deal of commentary at the time, mostly from those who speculated that Beauvoir felt swindled by Sartre. Beauvoir always denied this interpretation, and it is obviously the case that many other aspects of her existence as a woman also went into the formulation of this epilogue and its closure. What seems indisputable is that an end to her depression and despair, the final chapters of her life story, would have to come from sources other than Sartre.

The Coming of Age

Anne is a first step, to be followed by several other experiments with ambiguous outcomes in the stories of *The Woman Destroyed*. Although Beauvoir wrote *The Coming of Age* in 1970 after these last works and after the significant breakthrough of *A Very Easy Death,* it is certainly the work that sounds her darkest note of despair about aging. Perhaps this is because she wrote *The Coming of Age* at the beginning of Sartre's final, irreversible decline and, by her own admission to Deirdre Bair, writing the book gave her a reason not to be present at Sartre's bedside to minister to his needs during this time (529). Perhaps too its totally pessimistic tone was a last attempt to exorcise through writing the obsessive connection in Beauvoir's thought between aging and death, and between aging and her original view of femininity. In any case, it need not surprise us that the working through of such a long-standing problem should have produced a certain overlap among the late works: in some, she is clearly working towards a new way of considering aging and femininity; in others she seems still mired in earlier visions; in still others she is somewhere between the two positions.

   The Coming of Age is a long, encyclopedic work not unlike *The Second Sex* in its cross-cultural, historical, case-history approach. It is structured very much like *The Second Sex* in that the more general studies of myths and ideologies precede the discussion of the individual situation and the ways in which various Western individuals have assumed it. The French version, *La Vieillesse,* consists of more than six hundred tightly packed pages. In the introduction, Beauvoir justifies writing it by saying it is time to break the conspiracy of silence that surrounds the subject, a reason not unlike that which prompted her to write *The Second Sex,* though more explicitly stated now, twenty-one years later. By 1970, Beauvoir was after all well aware that *The Second Sex* had broken the silence surrounding women's fate, at least for many women. She alludes to her own former work when she says in the introduction that "the myths and clichés put in circulation by bourgeois thought all attempt to portray the elder as an *Other*" [Les mythes et les clichés mis en circulation par la pensée bourgeoise s'attachent à montrer dans le vieillard un *autre*](9). According to Deirdre Bair, *The Coming of Age* had originally been conceived as a work of fiction about aging women, and then became a project for a "nonfiction study about the physical changes that afflict aging *women*" (531; emphasis mine).

Yet once the reader is past the introduction, the sense of similarity to *The Second Sex* all but disappears. As Kathleen Woodward aptly puts it, in "Simone de Beauvoir: Aging and Its Discontents," "*The Coming of Age* is a manifesto for social action. Its tone is passionate, not balanced. But Beauvoir's salutary polemical purpose would not seem fully to account for her hostile and bitterly dark portrait of old age." Like Woodward, I also read *The Coming of Age* "as a symptom of personal concerns and obsessions, as a *figure* on which she has both projected her subjectivity and displaced her anxieties" (Woodward 91). And once again, I believe these have to do with femininity. In the introduction, we read apropos of the fear of aging: "There is something terrifying in any metamorphosis. I was stunned, as a child, and deeply troubled to realize that one day I would change into an adult" [Il y a quelque chose d'effrayant dans toute métamorphose. J'étais stupéfaite, enfant, et même angoissée quand je réalisais qu'un jour je me changerais en grande personne] (*Coming of Age* 11; emphasis mine). We have already seen how this first change was related both to her fear of losing her mother on the one hand, and the frightening prospect of becoming a woman like her mother on the other, with the fear and disgust that the changes of puberty (her "swelling chest") inspired in her. Here, this has become a most unusual and telling way of introducing a discussion of the fears inspired by the aging body.

This fear of femininity becomes even more clear after the introduction, where aging *women* are virtually absent from either the anthropological or the historical analyses. Beauvoir justifies this systematic omission with the curious statement, "Historic societies are dominated by men; young and old women may quarrel over authority in matters of private life, but in public life, their status is identical: they are eternal minors. On the contrary, the masculine condition changes over time; the young man becomes an adult, a citizen, and the adult becomes an elder" [Les sociétés qui ont une histoire sont dominées par les hommes; les femmes jeunes et vieilles peuvent bien dans la vie privée se disputer l'autorité; dans la vie publique, leur statut est identique: d'éternelles mineurs. Au contraire, la condition masculine se modifie au cours du temps; le jeune homme devient un adulte, un citoyen, et l'adulte, un vieillard] (99). This deliberate blindness, which stands in contradiction to many passages about the significance of women's aging in *The Second Sex*, is compounded in the sections on individuals and their assumption of their aging. Only one woman, Lou Andréas Salomé, is studied in the entire text, whereas there must be at least thirty case histories of well-known aged men. Yet there is absolutely no explicit mention of any aspect of Salomé's experience that might have been affected by her gender. In other words, women *per se* are absent from *The Coming of Age*, despite its purported resemblance to *The Second Sex*. However, there are constant comparisons between aging and femininity.

For these reasons, Woodward is certainly right to speak of aging as a "figure" for something else, and it is in that spirit that we must read the book, rather than as the scientifically verifiable study it pretends to be. Beauvoir cites a number of doctors in her first chapter, "Aging and Biology," whose statements she uses to support her implicit claim that aging is the same thing as dying and as becoming a woman. Yet only fifteen years later, French gerontologists were speculating that senescence is neither as generalized throughout the body nor as easy to ascertain from a medical standpoint as Beauvoir seemed to think. The body remains modifiable until death, and psychic aging, like muscular aging, is most closely dependent not only upon its exercise but also on early training and level of education. In fact, as Henri Péquignot asserts in *Vieillesses de domain*, the unevenness and unpredictability of psychic development have parallels in the body which ought to be somewhat reassuring: the progressive inability of the eye muscles to adapt to changing distance actually begins before adulthood, as does the loss of auditory memory, and there may well be other examples that deny the validity of the classic three periods of life: growth, maturity, and decline (104). Péquignot studies all the functional systems of the body in turn, noting that most are fully able to perform almost indefinitely in the absence of disease or trauma, and that because the simple passage of time multiplies the likelihood of accident and trauma, it is very difficult empirically to separate the endemic causes of reduced function from others. The female reproductive system is the only one to cease functioning, but it does not do so suddenly, as Beauvoir asserts, but gradually, and this does not shorten a woman's life.

If there has been a philosophic tradition in French medicine of this kind in France, Beauvoir apparently paid no attention to it, preferring to see the mark of doom on all human flesh. About the relative absence of aging heroes from twentieth-century literature, rather than to perceive that their absence might be due to the very taboo she has presumably set out to break, she makes the remarkable statement: "It is true that . . . the old man is not a good subject for a novel. He is finished, fixed, without expectation, without hope; for him the game is over, death already inhabits him: *therefore nothing that happens to him is important*" [Il est vrai que . . . le vieillard n'est pas un bon héros de roman; il est achevé, figé, sans attente, sans espoir; pour lui les jeux sont faits, la mort déjà l'habite: rien de ce qui peut lui arriver n'est donc pas important] (*Coming of Age* 224; emphasis mine). She attributes the power of the theater of the absurd to its pessimistic central insight, that if life is unbearable it is because it is really nothing but "old age in disguise" [(la vieillesse) est (la condition humaine) enfin démasquée](226). She praises the fifteenth-century poet François Villon for his "accurate" (and deliberately grotesque) portrait of an old woman's face, claiming that he at least had the courage to consider what is, after all, every woman's fate (159).

The woman, apart from these literary evocations, is almost entirely absent, yet metaphors of aging men becoming feminine (or even more direct comparisons between their condition and the condition of women) are everywhere and are traced along many of the same paradigms that Beauvoir established in *The Second Sex,* using Sartrian existentialism as her point of departure. Thus she claims that in primitive societies the old man is considered the "Other," "with all the ambivalence carried by that term. As Other, woman is treated in masculine myths as at once an idol and a doormat. Thus . . . the old man in these societies is both less than a man and a superman" [avec toute l'ambivalence qu'entraîne ce terme. Autre, la femme est traitée dans les mythes masculins à la fois comme une idole et comme un paillasson. Ainsi . . . le vieillard dans ces sociétés est-il un sous-homme et un surhomme] (94). The comparison is made more explicit, and the question of *dependence* is evoked: "The most important point . . . is that the status of the old man is never achieved by his efforts but is *granted* to him by others. . . . I showed in *The Second Sex* that when women derive prestige from their magical powers it is in fact men who have granted it. The same thing is true for the elderly" [Le fait le plus important. . . . C'est que le statut de vieillard n'est jamais conquis par lui mais lui est octroyé. J'ai montré dans *Le Deuxième sexe* que, lorsque les femmes tirent de leur pouvoir magique un grand prestige, c'est en fait aux hommes qu'elles le doivent. La même remarque vaut pour les vieillards] (94–95). Because they are necessarily more passive as they age, these formerly virile men are now devoured by worries, as women always are. Helpless in the face of danger, they think about it constantly; this dependence puts them at the mercy of others and they resent it, like women (489). Resentment and a desire for vindication characterize both women and the elderly (502); even if men in the prime of life behave correctly towards them, they are treated as *objects* rather than *subjects* (504).

These comparisons continue throughout *The Coming of Age*. There is no lack of transgressive images of decadence, senility, and loss of physical function and control. There is little compassion here, and the emphasis is as much on mental as on physical deterioration. Beauvoir apparently could not see that she was in many ways supporting the very stereotypes that underlay the widespread fear of the elderly and led to their mistreatment by society. This blind spot seems too great to be accidental. Perhaps Beauvoir was seeking to distinguish between herself and other aging people by leaving women out. (Among the men, the philosophers age rather well, suggesting that Sartre, though now infirm, will retain his mental faculties while others may lose theirs.) Or perhaps she was groping for another portrait for women, which she had not yet fully drawn. In mentioning their sexuality, for example, she cuts the discussion short by saying that we have little historical documentation, and "the subject is even more taboo than for aging males" [Le sujet est encore plus tabou que la sexualité des vieux mâles](371). This interpretation would explain their absence from a work that had first been conceived as a specific discussion of them.

A Very Easy Death

I want to return now to the early 1960s, when Beauvoir actually began the series of exorcisms and examinations of plots for aging women that culminated with the writing of *The Coming of Age* in 1970, but also included the more complex fictional works "The Age of Discretion," "Monologue," and "The Woman Destroyed," all three collected under the title *The Woman Destroyed* and finally published in 1968. This period also saw the creation of the deeply moving *A Very Easy Death* in 1964 and of a manuscript that Beauvoir decided not to publish in story form but which appears to have been ready for publication by 1965. This text, "Misunderstanding in Moscow," expresses the essence of Beauvoir's late-life revision of gender roles and of the values that might govern an older woman's existence. Large parts of it were reworked and integrated into the first chapter of *All Said and Done* in 1972 in the dream sequences, in a series of moves that provide the final insights into Beauvoir's womanhood as she lived it in her sixties and seventies.

Chronologically, *A Very Easy Death* precedes this other writing, and the psychological work involved in the experience of her mother's painful death from cancer and the writing about it were undoubtedly necessary to the creation of some of the later texts. Her mother's death forced Beauvoir to consider her mother as other than a mythic being: "For me, my mother had always existed and I had never seriously thought that someday, that soon I should see her go. Her death, like her birth, had its place in some legendary time" [Pour moi, ma mère avait toujours existé et je n'avais jamais sérieusement pensé que je la verrais disparaître un jour. Sa fin se situait, comme sa naissance, dans un temps mythique] (270). Of course, many people regard their parents' existences in this way, but for Beauvoir the mythic mother was especially fraught with an ambivalence that had contributed to her daughter's construction of gender. In this she had been helped, as we know, by the other mythic "mother figure" in her life: the "good" (and phallic) mother Sartre, whose existential philosophy provided a terminology and a structure that enabled Beauvoir to justify the rejection of many aspects of what she saw as her mother's femininity (Jardine, "Death Sentences" 104).

In *A Very Easy Death*, Françoise de Beauvoir's life is examined by her daughter with insight and, for the first time, with compassion. Despite her critical ideological judgment of her mother's bourgeois Catholic life, Simone is able to measure and appreciate the degree of autonomy, independence, activity, and zest for life that Françoise had exhibited after the death of her husband. The frustrations she had felt in her marriage are sensitively described, including the sexual ones. Identification is at last possible. In an often quoted passage, Simone sits watching at her mother's bedside and incorporates her mother into her own person: "I talked to Sartre about my mother's mouth as I had seen it that morning and about everything I had interpreted in it. . . . And he told me that my own mouth was not obeying me anymore: I had put Maman's mouth on my own face and, in spite of myself, I copied its movements. Her whole person, her whole being, was concentrated there, and compassion wrung my heart" [Je parlai à Sartre de la bouche de ma mère, telle que je l'avais vue le matin et de tout ce que j'y déchiffrais. . . . Et ma propre bouche, me disait-il, ne m'obéissait plus: j'avais posé celle de maman sur mon visage et j'en imitais malgré moi les mimiques. Toute sa personne, toute son existence s'y matérialisaient et la compassion me déchirait] (*A Very Easy Death* 43–44).

In a familiar paradox, it is because she feels at last her separateness from her dying mother that she can allow herself to feel merged with her. As Nancy K. Miller describes, Simone is "astonished at her own distress" upon seeing her mother's naked body in its suffering, dying state. She does not feel merged with that body but separated from it by the certainty of its impending death. Yet something takes her by surprise after so many years of thinking that she had finally judged her mother: "my despair escaped from my control: someone other than myself was weeping in me" [mon désespoir échappait à mon contrôle: quelqu'un d'autre que moi pleurait en moi] (43); "The 'Maman chérie' of the days when I was ten can no longer be told from the inimical woman who oppressed my adolescence; I wept for both of them when I wept for my old mother. I thought I had made up my mind about our failure and accepted it; but its sadness comes back to my heart" [La "petite maman chérie" de mes dix ans ne se distingue plus de la femme hostile qui opprima mon adolescence; je les ai pleurées toutes les deux en pleurant ma vieille mère] (147). In the few weeks that follow, she finds again in accomplishing the bedside routines the simple love she had felt as a child for her mother, before she was old enough to judge her mother's life as a mask of clichés. Even if certain areas of incomprehension remain, and though ultimately the story of Simone de Beauvoir and her mother "is one of failed connection between generations of women" (Miller, *Bequest and Betrayal* 355), one can nonetheless read this ability to recognize and to feel deeply both her love *and* her anger as a kind of resolution to the problem long posed by their relationship.

This is an important step towards the reworking of her feelings about femininity and aging. As Kathleen Woodward says in "Simone de Beauvoir: Aging and Its Discontents," Beauvoir feels for the first time the value of memory in understanding the present (103). Accepting dependence and nurturing another, and coming in touch with the presence of the past not only *as past*, as in *The Mandarins*, but as a permanent part of oneself in the present, were all dramatic changes in Beauvoir's feelings. The compassion which does not displace but coexists with criticism, and the growing acceptance of her own and others' connectedness and need for dependence, were to mark her works from this point on. In the description of Sartre's decline in *Adieu*, Beauvoir did not so much work out her hostility against him, as some have suggested, as she projected onto him her own difficulty in reconciling the need to discipline herself, to take responsibility for the way she aged, with the fact that we do become dependent and we must accept that in the end other people will have to care for us.

This experience of her mother's death and the writing about it both occurred at a time when the affective climate in Beauvoir's life was changing in other ways as well. In 1960, Beauvoir became close to several students, all of course much younger than she was, and out of this group one woman emerged as a lifelong, committed relationship. Given the gloomy passages that closed *The Force of Circumstances* in 1962, it is not hard to understand that Beauvoir felt reborn in this loving friendship with Sylvie Le Bon (later to become Sylvie Le Bon de Beauvoir after a legal adoption). Beauvoir had had the same feelings for Sartre when she was twenty-one and now recognized the parallel in her rapport with Le Bon, as she reveals when she says that "once again, I was given a great chance" [une grande chance m'a de nouveau été donnée] (*All Said and Done* 84), echoing her meeting with Sartre as recounted in *Memoirs of a Dutiful Daughter*: "I had been given a great chance: I suddenly didn't have to face [the] future alone" [Et puis, une grande chance venait de m'être donnée: en face de cet avenir, brusquement je n'étais plus seule] (*Memoirs* 345; Kirkup trans. 481). By 1963, Sylvie had assumed in Beauvoir's life the same kind of intimacy she had known with Zaza or Sartre: "She is as thoroughly interwoven in my life as I am in hers. I have introduced her to my friends. We read the same books, we see shows together, and we go for long drives in the car" [Elle est mêlée à toute ma vie comme moi à la sienne. Nous lisons les mêmes livres, nous allons ensemble au spectacle, nous faisons de grandes promenades en auto] (*All Said and Done* 92). But at this point in her life, accepting the change brought by such a relationship was simple to Beauvoir, whereas a few years earlier she might have experienced it as a rupture or an inconsistency. For the first time since her early twenties, she was willing and able to accept change in her personal life.

Sylvie also offered Beauvoir a new gift she had not needed before and might not have been able to accept before her mother's death: "There is such an interchange between us that I lose the sense of my age: she draws me forward into her future, and there are times when the present recovers a dimension it had lost" [Il y a entre nous une telle réciprocité que je perds la notion de mon âge: elle m'entraîne dans son avenir et par instants le présent retrouve une dimension qu'il avait perdue] (92). There appears to have been a dialectical relationship between Sylvie's intimate presence and the psychological work of putting her "intrusive" mother object to rest. In fact, the actual *writing* of *A Very Easy Death* might never have occurred if Beauvoir had not recounted the entire story out loud to Sylvie in a café one afternoon (Bair 506). The symbiotic union with Sylvie undoubtedly facilitated the writing of the new vision of her mother.

The merging that occurred with Sylvie, and that more than anything else enabled Beauvoir to reconfigure her ideas of what it was to be an aging woman, was perhaps also made possible by the final experience of acceptance and blending with her mother. Sylvie, like Sartre earlier, is represented in *All Said and Done* as Beauvoir's double, rather than as her daughter. Beauvoir and Sylvie both cautioned against interpreting their relationship as mother and daughter (Bair 509), despite their age differ- ence and Beauvoir's joy at recapturing a dimension of life that Sylvie's youth returned to her, and I am not at all suggesting that Beauvoir had only maternal feelings for Sylvie; in fact, Sylvie was represented as a double who seemed at times like a mother. It is characteristic of relation- ships between women, following the mother-daughter model of blurred boundaries between the self and other, that such distinctions are not always rigid or clear. There was considerable fluidity in the roles that both women played, and in her love for Sylvie, Beauvoir knew none of the fear of abandonment and loss that had formerly fueled her compul- sion to resist dependence and reject identification with women who might be abandoned. In her book of inerviews with Beauvoir, author Alice Schwartzer summarized her subject's reflections: "Whereas love affairs between men and women often do not last, by contrast great friendships between women often endure. . . . She asserts in complete confidence that, 'up to my death, I will never be alone'" (Schwartzer 21; trans. Woodward, "Simone de Beauvoir" 111).

These aspects of this relationship would seem to be more important to understanding Beauvoir's aging than the question of whether or not it was homosexual. We know now, since Sylvie Le Bon de Beauvoir's publication in 1990 of Beauvoir's war diaries and letters to Sartre, that Beauvoir had had physical relationships with a number of her female students during the time that Sartre and Jacques Laurent Bost, her other heterosexual lover, were away.[6] Toril Moi provides a detailed and sensitive analysis on the evidence of her correspondence of what these affairs may have meant to Beauvoir, concluding that Beauvoir seems from her correspondence to have had little emotional investment in these women (230–36). If there is a parallel to be drawn between Sylvie Le Bon and other connections, it is rather with Zaza Mabille and Sartre, both of whom were enabling, symbiotic love relationships. The vigor of Beauvoir's sixties, the fictional and autobiographical production that seemed to proceed from a burst of new energy after Sylvie entered her life, argue that this relationship allowed her to face and even to enjoy her old age. In any case, by 1964–65, when Sartre surprised the "family" by legally adopting Arlette Elkaïm and devoted himself to his study of Flaubert, and Beauvoir became increasingly involved in feminist action, a certain distancing occurred between them. This is not to say Beauvoir could ever acknowledge, even to herself, this growing apart from Sartre. But we can see gradual changes in the late style of writing that indicate a degree of separation from this long-standing relationship.

The Woman Destroyed

In 1968, when Beauvoir was sixty, she engaged with *The Woman Destroyed* in a study of the traditional French novelistic plot for women's lives and literature, as we saw in its basic outline in chapter 1: unhappy love for a woman, ending in death (often by suicide) or a loveless marriage, and by the loss of creative power and death for the woman artist. Beauvoir herself had never written this plot except in a highly self-conscious, sometimes self-reflexive manner. Neither had she been willing to live it, though surely she felt its undertow in her fear of abandonment by Sartre. What is new for Beauvoir in *The Woman Destroyed* is the highly critical, yet fair and often compassionate position that we are invited to take with respect to the three women. They belong to the family of *amoureuses* in Beauvoir's work, of whom Paule was an example, but here there is a different understanding of their dilemma. These are complex characters, each quite distinct from Simone de Beauvoir, although certain striking resemblances exist between each woman and the author. They are also new as heroines of this kind of plot in that they are older by the time the story begins and we meet them. The customary beginning age of courtship is long over. In literary terms, they are all older women: Murielle in "Monologue" and Monique in "The Woman Destroyed" are in their forties, and the narrator of "The Age of Discretion" is in her sixties.

In other words, here we have the story of what happened afterwards to several women who allowed their identities to be lost in conventional relationships with men or who otherwise conformed to a stereotyped role including an early marriage and children, or who, in the case of "The Age of Discretion," simply found that everything seemed to change as they grew old. Despite the variety of narrative techniques, when the three stories are read together, they appear more as an indictment of a certain plot for women than of the characters themselves. The critical reception of the book utterly missed this point, and even Bair seems not to have seen that our conclusions must at least be tentative. In the openness of their endings and in the very expression of the anger or dissatisfaction that offended the critics, the stories are not entirely passive or pessimistic. Especially in "The Age of Discretion," a possible plot for the future of an aging woman is sketched. In "Misunderstanding in Moscow" [Malentendu à Moscou], a variant of this story published posthumously in 1992, this vision is asserted in more detail. Beauvoir also recognizes it as autobiography in 1972.

"The Age of Discretion" is narrated in the first person by a woman who is a university professor of French literature. She is married to André, a research physicist, and has a son, Philippe, who had originally followed her in pursuing his literary studies. Despite the difference in age between this woman and Anne in *The Mandarins*, they face many of the same agonizing questions about aging, though the precipitating factor of the discovery and loss of erotic passion is not present here in the same way. The problems of loneliness, fear of isolation, loss of attractiveness, and fear of the empty future are obsessively repeated in these "cure" stories. For this woman, they are compounded by what she considers the loss of her son. When he disappoints his mother by accepting a job from his in-laws in the business world, she interprets this to mean that Philippe has passed from her influence to that of his attractive young wife, and despite her intellectual sophistication, she mourns the loss of a scarcely veiled erotic connection to him. This development quickly leads to the familiar Beauvoirian dismissal of maternity as a source of connection: "He left me at the moment he announced his marriage, from the moment of his birth: a wet nurse could have replaced me" [Il m'a quittée dès l'instant où il m'annoncé son mariage; dès sa naissance, une nourrice aurait pu me remplacer] (*Woman Destroyed* 31). This woman's problems in aging are further complicated by another, which Anne could not have known at forty: she has written a new volume of literary criticism that she considers her most original to date, but the critics unanimously agree it is nothing but repetition of the ideas of her youth (59).

The quarrel with Philippe and the anguish over her work precipitate a full-fledged crisis over aging. Certain underlying elements were already present, familiar not only from *The Mandarins* but also from *The Force of Circumstance*. Thus she notes her loss of perspective on the world of human relations that results from her self-imposed loss of sexuality: "I have a tendency to underestimate the importance of the link created between two people by sexual happiness. Sexuality no longer exists for me. I used to call this indifference 'serenity'; suddenly I understood it otherwise. It is an infirmity, the loss of a faculty" [Ce lien que crée dans un couple le bonheur physique, j'ai tendance à en sous-estimer l'importance. La sexualité pour moi n'existe plus. J'appelais sérénité cette indifférence; soudain je l'ai comprise autrement: c'est une infirmité, c'est la perte d'un sens] (*Woman Destroyed* 27).

She is also greatly troubled by André's aging process, which seems to follow a different course from her own in some ways, though at the end of the story André admits that he is haunted by physical decrepitude as well, and especially by losing his teeth. This woman is initially terrified by what she perceives (though does not articulate) as a certain loss of masculinity in André. For example, she resents the way he seems to "abandon" himself to the aging process without a fight, becoming passive and attributing less and less importance to things that go wrong (47). Formerly, her relationship with André, like Anne's with Robert or Beauvoir's with Sartre, had been like "Siamese twins" (41), but now she begins to feel that they live in isolation from each other even when they are together (51), and to her this separation is a foretaste of death.

It is important to note that if this woman finds herself in crisis at this point in her life, it is not primarily because she has made the obvious errors of dependence and inauthenticity of someone like Paule. Like Anne, she has a professional life that matters greatly to her, students with whom she has meaningful friendships, and a husband with whom a symbiotic kind of relationship functioned well for her and protected her from feeling painful loss in middle age. She has admittedly been blind and egotistical in certain ways, but she is still a healthy woman who now has no erotic objects and can no longer be one, and who feels increasing isolation as André's aging seems to distance him from her. For these reasons we can feel compassion and identification with her.

The key to understanding the role of this story in the corpus of Beauvoir's works about aging is precisely the structuring of the narrative as a crisis, or even a brief breakdown, from which the character recovers in a convincing and reassuring way at the end. This technique confers value on certain of her conclusions and reveals others as the errors of a temporary delirium, and the schema that emerges is not consistent in some important ways with the findings of The Coming of Age.

The woman's anxiety mounts and with it her anger, lending the aggressive tone to this story that offended critics. After she tells Philippe she never wants to see him again and refusing André's entreaties to repair the situation, the summer vacation begins. She insists that she prefers to remain alone in Paris for a while before joining André at his aged mother's country home. Once alone, she wonders why she has done this, since solitude is what she most dreads, but she still lacks the insight to perceive her own rigid need to triumph over other people's wills. When the negative criticism of her book appears, although it is unanimous, she refuses to believe it. Finally she concludes that her age alone is responsible for her failure to have created something new. Her younger friend assures her this assumption is not so, but she becomes increasingly convinced that for herself, and for André, there is no meaningful work left to do. These ideas of course reappear in The Coming of Age.

In a similar way, the woman's attitude towards change and the value of the past *as a part of the present* undergoes a radical transformation during her crisis. Before André's departure, the couple takes a day trip to a village near Paris where they had pleasant memories from their younger days. Naturally they find it radically changed, with large chain stores and high-rise buildings. She has the following exchange with André on her feelings about modernity and change:

> "There. When you see the world change, it's both miraculous and devastating."
> I thought this over. "You'll probably laugh at my optimism again, but for me it's mostly miraculous."
> "But for me too. What's devastating when one ages is not in *things,* but in oneself."
> "I don't agree. There too you lose something, but you gain as well." (49)

> [Voilà. Voir changer le monde, c'est à la fois miraculeux et désolant.
> J'ai réfléchi: "Tu vas encore te moquer de mon optimisme: pour moi c'est surtout miraculeux."
> "Mais pour moi aussi. Le désolant quand on vieillit n'est pas dans les choses, mais en soi-même."
> "Je ne trouve pas. Là aussi on perd, mais on gagne.]

At this point, before her crisis, she feels enriched by her long past and her memories. André is skeptical that one can really *possess* one's past; she answers: "I know it's there. It gives a certain consistency to the present. . . . Intellectually, you're more on top of things. You forget a lot, I know, but even the things you forget remain available to you in a certain way" [Je sais qu'il est là. Il donne de l'épaisseur au présent. . . . Intellectuellement, on domine mieux les questions; on oublie beaucoup, d'accord, mais même ce qui est oublié reste à notre disposition, d'une certaine façon] (49).

As the crisis sets in, she becomes convinced after all that the past is as empty as a desert behind her (65). Memories are worthless and wisdom a meaningless notion. At the height of her crisis she tells herself that she had been wrong earlier that summer to think that Valéry had spoken the truth about aging as "ripening" in his lines: "Each atom of silence / is the chance of a ripened fruit" ["Chaque atome de silence / Est la chance d'un fruit mûr"]; now it is Sainte-Beuve who has captured the truth: "One hardens in places, one rots in others, one never ripens" ["On durcit par places, on pourrit à d'autres, on ne mûrit jamais"] (71).

She now also feels that change is fraught only with danger. For the first time she wonders whether André's feelings for her have undergone change over the years, and she feels superfluous in his life now. When she joins him at his mother's house, everything goes wrong between them and she feels totally estranged. Increasingly, the focus of the story is on the connection between her and André.

And the crisis is indeed resolved with the restoration of their understanding, in which André's eighty-year-old mother also constructively participates. The protagonist is at last struck by the genuine sorrow and political commitment that André still feels towards mankind and that had always united them in the past. She realizes all over again that they will never be strangers (78). Later, they sit on the grass and really talk: "again, we could really talk to each other and something was released in me. For the first time I thought about Philippe without anger . . . perhaps because André was suddenly so close to me" [de nouveau nous pouvions nous parler et quelque chose s'est dénoué en moi. Pour la première fois je pensais à Philippe sans colère . . . peut-être parce qu'André m'était soudain si proche] (79). She looks at the moon and a star and recites a little poem from "Aucassin and Nicolette" that she feels unites her in a continuity with past centuries and returns the treasures of her own memory, and as she holds his arm against her, the natural world regains its beauty (80, 83). Love, or a form of eroticism, and the pleasures of the earth are restored together. They decide together to continue their life, not without fear of the future and perhaps with more modest expectations of themselves intellectually. The phrase recurs as in *Memoirs of a Dutiful Daughter* and *All Said and Done*: "We are together, that is our great chance" [Nous sommes ensemble, c'est notre chance] (84).

This ending is not only open but also relatively optimistic in its depiction of the power of intimacy to make aging fully tolerable. The woman has had to abandon her rather ferocious individualism, but she has not been abandoned. Most important of all, from the perspective of *The Coming of Age,* the darkest thoughts about change, memory, and the value of the past are shown here to have been delusions. This story can thus be seen as existing in dialectical relationship to the treatise written two years later. The ending is tentative, yet this account of a crisis resolved could not be called pessimistic or a "decline narrative," and it certainly charts new territory for the aging woman in more ways than one.

If the aging woman in "The Age of Discretion" is not punished for her anger, one cannot say as much for Murielle in "Monologue." Of her, the critic André Billy said: "I won't discuss the second story, scurrilous and slangy. It offended me. I hardly know why. I am probably a little behind the times."[7] Deirdre Bair calls Murielle a "Molly Bloom out of control," but James Joyce's Molly Bloom should have prepared critics half a century later for this kind of unbridled stream of consciousness monologue, unless they feared it might in some way represent the feelings of a real woman. "Monologue" is obviously excessive, out of control, and Murielle knows it. In a commentary on the text which is also one on some of Beauvoir's other writings, Murielle sums up a number of epithets about herself by saying, "People can't stand it if you tell them the truth. . . . I'm lucid and frank and I unmask everyone. The lady who murmured: 'Don't we love our little brother?' and I said with poise: 'I hate him.' I'm still that little lady who says what she thinks and doesn't cheat" [Les gens n'acceptent pas qu'on leur dise leurs vérités. . . . Moi je suis lucide je suis franche j'arrache les masques. La dadame qui sussure: "On l'aime bien son petit frère?" et moi d'une petite voix posée: "Je le déteste." Je suis restée cette petite bonne femme qui dit ce qu'elle pense et qui ne triche pas] (*Woman Destroyed* 102). The text is peppered with slang and obscenity, but then so are a number of Beauvoir's other texts: one thinks of the epilogue to *The Force of Circumstance*, where she casually says, "I learned in my youth not to give a damn about public opinion" [Je me suis entraînée dans ma jeunesse à me foutre de l'opinion] (495). Murielle is, in her unrestrained verbal outpourings, most of which are invective, typical of the excessive, out of control female body fearfully described in *The Second Sex* and *Memoirs of a Dutiful Daughter*. In other words, she is verbally "incontinent," but she is also right when she says that she takes pleasure in saying out loud what others dare only to feel (90), as in many of her accusations of the men in her life and of the way she has been treated. And she knows that her difficulties as a woman alone will worsen as she ages. It is the complexity of her clear-sightedness and the paranoia induced by mistreatment that make it impossible to judge her; even her maniacal desire to wield power over others is clearly a reaction to her real powerlessness (103). The traditional plot for women has here been fulfilled in all its unhappiness and now, afterwards, this woman refuses to languish or keep silent.

"The Woman Destroyed" has undoubtedly been the most discussed of the three, perhaps because it best exemplifies the classic Sapphic plot of abandonment and unhappiness. Monique was married at a young age to a doctor with whom she was in love. At a point about ten years before the beginning of the story, Maurice begins to change, but his wife is unaware of it. When the children have grown up and left home, he tells Monique he is in love with another woman who is in every way Monique's opposite: an ambitious, worldly lawyer with the festive name "Noëllie." Moique is totally unequipped to deal with the schism between the past as she understood it and the present. We recognize a variant of Paule beneath this banal story of a woman whose husband leaves her in middle age. Monique has refused to live for herself. Her entire existence has been alienated in the life of her husband and family. But her greatest error has not been her failure to project herself into the future by means of activity outside the domestic sphere, although that is serious enough, as Beauvoir would have suggested in *The Second Sex*. Worse yet has been her unwillingness, now become her inability, to realize that time passes and everything changes, that change must be accepted, that the past only has lasting value when it is accepted as past and also integrated into the present. This is the problem of "femininity," which haunts Beauvoir's works most doggedly and which proves to be the most threatening in advancing age. Because Monique's existence has been limited to one relationship, her blindness and failure to adapt have cost her the intimacy that is absolutely necessary to the aging. In "The Woman in Love" in *The Second Sex*, Beauvoir asserts: "Yet there are few crimes that entail worse punishment than the generous fault of putting oneself entirely in another's hands" [Mais il y a peu de crimes qui entraînent pire punition que cette faute généreuse: se mettre tout entière entre des mains autres] (740–41; Parshley trans. 413).

Thus the traditional plot for women, seen through the lens of Beauvoir's existentialist beliefs but also from the perspective of her own evolving view of a "successful" femininity for late life, is doomed to failure, not so much because men are inconstant as because the plot deprives the woman of agency, projects, ability to adapt. "The Woman Destroyed" is written in journal format, like the personal writing Beauvoir herself engaged in when she was most anxious about Sartre's behavior (Moi 247). Monique tries one strategy after another, but the outcome is overdetermined and on the last page she is alone and contemplating suicide. Just as Beauvoir wanted to criticize and distance herself from this plot, as a writer she will not actually reproduce it. Again there is an open ending: "A closed door, something waiting on the other side. It won't open if I don't move. . . . But I know I will move. The door will open slowly and I'll see what's waiting for me on the other side. . . . I'm afraid. And I can't call anyone for help. I'm afraid" [Une porte fermée, quelque chose qui guette derrière. Elle ne s'ouvrira pas si je ne bouge pas . . . Mais je sais que je bougerai. La porte s'ouvrira lentement et je verrai ce qu'il y a derrière cette porte . . . J'ai peur. Et je ne peux appeler personne au secours. J'ai peur] (The Woman Destroyed 252).

All Said and Done

In 1972, in yet another supposedly final volume of Memoirs, Beauvoir announces in the prologue that she no longer feels the same need to write in strict chronological order. In All Said and Done she is sixty-four and in excellent health, and although she hasn't changed in any profound way and is still totally devoted to her projects, she no longer feels constrained by the linear drive towards a fixed goal that made the flat, chronological account necessary to The Prime of Life and The Force of Circumstance. She feels much freer now to organize her material thematically, since she is "slipping ineluctably toward the grave" [l'impression . . . de glisser inéluctablement vers ma tombe] (10), without feeling depressed about it. And yet, it is only in the first chapter of this book that she will abandon the dry, extremely linear style of the earlier volumes. Although the entire book does not live up to the new organization promised in the prologue, it is interesting that Beauvoir draws our attention to this change. The first chapter, about 150 pages in the French edition, is perhaps the most personal, confessional writing Beauvoir has left us, along with A Very Easy Death and Memoirs of a Dutiful Daughter. It is organized into four sections, according to a kind of metonymy that reveals much about Beauvoir's final feelings about aging and femininity.

It is full of logical inconsistencies; that is, she rarely thinks about the past but needs to remember everything that ever happened to her (60), she worries less about death (9–10, 60) but still wakes up from anxious dreams, bathed in a sweat of fear and she says "I have a fascination with death in my bones" (61). These inconsistencies may be seen as proof of the fragility of a euphoric facade in the first part, or—in a reading I prefer—as evidence of the complex and still imperfect resolution of certain fears, which are dealt with differently here in that she accepts dependency, change (including the death of those close to her, the ultimate change), the loss of the future, the pleasure of retrieving the past.

In the first part of *All Said and Done*, we find Beauvoir feeling relieved to have come through the difficult time of middle age and looking back with evident satisfaction on her life. Comparing this section to the ending of *The Force of Circumstance*, the reader is almost shocked by a euphoric note that hasn't been heard since Beauvoir was quite young, and indeed on page 47, Beauvoir is struck by her own feeling of not having aged any further since 1962. In the first pages, Beauvoir gives free rein to her familiar narcissism, asking, "Why am I me?" [Pourquoi suis-je moi?] (11). She examines her childhood and youth to discern what was predetermined by her social class and family situation. Bit by bit, she describes the way she turned these given circumstances to her advantage in the exercise of her freedom by making choices, expressing preferences, etc., which then in their turn narrowed the field of possibilities. Encounters became less and less a matter of pure chance. Her life, constructed by the exercise of her free will, became more and more individuated. She misses her youth only to the extent that it was the time when all her choices were still before her.

Late life is also a time of satisfaction because of her involvement with feminism, and her new relationship with Sylvie Le Bon proves to her that one does in fact continue to invent oneself until the very end. She goes through an interesting exercise of wondering "what if:" what if her family had not lost its money, what if her father had been more supportive in her adolescence, what if she had married her cousin Jacques, etc. And the conclusion is almost always the same: "Of one thing I am sure: I would have come out all right." [Ce dont je suis sûre, c'est que je m'en serais sortie.] (31) She acknowledges the striking continuity of her life and its relationships and says that two things in particular have unified (and we are entitled to read "justified") her existence: Sartre's place and her fidelity to her original project of becoming a writer. Whatever we may think of this display of narcissism, I am convinced of the authenticity of the narcissistic satisfaction that she felt, perhaps because of her very insistence: she also wrote, she claims, in order "to be materialized in books that would be, like the ones I had loved, objects that existed for others but that would be inhabited by a presence: mine" [me matérialiser dans des livres qui seraient, comme ceux que j'avais aimés, des choses existant pour autrui mais hantés par une présence: la mienne] (45).

In the second part, now that she is "no longer aging," she has stopped thinking about her physical attractiveness, and this freedom from worry is a great relief (48). She speaks explicitly about her new position with respect to the future and to the past, both terms that were originally so laden with masculine and feminine connotations in *The Second Sex* because of their respective identifications with the Sartrian notions of transcendence and immanence. The future had always been her source of passionate inspiration, but now she is at peace with the idea that she cannot project herself indefinitely into the future and that no matter what else she writes, her oeuvre is essentially finished (53). She enjoys the idea that the past is present in her, though she doesn't think about it very often, since there have been so few breaks in the continuity of her life (49–50). However, in one of the self-contradictions referred to above, she says she is in fact preoccupied with remembering, with filling in the gaps in her memory, "as though there were a moment when all my experience would have to be added up, as though it were important to arrive at this total" [Comme s'il devait y avoir un moment où mon expérience serait totalisée, comme s'il importait que cette totalisation fût effectuée] (60). This reverie might seem like entirely normal behavior for an elderly person, especially to those who have read Robert N. Butler's article "The Life Review" in the journal *Psychiatry*. But we have seen to what extent Beauvoir resisted taking this stance throughout her life, associating this orientation towards the past with a kind of behavior that was often a woman's undoing, and curbing any such tendencies by an obsessive writing of autobiography without much commentary or expression of feeling. She is ready now to mark this difference with Sartre's early philosophy and to assert her love of her personal past, *particularly* when she can integrate it into the present and watch the progressions. Thus in this section Beauvoir is moved to see her girlhood friend Stépha, who is now an old woman with arthritis and who has aged magnificently. She defends the permanence of her circle of friends that she and Sartre have always called the "family" against charges of stagnation (62). They are mutually supportive, a community of the kind Betty Friedan describes and recommends to the aged (293). With great affection Beauvoir describes the end of Violette Leduc's life and her dignified death despite the menace of madness. Finally, before introducing the relationship with Sylvie, she emphasizes how much she is enjoying the company of the young. A picture of remarkable stability and serenity is emerging.

Sylvie is then presented as a double. Beauvoir stresses that Sylvie's relations with her mother were even more difficult than those of Simone and Françoise de Beauvoir. The impossibility of deciding the mother-daughter aspect of the relationship is forcefully stated. Obviously, Sylvie is thirty-three years younger, and she allows Beauvoir to project herself vicariously into the future in the way that a child would allow. It is as if Sylvie as her double makes it possible for her to live her old age fully while ignoring the specter of her death. Like a daughter, Sylvie also sometimes appears as a reincarnation of Simone's younger self, as when she teaches in the same lycée in Rouen where Simone began her career and arranges to sleep in the same hotel and frequent the same bar.

But Sylvie as double is also a mother figure, and the acceptance of dependence on Sylvie may have been more significant to Beauvoir's development in late life than her feeling of having a daughter. Sylvie comforts Simone when Françoise dies and—most important—she enjoys listening to Simone talk about herself (91). Here again, one cannot help but think of the earlier signs of affinity between the twenty-one-year-old Simone and the twenty-four-year-old Sartre, who loved to talk with Simone about her favorite subject: herself (*Memoirs* 340). Beauvoir dreamed of a lifelong union with Sartre that would ideally have allowed her a greater dependence on him. She had to come to terms with the fact that the price of their permanent connection was his dependence on her in many ways but that her own similar dependence would have meant abandonment. She saw reflections all around her of the price of female dependence, which is also of course the fate of women in literature. Her mother's example had led to frustration in every domain and to sexual abandonment. The autonomy she wanted for women in *The Second Sex* was mingled in an earlier period with a fear of dependence that was in fact a confusion between dependence and femininity; I have tried to show how this obsessive theme was reworked throughout her life, starting with *The Mandarins*, as she struggled with advancing age to reconcile a deeply felt need for greater dependence and connection with her hard-won autonomy. This was precisely what the relationship with Sylvie allowed. It is not surprising that her sense of the aging process seemed to stop, because the fear of aging did stop with this acceptance of dependence as a part of femininity and the assurance that she would not be abandoned.

Yet if in the end the body in old age is a female body, as Elaine Marks suggests, the end is also death. The female body remained to the end for Beauvoir the changing body, the Real of the human condition that always imposes itself and shapes our lives, and which Beauvoir must scrutinize and write about. In the third part of chapter 1, the women who were omitted from the minute accounts of deterioration in *The Coming of Age* appear at last. Their juxtaposition to the happy account of Beauvoir's own old age is striking. In this brusque passage from a euphoric to a dysphoric register, I read an attempt to distance herself. Her own death, she seems to indicate, will be more like Violette Leduc's, whose body never changed as she aged (apart from her face) (73). There is something left to exorcise after all.

A great deal of attention is paid to the changes in physical appearance in the various women who have died: Camille, Lise, Madame Lemaire, and Sartre's mother, Madame Mancy. This detail is especially true of Camille and Lise, who had been young and attractive when Beauvoir first knew them and towards whom she had felt some hostility. The example of Camille is interesting because of the degree of detail in the description of her final abject state. Camille had been one of Sartre's lovers before Beauvoir and lived for a long time with the theater director Charles Dullin. Beauvoir begins by describing at length her failure as a writer. Without entering into the entire narrative, it is worth remembering that Camille was one of the examples chosen by Elaine Marks to illustrate the feminine metaphor of aging: Camille arrives one day at Beauvoir's apartment disoriented and staggering, and goes immediately to the bathroom upstairs where she urinates loudly, leaving the door open (78). Marks observes: "Here the move from sexuality to urination and back to sexuality is explicitly made. Urination, abundant, excessive urination by women becomes the metaphor for everything that is embarrassing in sexuality. The body grows on its own, so to speak, proliferates without permission, makes noises, in the same way as incontinence takes over the body in decline" (192). Camille becomes a hopeless alcoholic, lying all day in her own filth, shocking even the doctors and nurses who come to hospitalize her. In the hospital she develops bedsores. Her face and body swell to unrecognizable proportions, and she dies. This horrifying narrative, when placed next to the account of the physical decline of Françoise de Beauvior or Sartre, is both the same and different. Beauvoir doesn't have the same compassion, but the context for *Adieu: A Farewell to Sartre* not only existed but furthermore was such as to make her description of Sartre's decline a much more normal case within the corpus.

Lise, the next woman to be described, appears after a long absence and illness with a "monstrously swollen" body [monstrueusement enflé](116) and physical gestures that "escape her control" (*All Said and Done* 117). Her behavior during her long life in America has become ridiculous, her expressions "outrageous" [expressions outrées] and "exaggerated" [exaggérées]. She dies soon after this reunion with Beauvoir. The deaths of Giacometti, Madame Mancy, and Madame Lemaire are treated with more restraint. Beauvoir will not even talk about the one death that has really moved her, that of Claude Lanzmann's sister Evelyne, but she feels compelled to tell us so before moving rapidly on to observations of a more general nature. There is evidence of considerable anxiety in this portion of the text.

How to escape these fates? How to be another kind of aging woman? Beauvoir has already provided her rational account of her difference in the first two parts of the chapter. In the last, she gives us her dreams, without attempting analysis and without really explaining her motivation. She simply says that she has never spoken of them before and would like to do so before speaking of her recent activities, because they are one of her favorite recreations. This is mostly because the dreams exist outside of time in a "perpetual youth" [une perpétuelle jeunesse] (139).

Beauvoir claims that these dreams are those she has written down between 1969 and 1971. But much of the material must be older even than that, since some of the dreams and some of the elements of action and decor can be found in "Misunderstanding in Moscow," which was written between 1965 and 1967. This story resembles "The Age of Discretion" in that there is a sixty-year-old woman university professor, Nicole, who is married to André, now also a university professor of literature. They have a son, Philippe, and certain passages of the text are identical in the two stories. But here, both are retired and have taken a trip to Moscow to visit André's forty-year-old daughter, Macha, by a previous marriage. During their stay there is a crisis, as there was in the published story. But the narrative is changed radically by the fact that both Nicole and André are narrators. The point of view shifts constantly between them throughout the text, sometimes slipping briefly into the first person, more often into free indirect discourse. The two are given equal time and neither is dominant. The crisis here is a breakdown in the communication between them. In fact, these "Siamese twins" [des frères siamois] (162) resemble each other in many ways that might have been more differentiated by gender in earlier stories: each feels old and is reluctant to say so to the other, each worries about physical deterioration, each worries about becoming "asexual." (Nicole has decided she is too old for sex, and although André finds her as desirable as ever, their relations cease and after a while he too thinks of himself this way.)

Only the reader is omniscient during their crisis of communication, which is exacerbated by their terror of solitude. In the last pages, as in the published story, they find each other again. Their reconciliation is all the more moving in that André explicitly says that he had never considered abandoning Nicole, whom he loves; her fears were groundless. And the "great chance" here is defined somewhat more precisely: it is having someone with whom to talk about what matters most, to make the "disclosures" that are "the glue of true intimacy" (Friedan 290). Here the decision to continue together is less reserved, more confident than in "The Age of Discretion." The story's open end is a question: "He would ask questions, she would answer. 'Why did you feel old?' he asked" [Lui il poserait des questions, elle répondrait. 'Pourquoi est-ce que tu t'es sentie vieille?' demanda-t-il] (All Said and Done 188). To borrow André's phrase, "Finally . . . it was a misunderstanding" [En somme . . . il y a eu malentendu] (187). The reader who has known their almost identical concerns knows that gender difference here need be no barrier to communication. In the interchangeability of much of their interior monologue, one sees that their sexual difference is no longer as great as in their youth, but the presentation and resolution of the crisis prove that this is no longer to be thought of as a catastrophe.

And indeed, Beauvoir's voice in the first part of *All Said and Done* borrows first from Nicole, who asks herself why she is the person she is (162) and then from André, who enjoys his dreams as an "eternal novelty" [une éternelle nouveauté] (147), and so on. It is not without significance that Sartre and Beauvoir made seven trips together to the Soviet Union between 1961 and 1966, and in most of the dreams there is a journey of some kind, often involving Russia. She is afraid of losing Sartre in these shifting surroundings, as indeed she frequently does. He does little to help, leaving the map at home or behaving indifferently. She is angry with him and he knows it, because he drinks too much and refuses to take his medications. Unlike André, Sartre refuses to attend to her needs. In one dream, they stop at a restaurant where Sartre leaves her alone in the car in order to go in and eat. "Suddenly furious" [Furieuse soudain] (148), she decides to eat too. She finally finds Sartre sequestered in a corner, but when she has caught sight of the appetizing food, Sartre nastily announces that he's eaten enough and returns to the car (148).

In these dreams Beauvoir is frequently disoriented, lost, missing a train, or losing her luggage. All of these elements are also found in "Misunderstanding in Moscow." Upon their arrival, Nicole obsessively repeats, "Is the baggage going to arrive?" And André answers: "It will arrive in the end" [Ils finiront bien par arriver] (139). This question of baggage seems important. It is sometimes related to another dream problem, the question of what she should wear, which surprises Beauvoir because it is so different from her waking life (143). Even if she can decide, the baggage may get lost anyway. Or something is wrong with her suit, but her mother will repair it (153). One automatically thinks of the passage from *The Second Sex* in which Beauvoir describes her own femininity in 1949 as not yet a "new woman," but "an independent woman": "The woman of today is torn between the past and the future; she feels herself as ill at ease in her flesh as in her masculine garb. *She must shed her old skin and cut her own new clothes*" [La femme d'aujourd'hui est écartelée entre le passé et l'avenir; elle se sent mal à l'aise aussi bien dans sa chair de femme que dans son habit masculin. *Il faut qu'elle fasse peau neuve et qu'elle se taille ses propres vêtements*] (II 807; Parshley trans. 495, emphasis mine). The "old skin" in question could also refer to the pejorative expression Beauvoir used in her youth to describe aging women: "des vieilles peaux" (literally, "old skins"). She is not an "old skin" like Camille, though she is anxious about it: in one dream she needs desperately to urinate but can't find the toilets. When she is finally seated, she is suddenly surrounded by many people. Sometimes this upsets her; sometimes she doesn't care (158). But what skin has come to replace the "old" that has been shed? And will she be able to hold on to her baggage? Or perhaps it would be just as well to lose some of the baggage containing the old-style clothes? An earlier kind of femininity is also a source of anxiety in her dream in which a "stupid girl" her own age claims to be a "woman" because she has a husband and a baby. Beauvoir herself in this dream has just come from a pro-abortion demonstration (156). This "stupid girl's" model doesn't fit, yet it is she who claims to be a woman.

"Losing the baggage" is changing her way of being a woman and is necessarily charged with anxiety. But in her dreams she keeps traveling, often in the reassuring company of Sylvie, whatever the risks. Within herself she carries Nicole and André, whom she created in order to get beyond the misunderstandings and failures of intimacy generated by the masculine and feminine roles of her youth. Beauvoir's reaction against the traditional plot for women came early in her life with her refusal to live a bourgeois Catholic existence including marriage and motherhood. This reaction against the traditional womanhood of her mother and female relatives made it possible for her to make one of the most important philosophical and sociological breakthroughs of the century in writing *The Second Sex*. But it also placed her in a position of extreme reaction against the very real needs for dependence and attachment to her past which increased, as they do for all people, as she aged. For Beauvoir, the discovery of a late-life femininity was a reconciliation of these values with the freedom and autonomy she had acquired and which she still thought of as masculine. And thus it was only in her late years, with the assumption of a position outside of society's traditional sexual definitions, that she could begin to free herself entirely from the limiting effects of the original plot.

MARGUERITE DURAS: LOVE AND INTIMACY AT EIGHTY AND BEYOND

Marguerite Duras begins *The Lover* [L'Amant] with a passage that has no equivalent in French literature. A woman of seventy, writing a book about her first experience of love and sexuality at age fifteen, says, "One day when I was already old, in the hall of a public place, a man came up to me. He introduced himself and said, "I have known you forever. Everyone says you were beautiful when you were young. I have come here to tell you that I find you more beautiful now than when you were young, that I liked your young face less than the one you have now, devastated," [Je vous connais depuis toujours. Tout le monde dit que vous étiez belle lorsque vous étiez jeune, je suis venu pour vous dire que pour moi je vous trouve plus belle maintenant que lorsque vous étiez jeune, j'aimais moins votre visage de jeune femme que celui que vous avez maintenant, dévasté] (9). Duras presents her "devastated," "cracked," "destroyed," and wrinkled face without masquerade, claiming she prefers it that way, and her feeling is corroborated, in our cultural terms, because it is echoed by a man. This is already an alteration of what we expect: the "psychic body" does not seem to coincide with the physical or social body.[1] But then she goes on to remember her youthful body at fifteen, which masqueraded as *older* precisely because her psychic body (that is, the way she felt about her body) was older. Thus Duras effects in *The Lover* a double reversal with respect to the specular economy of our society as it represents women and aging.

But how does the reader react to this woman's preference for her ravaged, devastated face? What sense does Duras give to "devastated"? She looked physically different forever, we are told, after she had first known sexual pleasure, which is the reason the incident is placed at the very beginning of the novel: she is now going to tell us about her experience of love and also about love in relation to aging. The connection is not one of renunciation, waiting for death, or ending one's life in a radically different erotic and emotional posture from that of youth. The love of her first lover devastated her face, but it also made her more beautiful in her own eyes because it marked her with erotic capability and experience, and now the old woman who has learned how to touch the beloved other through the medium of words is still more desirable. Thus she feels that physical aging is actually a physical enhancement, a particular kind of feminine beauty. Duras did, in fact, live her life to the age of eighty-one according to these notions, although she was of course aware of social stereotypes of aging women.[2]

The Lover was acclaimed by the reading public as a literary breakthrough. Duras received the Prix Goncourt for it in 1984, when she was seventy and the author of a truly vast corpus, although this prize is normally reserved for a young writer. As both Jean-Laurent Del-Bono and Philippe Sollers observe in *Le Nouvel Observateur*, the success of *The Lover* consecrated Duras as the French author most widely studied at the university level today, both in France and abroad. I also think that *The Lover* represents a dramatic moment in Duras's work from the perspective of the changes brought by aging. Of the several repeated, incantatory phrases that loosely structure the book, "look at me" is perhaps the most haunting, along with the descriptions of herself, and her insistence on *telling* the reader: "On the ferry, look at me again, I still have [my] long hair" (24); "Look at me again, I am fifteen and a half" (11). "Look," she seems to be saying, "and the woman character will finally be revealed, and she will be *me*." Thus this late work obliges the reader to reevaluate the much-discussed notion of the Durassian woman as silent, empty, sleepy, and unknowable. For that matter, her style also requires reevaluation here, by those who had come to expect to find it located always slightly beyond the reach of the reader's intellectual comprehension, silent like the women characters, referring to the unspoken rather than speaking, never disclosing.

The silent women of Duras's middle period in the 1960s reveal her own extraordinary difficulty in finding an individuated identity, certainly a result of the circumstances of her early relationship with her mother in colonial Indochina, and in her sixties Duras overcame this problem to the extent of becoming a writing subject who is able at last to reveal her women characters psychologically, and thus to reveal her *self*. Most interesting is the connection between aging and the need and desire for disclosure, and the ways in which this connection can inflect the development of the older woman's personality. Betty Friedan in *The Fountain of Age* correctly identifies disclosure, the tendency to tell stories about one's life, which has long been recognized informally as a characteristic of older people and more formally in Robert N. Butler's "The Life Review" and related works, as the essence of intimacy: "For the process of disclosing oneself to another is the essence of intimacy. It may be experienced or enhanced by physical touching, but the touching of the human heart is through words" (Butler 266). In several important ways, in fact, Duras presents more marked evolution with advancing age than the writers considered in preceding chapters. She shows a greater acceptance of her own aging as a positive process, or perhaps one should simply note that nowhere does she record her feeling that it was a negative one. This view of the older woman, along with Duras's social marginality and perhaps her less disciplined childhood outside of France, seems to have led to more emphatic rejection of the plot for women's stories. To a degree that is perhaps unparalleled in French women's literature, Duras dealt explicitly with sexuality and eroticism in her late writing, both with respect to her own past and present desires and more generally in the name of all women. These writings include the familiar eroticism of *The Lover* (1984), the later *Lover from the North of China* [L'Amant de la Chine du

Nord] (1991), and the explicit description of incestuous love between herself and her brother in *The Summer Rain* [La Pluie d'eté] (1990). They also include the woman-centered, singularly explicit erotic text *The Man Sitting in the Corridor* [L'Homme assis dans le couloir] (1980) which was written when she was sixty-six and involves fellatio, exhibitionism, and sado-masochism. It would be hard to imagine an intellectual woman writer more outside the bounds of conventional propriety. Desire, we learn from Duras, does not belong to any particular age. And the writing of the 1980s and early 1990s suggests, perhaps even more surprisingly, that it does not necessarily find its most potent expression directly through the body.

Duras also completely and finally upsets any received notion of a distinction between autobiography and fiction. She first achieved wide public recognition in 1950 with the publication of *The Sea Wall* [Un Barrage contre le Pacifique], a highly fictionalized account of her early years. With this work she invented a kaleidoscope of images and relationships that she would shift several times until as recently as 1991, in *The Lover from the North of China. The Lover* was understood in 1984 to be her first real "autobiography," but it does not follow the rules that ordinarily define the autobiographical genre. Duras is very clear about rejecting autobiography of the usual sort, which is presumed to be entirely nonfictional, because it seems to her to be totally inauthentic:

> I have no story. In the same way, I have no "life." My story is pulverized each day, at every second of every day, by life in the present, and I have no means of perceiving clearly what is called "her life." Only the thought of death assembles all the parts of me, or the love of this man and of my child. I have always lived as though it were impossible for me to come close to any preexisting model for my existence. I really wonder how people go about recounting the story of their lives. It's true that there are many models based on chronology, external events. Those are what most people use.

> [Je n'ai pas d'histoire. De la même façon que je n'ai pas de vie. Mon histoire, elle est pulvérisée chaque jour, à chaque seconde de chaque jour, par le présent de la vie, et je n'ai aucune possibilité d'apercevoir ce qu'on appelle ainsi: sa vie. Seule la pensée de la mort me rassemble ou l'amour de cet homme et de mon enfant. J'ai

toujours vécu comme si je n'avais aucune possibilité de m'appro-
cher d'un modèle quelconque de l'existence. Je me demande sur
quoi se basent les gens pour raconter leur vie. C'est vrai qu'il y
a tellement de modèles de récits qui sont faits à partir de celui
des faits extérieurs, de la chronologie. On prend ce modèle-là en
général.]

(*Material Life* [La Vie matérielle] 88)

For Duras, the mythological and fictional universe she has created is
every bit as much "her life" as any historical account, and while certain
autobiographical facts are verifiable and recognized by her, in the case of
her writing we are more than ever entitled to consider fiction and autobiography together. Duras herself explicitly encourages the reader to make
a connection between her life and her work in various interviews, in
Places [Les Lieux] (1977) and *Women Speaking* [Les Parleuses] (1974), or
in her dialogue with Bernard Pivot in 1984 on the French television program *Apostrophes*" (Ironically, perhaps, these discussions, with their rev-
elations in response to direct questions, are in some ways the most traditionally autobiographical texts for which she is responsible). Thus
in one of the conversations with Xavière Gauthier that constitute *Les
Parleuses,* Duras describes her first break with her early classical narrative
style as the direct consequence of a tragically unhappy break with a man.[3]

The previously cited passage from her late-life text *Material Life* (1987)
makes explicit what her writing suggests with increasing insistence as
she ages: that the unified, independent subject necessary to the writing
of traditional autobiography depends upon the gathering up and bringing
together of her "pulverized" parts, which in turn depends on the transfor-
mational experiences of love and writing. In fact, the late psychological
perspectives of her work, when considered in relation to her writing
through the 1970s, pose questions about female subject formation. The
problematics of Duras's relationship with her mother were in some important ways different from those experienced more generally by all
daughters who write. The political and social realities of her childhood
and youth in French colonial Indochina and her mother's complex participation in that society seem to call for a revision of the way we consider
social and political reality as potentially entering into and marking the
outcome of the symbiotic mother-daughter dynamic.

To the extent that Duras remained locked in this dynamic, incapable of individuation and subject formation, her work reveals an interchangeability and uncertain identity among characters, especially women, and above all a dynamic of symbiosis, or attempted, frustrated fusion, with the reader. But with the development of her late style by her mid-sixties, Duras's relationship to the reader changes as she increasingly achieves a form of subjectivity. And although this subjectivity always bears the stamp of her early difficulties, in some ways it will be the stronger for the value it places on connection. If there is to be true intimacy in the late years, or at any time, there must be a hard-won subjectivity, but in Duras's work the opposite is also true: subjectivity does not exist without intimacy and relationship. This dichotomy is what sets the Durassian subject apart from the usual definition of the subject as autonomous, fully individuated, and separate. And the shifts between subjectivity, its collapse into fusion, and its reconstruction through writing oblige us to reconsider the very nature of the subject, modern or postmodern, and its possible gendered modalities.

Multiculturalism in 1920: The Complicated Story of Marie Legrand Donnadieu and Her Daughter in Indochina

Marguerite Donnadieu was the youngest of three children and only daughter of Marie Legrand and Emile Donnadieu, both French schoolteachers who had emigrated to the Indochinese colony. They had come in order to seek their fortune but also in response to government propaganda about bringing the moral and intellectual benefits of French civilization to the Third World. Marguerite was born in a village outside Saigon in 1914, long before any discourse about the contradictions of colonialism could be available to her or to her family. When her father died in 1918, her mother undertook a life of almost absolute self-sacrifice in the name of raising her children and imparting to them the certainty that they were superior because they were French and white.

And yet, quite unlike the wealthy French colonials presented in Duras' novels like *The Vice Consul* [Le Vice-consul] or her film *India Song*, who lived in luxury and in isolation from the native inhabitants, Marguerite and her brothers, Pierre and Paul, were children of the bush. Their mother's financial circumstances were drastically reduced for years after her husband's death, a situation that produced a way of life teeming with contradictions. Poor and shunned by the French, the Donnadieu family nevertheless had Vietnamese servants, even when there was very little dinner to be served. In total ignorance of the history and vast culture of the colonized country, Marguerite and Paul were perfectly bilingual and, in the manner of children, totally absorbed in their daily life in Vietnam, swimming in the muddy Mekong River, wandering barefoot, adept at avoiding the wild animals in the tropical forest. Marguerite presented Vietnamese as her second language when she passed her *baccalauréat*, for, unlike her brothers, she was a good student and interested from childhood in becoming a writer. Her mother recognized her intelligence and looked to her somehow to deliver the family from its dire circumstances. Her plans for Marguerite included a return to France, marriage to a French man, preferably wealthy, and a solid intellectual career. Thus this mother, who worked all her life outside of the home, distinguished herself from the two others we have seen with respect to her daughter's professional future, but only up to a point; she utterly rejected the almost indecent notion of becoming a writer. For Marguerite, although she was desperate for her mother's approval, the desire to write was nevertheless "stronger than anything" (Duras, qtd. in *Apostrophes*).

Among the other historically verifiable facts of her existence was the catastrophe that befell Madame Donnadieu when she entrusted her life's savings to the colonial cadastral agents in exchange for a parcel of land. Her naiveté with respect to the very colonial administration she herself represented and fervently believed in cost her both her savings and her youth: because she failed to bribe the agents, she was granted land that was flooded annually by the salt waters of the Pacific and therefore useless for cultivation. She bravely inspired the native population of the peninsula and enlisted them to help her build a dam to hold back the waters, and the inhabitants joined with her in a common cause against the cadastral agents—but the Pacific inevitably invaded the land. Marguerite and her brothers grew up in the shadow of this colossal injustice to their mother and the resulting misery. The older brother, Pierre, very early became something of a petty thug, tyrannizing the younger brother in ways that seemed like serious threats. Marguerite and Paul spent much time together, united by a fierce love that almost certainly, according to the evidence of Duras's fiction, was also incestuous. Slightly retarded, Paul appeared to his sister as the gentle victim of much oppression. Finally, at age eighteen, Marguerite left for France to pass the final portion of her *baccalauréat* and pursue her university studies, and she never returned to Indochina.

When we examine the evidence of the various novels and plays written about the family, certain thematic and symbolic material relating to Duras's early life is present from her early work, *The Sea Wall* (1950), until almost the latest, *The Lover from the North of China* (1991). As mentioned earlier, the treatment of these elements changes over time and is actually an interesting barometer of the changes that occurred with age and increasing distance. Repeated accounts seem to have allowed Duras to explore several obsessive concerns, including the distribution of power in relationships and in society. It already emerges clearly from the simplest statement of her early circumstances that her lifelong personal sensitivity to suffering was necessarily linked to her life in a harsh political climate in which it was dangerous, even deadly, to be among the colonized or to be poor, but also very difficult to identify with the colonizer. This primal story of the family's dilemma was the only possible vehicle for Duras's entry into a literature of self-revelation or disclosure.

Here, I would like to consider the early novelistic presentation of this childhood in *The Sea Wall*, although this work was not written until Duras had already been in France for eighteen years. The novel reorganizes certain verifiable autobiographical materials and seems to emphasize others in ways that will change in subsequent renditions. The style is one of social and historical realism, quite unlike Duras's late work and to some extent a response to pressure from her publisher Gallimard and her mentor and protector, Raymond Queneau. In addition to the stifling despair of the family, we are given a panoramic view of the disaster of French colonialism in Indochina. The inevitable connections between this family's life and this political environment are made clear, and in this way *The Sea Wall* does announce all of Duras's writing to come: the world at large is portrayed in terms of the young girl Suzanne's formative family experience, in what Julia Kristeva calls "the absorption into the microcosm of the individual's experience of all the political horror of our time"(*Soleil noir* 242).

Briefly, *The Sea Wall* is the story of "the mother," her daughter, Suzanne, and her only son, Joseph, who live in the flat, hot, and wet Cambodian Plain of the Birds among peasants who cultivate rice and hunters who frequent the surrounding high forest land. Ruined by her project of building a dam to protect her concession from the floodwaters of the Pacific, the mother is portrayed from the first pages as old at age fifty, spent, and near madness and death, like the dying old horse in the opening scene. Her children, however, are young and vigorous adolescents. Early in the story, the family makes the acquaintance of Monsieur Jo, the wealthy son of a Chinese developer in Saigon, who would like to marry Suzanne but whose father forbids the marriage. His desire for her, coupled with his general ineptitude, make of him a pathetic figure from whom Suzanne finally manages to extort a large diamond. The first half of the novel ends on this note of hope: the family will sell the diamond in Saigon, pay off their immense debt to the cadastral agents, and regain their dignity and the possibility of a new life. In the second half, Suzanne, Joseph, and the mother all awaken to certain truths about money, power, and their relationship to sexuality. The narration is in the third person but centered within Suzanne, so it is her dawning awareness of female sexual desire and power, including issues of marriage and prostitution, that are fully explored. In the end, the diamond proves to be worth much less than expected. Half defeated, but with new ideas about their futures, the son and daughter return briefly to the Plain. The mother returns only to die there, for she has come to the end of her story and there is no other possible ending for her.

The plot appears at first glance to turn on the sale of the diamond and the importance of this change in material status. But even more essential questions posed by the novel lie elsewhere. The winning of the diamond, Suzanne's ruses to avoid sexual relations with Monsieur Jo, the children's decision to sell the diamond rather than to continue with Monsieur Jo, Suzanne's discovery in Saigon of her sexuality, and her affair back on the Plain with Agosti, a young friend of the family, do not lead to marriage, as the mother would like. Suzanne is questioning marriage as an ending for her story throughout the novel. For her, the real question becomes how to leave the Plain and how to avoid the mother's fate. Marriage to the attractive Agosti is not seen as deliverance from this fate in that it would probably leave her with children, older, and perhaps abandoned, according to her experienced friend Carmen in Saigon. Marriage to Monsieur Jo is both unthinkable and impossible. Thus I read *The Sea Wall* as an early yet definitive moment of rejection of certain traditional plots for women, as well as an examination of the ways in which these plots are inevitably enmeshed in the realities of a particular political situation.

As always, it is the mother who presents the daughter with the example of her own story and with instructions about how to live her life according to established codes of sexual conduct and marriage. In *The Sea Wall,* the mother is doubled in part 2 by Carmen, a prostitute turned hotel manager who takes Suzanne under her wing while the mother is vainly trying to obtain the expected price for the diamond. The question of prostitution is raised almost immediately after Suzanne meets the wealthy Monsieur Jo in part 1. It is a recurrent theme throughout Duras's works, always related to the question of letting oneself be *seen* ("se faire voir" in French) and hence, by association, to writing and publication and also to disclosure. It is important to note that in *The Sea Wall,* as elsewhere in this corpus, not all female prostitution is the same. Distinctions are made according to whose pleasure or whose desire for power is being satisfied. Thus Suzanne is briefly tempted to expose her naked body to Monsieur Jo in the shower, as she suddenly recognizes her own beauty and desire to make love and realizes that her body "was not made to be kept hidden but on the contrary to be seen and to make its way in the world" [Ce n'était pas fait pour être caché mais au contraire pour être vu et pour faire son chemin de par le monde](73). But Monsieur Jo attempts to buy this favor with still more gifts, and "it was thus at the very moment when she was about to open the door and let the world see her that the world made a prostitute of her" [C'est ainsi qu'au moment où elle allait ouvrir et se donner à voir au monde, le monde la prostitua] (73). From this point on, Suzanne insists upon choosing.

In Saigon, Carmen repeats the advice that Suzanne must leave her mother, that she must walk in the streets of the elegant white neighborhood of Saigon until she meets a wealthy man. After one try, Suzanne abandons this pursuit, which she doesn't really understand. She prefers to go to the movies alone, where she is enthralled by idealized visions of love and lovemaking. Or she takes a ride in Monsieur Jo's car, and when he tells her she has beautiful breasts, she imagines herself reigning over the entire city in her newfound power, "her hardened nipples standing higher than all that was standing in the city" [l'érection de ses seins plus haut que tout ce qui se dressait dans la ville] (226).

By the end of their stay in Saigon, the reader is left wondering whether Carmen and Suzanne's mother are really different from each other, as the mother tries to arrange a marriage between Suzanne and a rich but unknown traveling businessman, and when in her chasing after Monsieur Jo in Saigon the mother is compared by Suzanne to "a kind of old whore who didn't even know it" [une sorte de vieille putain qui s'ignorait] (193). It becomes clear that Suzanne has refined the notion of prostitution according to her new understanding of sex and power. Even earlier, armed with her dawning awareness of these distinctions after the encounters with Monsieur Jo, Suzanne had been able to endure two hours' worth of beating by her mother, who is infuriated by what she imagines to be Suzanne's "prostitution" with her Chinese suitor. The beating ends as Suzanne's brother, Joseph, intervenes as her defender and accomplice. "The only sweet thing in life was Joseph" [La seule douceur de la vie c'était lui, Joseph] (141). Through her brother, Suzanne attempts to understand their mother, as he seems able to do, and first learns the value of love and, ultimately, how to leave the Plain. By showing her a way to direct her will and, by implication, a way to fulfill her sexuality, he stands as an alternative to the mother's imagined plots for the daughter, all of which involve a subordinated status of some kind.[4] By the end, Suzanne has lost her virginity to Agosti but has refused marriage, saying to her astonished lover that what she truly wants is to *leave* [C'est partir que je veux], both the Plain and the matrix of possible stories and outcomes for herself if she were to stay (353). Joseph and his lover then take Suzanne away with them. The reader is not sure where she is going but feels that the ending is unusual and open.

Shortly before the end, the mother writes a letter to the cadastral agents, setting forth the full extent of their crime against her and promising revenge in the event that they do not grant her a small, arable portion of land. Joseph gives a group of mourners explicit instructions to murder the agents and furnishes them with rifles. As he has promised Suzanne earlier, now that he is in a powerful position he will crush the colonial enemy without compassion, in essence by using their own tactics (164). Thus he positions himself on the side of his mother, but he seeks all the same to resemble the enemy; he advises his sister to follow the same conflicted course (284). What are we to make of this complicated relationship between unending compassion for the victimized mother and a refusal to be like her, to the point of adopting the tactics of the enemy? For Joseph's voice, as I have indicated, is also Suzanne's. She is fleeing not only political exploitation in the form of the wretched bungalow and useless land, but other possible exploitation as well in the plots of marriage and undesired "prostitution," which reflect the same power dynamic. Most complex of all is the relationship to colonial reality of white and nonwhite. The mother has been ruined, after all, by her own people. In future versions, more will be made of this, for in fact Duras's mother clung to her French, white identity, and in her interview with Pivot, Duras claimed it would have seemed to her mother an even worse calamity than the flooding if she had known her daughter had slept with a Chinese man, as recounted in *The Lover*.

In *The Sea Wall*, we are essentially in the grip of a social and political situation in which there are only two terms: the powerful and the powerless, the white French and the nonwhite Vietnamese, the rich and the poor, men and women. For the moment, it is impossible for Joseph or Suzanne to articulate a third term, and this of course prevents them from moving forward to the considerations of new alternatives. Suzanne, like her brother, has discovered one potential for difference from her mother's fate through the exercise of her own eroticism, and she also restlessly rejects the standard plots that are proposed to her. But these are not replaced by another project. The only value in her universe is her love for Joseph. And more than Joseph, who can at least embark on a specific adventure at the end, she is locked into the alternatives of identifying with her mother as a powerless victim or with the all-powerful colonial regime, also represented by her mother, which ruthlessly exploits and murders the Indochinese to the point where the mud of the Plain is described as full of children's corpses in references that recall the mass graves of World War II (296).

The question for a daughter of how to identify with such a mother in these circumstances was absolutely central to Duras's psychic development over the entire course of her life. We have seen in the preceding chapters and in countless other histories of women writers what we already know to be the case for women in general: that the work of differentiation and subject formation is different for girls, that it is never fully realized, and that the mother-daughter relationship is often a continuing preoccupation into a woman's late years.[5]

Julia Kristeva in her book *Soleil noir: Dépression et mélancolie* has addressed the complex question of Duras's "impossible mourning," "a quest forever nostalgic," of her mother as the lost object. Kristeva sees Duras's work from *Hiroshima mon amour* onward as pervaded by an aesthetic of pain and suffering that is a consequence of maternal abandonment. Because this pain is by its nature impossible to describe verbally (Kristeva, *Soleil noir* 241) since it belongs to a time before the child possessed language, Kristeva believes that Duras's writing is marked by silences and pre-oedipal figures of doublings of characters and situations. She does not altogether deny the political dimension of Duras's work, but she insists that it becomes secondary to, an echo of, the personal depression of the author that has its true origins elsewhere, in the early psychic drama between mother and child (242). The individual thus becomes the focus of a drama that is nevertheless unique to our time. Kristeva does not credit the specificity of Duras's childhood with her inability, for a long time at least, to move beyond a fixation on the mother-daughter bond, the "crypt of reflections where identities . . . are destroyed" (262). She does go so far as to speculate: "Perhaps there had to be the strange adventure of a cultural uprooting, a childhood spent in Asia, the tensions of an arduous life with a brave and hardened mother . . . the early encounter with . . . the misery of all people, in order that a personal sensitivity to suffering join together so fervently with the drama of our time" (245).

As I have suggested, I do not altogether agree with Kristeva's assessment of the nature and source of Durassian problems with subject formation, suffering, and what she diagnoses as a "lack of catharsis" in her work (234). I would contend that Duras's example suggests another possible conclusion: the sociopolitical dimensions of women's lives, as of men's, enter into the early formation of psychic structures in ways that are not simply superimposed on an inevitable, biologically based unfolding, but that condition that unfolding as surely as the child's sexuality or the inevitability, for the girl, of the persistence of the archaic mother-child bond.

I also think it is possible to tease out of some of the apparently contradictory structures of Duras's life and work a good deal of evidence that the daughter was increasingly aware, with the passing years, of the need to find an alternative to the impossible identification with the mother as she had seemed to her children. Marie Legrand, the mother's maiden name, was "grand" indeed as she set off from France to bring the superior culture of her country to its colonies and increase her personal fortune at the same time. But Marie Donnadieu, the mother's married name, which she kept when she was a ruined widow, meant "Mary give to God," or perhaps "Mary gives to God," an ultimate epithet of self-sacrifice that described her martyrdom. For her daughter, identification with either of these figures of the mother, both products of colonial society, was unbearably painful, certainly as painful as the mother's supposed abandonment of her daughter. It is true that Marie Donnadieu preferred her older son to her other children and that Marguerite suffered from this predilection, particularly in view of her mother's depressive personality. But it is unclear to me that this degree of frustration could have created, in the absence of other factors, the need for fusion that is so striking in her work.

In *The Sea Wall*, the mother's suffering, her *déveine* (bad luck, or curse), contributes much to the impression of social and historical realism. The mother's pain is larger than life, and certainly Suzanne and Joseph will carry it with them always. But there are also interesting cracks in the compassionate accounts of the terrible destruction of the dams and of the mother. There is in fact an oscillation between two points of view, one more explicitly stated than the other, which are in fact two frightening visions of the mother. The most striking of these moments of ambiguity concerns the contest between the sea and the wall:

> The mother's dams in the Plain were the great sorrow and the great joke all at once, depending on what day it was. They were the great joke and the great sorrow. They were terrible and they were funny. It all depended on which side you took, the side of the sea that had knocked them out, these dams, in one fell swoop, the side of the crabs that had filled them with holes, or, on the contrary, the side of those who had spent six months building them in total forgetfulness of the damage, which was nevertheless certain, that would be inflicted by the sea and the crabs.

> [Les barrages de la mère dans la plaine, c'était le grand malheur et la grande rigolade à la fois, ça dépendait des jours. C'était la grande

rigolade du grand malheur. C'était terrible et c'était marrant. Ça dépendait de quel côté on se plaçait, du côté de la mer qui les avait fichus en l'air, ces barrages, d'un seul coup d'un seul, du côté des crabes qui en avaient fait des passoires, ou au contraire, du côté de ceux qui avaient mis six mois à les construire dans l'oubli total des méfaits pourtant certains de la mer et des crabes.] (53)

The irony here is so strong that one realizes that the daughter cannot be squarely on one side or the other. Suzanne betrays a similar ambivalence in other passages about the sea, even without explicit reference to the mother, in which she identifies with its destructive acts against the innocent; for example, the annual arrival of unwanted and short-lived Indochinese babies is described as brought by the tide (117). The point is that whichever side Suzanne takes, she has taken the side of the mother, but she has simultaneously taken a position against her as well. The mother is always *both* victim *and* the one who has power and inflicts harm. Neither identity is viable; neither exists without the other, in a reverberation that precludes moving beyond this phase, of finally assuming a stance and an identity.

In Duras's writing, this problem of subject formation can be seen in the well-known silences or blanks. It is personified in the haunting female double of the Beggarwoman from Savannakhet, the powerless, rejected wanderer who ends up in Calcutta, and Anne-Marie Stretter, the pale femme fatale who exercises such power over men that, in a reversal of the abandonment plot, her lover kills himself when her husband is assigned to a distant post. For a long time, like Suzanne on the side of the sea or Joseph arming the peasants to kill the cadastral agents, Duras was fascinated, even enthralled, by the power of Anne-Marie Stretter, a fictionalized variant of a colonial French woman she had occasionally seen from a distance in Saigon. Stretter seduces Lol V. Stein's fiancé in another work, reducing Lol to madness and alienation, and yet Stretter is not, when we see her again in Calcutta, a fulfilled or happy woman. Every bit as much as the oppressed women who are her counterparts, she is empty and lacking an identity, which she hopelessly seeks in love. In the end, Duras kills her off by having her walk into the waters of the Ganges in her film *India Song* (1975). This was in fact one of a series of gestures that indicated her readiness, late in life, to move on to a position beyond this binary trap. Only with age did she achieve understanding of how pointless the exercise of such power per se can be, for herself or for characters like Anne-Marie Stretter: reversing the plot is not a solution, though seduction and eroticism in the name of connection and one's own pleasure are steps in the right direction.

Duras's life as a young woman in France also reveals her inability to align herself unambiguously with a cause, although she did finally militate ardently in the Resistance after she had personally felt the effects of the war when her husband was deported. In her book *The War*, written in 1947 and published in 1985, Duras's character Thérèse actively participates in the postwar torturing of captured collaborators. In "Ter the Militiaman," Thérèse and her husband stand guard over the childlike Ter, whose name implicates him in a doubling with Thérèse. She feels strong desire, even love, for this man she is supposed to torture. At once or alternately victim and executioner, Duras at this point is still unable to take sides in the power dilemma first presented by her earlier life, though she has learned by the 1940s that her primary task is to fight abusive power. The problem will always be one of comfortable affiliation. And it is no accident that some of her power is the power of seduction over men, as in the story of Pierre Rabier. Her older brother Pierre, whom she identifies throughout *The Lover* with the Nazis, found power seductive and seduction to be his only power. By the time she wrote *The War*, Duras already knew that as a young woman, seduction was a means of power for her as it was for Suzanne on the Plain.

Kristeva is clearly correct in diagnosing this difficulty of finding an identity outside of a symbiotic bond as essential to Duras's writing. She notes that identity, or subjectivity in both the psychological and the literary sense, can only come when one has moved beyond the stage of symbiosis into a stage in which the self recognizes itself as a separated individual and no longer seeks its identity as reflected in a double (*Soleil noir* 263). Kristeva observes that entering this phase requires the intervention of a third element. We shall see that the Durassian writing subject emerged via a transformative process involving a third term, though in a unique way and at a particular time in her life. As Kristeva astutely adds, Duras's most radically innovative aspect will always remain the testing of the limits of subjectivity, as she dissolves, recreates, and contests the very notion that a fully autonomous subject is possible: "But even the most solid and integrated among us recognize that a firm identity remains a fiction . . . thus she takes hold of us and carries us to the dangerous limits of our psychic lives" (263–64).

Kristeva is pointing to a connection between a postmodernist view of the subject and certain essential tenets of feminist revisions of psychoanalysis, which were largely inspired by object-relations theorists. In psychoanalytic terms, subject formation depends on a separation from the mother that is fully accepted by the child. But this process is never accomplished altogether for girls and women, and in cases as difficult as Duras's even the female writing subject addressing itself authoritatively to the reader in a traditional manner, presenting its *jouissance* in its own name, requires understanding in different terms. It is useful to examine the dynamic between writer and reader over the course of Duras's long lifetime, in order to trace the emergence of the Durassian subject, which occurred in response to Duras's deep emotional need for a new kind of connection with her reader. Duras explored these problems in a series of "cure stories" in the 1960s, which she sometimes experienced as painful and threatening. Years later, when she returned to writing in the late seventies after a period of filmmaking, changes began to occur. Kristeva's analysis would have been stronger had she taken the effects of aging into account. Having traced here the origins of Duras's fundamental psychic drama, I propose now to examine the unfolding of that drama over time and into old age.

France: A Stranger in Her Own Country

Marguerite Donnadieu's first contact with France when she returned at age eighteen was in the Duras region of the southwest, where her father's property remained. Although she moved on very soon to Paris to resume her studies and was permanently separated from her brother Paul and from her mother, her sojourn in Duras obviously provided her with a means to escape her name. In *Women Speaking* (Les Parleuses), Duras says that she was unable to write under the name Donnadieu because she had "such a horror of my name that even now I can hardly manage to pronounce it" [je tenais mon nom dans une telle horreur que j'arrive à peine à le prononcer] (23–24). Although Marguerite hardly knew her father, in choosing "Duras" as a name she reconnected herself in fact to the paternal line. It seems to me that in abandoning "Donnadieu" she abandoned a certain identification with her mother that might have hindered her writing. It is interesting to compare this move with Colette's assumption of her father's name and her dropping of "Sidonie Gabrielle," first names that inevitably recalled her mother. Both writers finally created unambiguously feminine names for themselves all the same, unlike many of their nineteenth-century sisters in both England and France. By the end of World War I, a woman could hope for recognition without falsifying her gender, even if certain very real difficulties remained.

In Paris, Duras was bewildered at first by the European environment wherein the claims of colonial powers, which she had been conditioned to regard as "legitimate," were considered by French intellectuals to be fascist. As the Second World War approached, Marguerite went to work for the Ministère des Colonies. With a friend from the Ecole Coloniale, she coauthored *The French Empire* [L'Empire français] in defense of French colonialism, justifying the civilization of "inferior" races by the "superior," glorifying the French administration in Indochina, although she was intimately familiar with its injustice, as readers learned ten years later in *The Sea Wall*. She went so far as to point out that if war seemed imminent in Europe, France could only benefit from the participation of the colonized in its army. It seems evident in view of her subsequent political evolution that Marguerite was intent at this point in burying any memories that could remind her of the victimization she and her mother had experienced.

Duras worked at the Cercle de la Librairie, a Gestapo-controlled agency where she was responsible for deciding which books deserved a share of the paper available for publication. Her husband, Robert Antelme, worked at the police prefecture, where he was sometimes able to intervene in discrimination against Jews. But neither one rose above a kind of ambiguous collaboration at the beginning of the war. In 1942, their baby died at birth, and within the same year, Marguerite's beloved brother Paul died in Indochina. A short while later, she met Dionys Mascolo at the Cercle, fell in love, and arranged a ménage à trois that was to outlast the war. Marguerite and Dionys already planned to have a child, but Robert and Dionys became fast friends all the same. There was nothing conventional in Marguerite's personal situation, even if the trio's easygoing way of living through the Occupation was typical of many Parisians.

Under the influence of their friend François Mitterand, they awakened to the moral necessity of resistance. Yet even at this point, the ambiguity of Marguerite's position, her unwillingness to align herself thoroughly with respect to prevailing power relations, is striking. We read in *The Lover,* for instance, that she frequented the Fernandez's apartment just above her own in the rue Saint Benoît, although Ramón Fernandez was the minister of culture of the French fascist party. In this murky period when many French writers refused to publish on the grounds that their work was necessarily censored by the Germans, she wrote and published a first novel, *Les Impudents,* for which she received the important recognition of Raymond Queneau.

Then she fell silent and published nothing further until 1950, as full political awareness and commitment came to her with the deportation of her husband. The terrible sorrow of her early life, the death of her baby and of Paul in Vietnam, and the atrocity of the German camps mingled and forced her to feel the pain and suffering she had tried to leave behind. Robert returned from Buchenwald on the point of death, and Duras's account in *The War* of the Nazis' failed attempt to dehumanize him and of the weeks in which he hovered between life and death is one of implacable realism and refusal to avert her eyes from horror and her own inconsolable grief. With this work, though she only published it forty years later, Duras proved that for her, as earlier for Simone de Beauvoir, writing had become a space of transgression, where no subject or aspect of human physical suffering was taboo. And she began to realize what had always been implicit in the complicated relation between suffering and politics in her early life: the dreadful capacity to victimize other human beings no longer belonged to her past or to any one situation, but rather it was everywhere and in everyone. From this point until the present, Duras would identify strongly with the powerless.

After the War

In the immediate postwar years, Duras, Antelme, and Mascolo became members of the French Communist Party. The excessive discipline, intolerance of individual creativity, and submission to the Soviet Union put an end to the experiment when the three were expelled or felt obliged to resign. Yet out of it grew the "group of the rue Saint Benoît," an intellectual circle that for a time rivaled that of Sartre and Beauvoir and over which Duras presided. The three remained firmly on the left politically, communist in spirit and committed to the victims of war and social injustice, despite the bitter realization they shared with many other French ex-communists that communism was not a viable political solution to the problems of the twentieth century.

For Duras, this disillusionment was to have particular consequences. Unlike Sartre, Camus, or Malraux, who were still seeking a literature of political engagement, she began to contest the necessity of a relationship between writing and politics, the very premise of writing as a political act in a conventional sense, and she wondered whether the time would ever return for meaningful political activism. She was hardly alone in turning away from commitment by the late 1950s, and for a time she found herself associated with the authors of the formalist "new novel": Michel Butor, Alain Robbe-Grillet, and Claude Simon, among others.

It was at the beginning of this period that she published *The Sea Wall*. We have noted its ambiguities with respect to power and what they implied about her relationship with her mother. In life, despite the consecration the book brought to her daughter, the mother was horrified by so much revelation or "publication" of herself and the family.[6] Pained by her mother's reaction, Marguerite nonetheless continued her scandalous existence, which followed no recognizable model for a wife and mother. Her writing became increasingly transgressive, disobedient, outside of any social, political, or aesthetic law. She had come in touch not only with sorrow but also with anger through her experiences of the war and of Communism, and her increasing willingness to express her anger directly sets her work apart from her major compatriot women writers, including Simone de Beauvoir.

Between 1950 and 1962, Duras published eight novels or collections of short prose, one play, and two film scenarios, including *Hiroshima mon amour* (1960). Even in this early work, there is no story for a heroine that follows either an abandonment plot in any conventional way or any other traditional love and marriage plot. Several, though not all, of these texts are remarkable for the sexual freedom of their female characters. Their style remains essentially realist, the narrator in control of her/his story, the reader easily able to construct her/his position as reader-subject in relation to them. The Durassian "silence" within the text had yet to appear.

The theme of aging in Duras's work is most explicitly treated in one of these novels, *Ten Thirty on a Summer Evening* [Dix Heures et demie du soir en été] (1960). Maria, a woman in her thirties, is aware that her husband, Pierre, desires a younger woman. Maria is an alcoholic, and under the influence of alcohol she tries to invent an alternative form of plot for herself by coming to the dramatic rescue of a jealous criminal who had killed his wife and her lover. But the criminal ends by committing suicide, and this effort to construct a different outcome fails. Maria learns to accept her husband's love of her rival, Claire, as inevitable. Although her original anguish appears to be spent with the failure of her attempt to save the criminal's life, she remains preoccupied by the question of men's attention: is it directed towards her still, or not? Is it directed towards Claire instead?

At one point, Maria notices that a permanent change has occurred in her: "It is when she touches her face with her hand that she feels it, that she knows that was beautiful, but that she has begun to be less beautiful now" (98). Aging and the passing of time are inscribed in her face for all to read, and it is there that she herself becomes aware of them. Maria finally fully accepts these changes too, and at the end, Pierre also seems to have changed with time. He will not give up his new adventure, but it is no longer enough for him; he wants Maria too (150). However, Maria does not accept her husband's genuine offer to be part of his life with Claire. Determined to be the author of her own destiny, she decides to leave rather than stay in a situation that was not her own creation, and that is, in fact, a variant of the abandonment plot. This courageous and basically serene depiction of the problem of aging in *Ten-Thirty on a Summer Evening* contrasts with other treatments of the theme that we have already seen. Its honest portrayal of Maria's initial disarray on the brink of middle age and then of her coming to terms, especially in the absence of subsequent explicit discussion of age as an obstacle to women's happiness in Duras's writing, seems to suggest that the essential problem of middle and late age for Duras did not lie in the loss of physical beauty. A changing body image was a problem to her to some extent, as to all sexually active women. But the most compelling issue for her lay instead in the resolution of her problem of identity and subject formation and its impact on her intimate relationships.

In 1958, with *Moderato Cantabile,* an important shift in narrative style occurs, as Duras herself noted in a quotation at the beginning of this chapter. She was forty-four and had been abandoned by Gérard Jarlot, to whom she had been passionately sexually attached. Like Maria, she began to drink heavily. Her son moved out of the family apartment in the rue Saint Benoît and Dionys Mascolo became involved with a younger woman. She felt the pain of abandonment that came to her with increasing age, even if her response to it was somewhat different from that of most other women. By 1964, at the age of fifty, Duras published *The Ravishing of Lol V. Stein* [Le Ravissement de Lol V. Stein] inaugurating a cycle of "cure stories" that are among her best-known works. In her fifties, Duras withdrew into her writing, though she continued to receive occasional lovers in her home in Neauphle-le-Château in the Paris region. She experienced the period between 1962 and 1971 as essentially one of solitude.

Blanking Out

French critics of Duras, in particular French feminist critics following Luce Irigaray and Marcelle Marini, have stressed that certain missing links or blanks in her works of the 1960s are crucial to the view that Duras's writing is "feminine" (Selous 12). Such a view is conditioned by the Lacanian framework within which many French intellectuals have written about a theoretical association between gender and language. Duras agrees with Xavière Gauthier's statements that her blanks are "sexual" and "feminine," and that a man could not have written them (*Les Parleuses* 19), a position she reiterates in *Material Life* (104).

It is not my intention here to reinvestigate the question of a "writing of the body" (l'écriture féminine), except perhaps to remind the reader of my assessment in chapter 1 of this movement in France as a recent reassertion of essentialist difference between the sexes, and hence a contradiction of an earlier, politicized form of feminism. I prefer to concentrate instead simply on Duras's writing. Trista Selous, who retains a Lacanian psychoanalytic framework herself, has made a thoughtful analysis of

Durassian blanks. She does not find them to be "specifically feminine" nor even "disruptive of the rules by which masculine language or literature work" (137). She catalogues the blanks as textual effects: the missing event that triggers the story; the restriction of the narrator's knowledge where she/he seems not to have a point of view at all and finally disappears, as in *Moderato cantabile*; empty but recurrent symbols that resist all interpretation; and finally the withering away of character, motivation, and desire, particularly among the women (127–37). Selous believes that these various narrative obstacles to intellectual understanding, or to solving a puzzle most often presented by a woman's behavior, work according to the same mechanism as innuendo, or jokes; that is, they trigger unconscious links among signifiers in the reader's mind in the effort to *fill in* the blanks. The rules of signification, she feels, are resilient to omissions, and while "Duras's blanks may require that the reader assume meanings on an unconscious or preconscious level, they do not break meaning down. The power of her writing comes from understatement and interpretation, rather than the eruption of the unconscious into the conscious"(137).

Thus Selous makes the radical move of situating Duras's own radical departure not at the level of meaning itself, but rather in the relationship she sets up with the reader by way of the text, and with this I fully agree. I would add, with Sharon Willis, that the greatest blanks or lack of information in the texts, and hence the greatest effort required of the reader, increasingly concerns the central woman character. This confirms that the problem Duras was grappling with during this period was indeed woman's identity. And this riddle of femininity concerns Duras as much as her characters.

Like Duras, Selous locates the beginning of a new kind of narrative in *Moderato cantabile*. And she observes that as early as *The Sea Wall*, there is an ironic tone produced at the "points of conflict in its discourse," where the narrator's position seems suddenly uncertain (92). I have noted these ironic cracks as indicative of the narrator's inability to maintain a coherent commitment with respect to the colonial system. Selous notes an example in the story of Monsieur Jo's father's rise to riches by the exploitation of the Vietnamese. The son will not be able to run this business in his turn, of course, because of his gentle nature, here portrayed as simple inadequacy and a source of ridicule. The reader is left wondering about the narrator's position with respect to the father, whose career has been like that of French colonials. (In subsequent versions of her early life, Duras will more fully develop these contradictory aspects of the Chinese suitor as revealing of his position outside the Franco-Vietnamese dichotomy, rather than of anything ridiculous in his character.) Selous's diagnosis of the fragility of narrative authority does not accidentally concern a question of power relations in the colony. And in a further enactment of the dilemma, the reader of this early text is unsettled in turn *as a subject*. Durassian texts are often concerned with crime and detection, just as they are narratively *transgressive* (*The Sailor from Gibraltar* [Le Marin de Gibraltar], *The English Lover* [L'Amante anglaise], *Ten-Thirty on a Summer Evening,* etc.) By posing insoluble riddles, they deny the subjecthood to the reader that the latter expects to acquire through the act of reading.

With *Moderato cantabile,* the illusion of a solidly constructed narrator and reader more obviously begins to fall apart. The scenes of story-making between Anne and Chauvin in the café are described in all their strangeness without any explanations: Why, for instance, is Anne so curious about the woman who wanted to die? What are her feelings about Chauvin? Why has she started to drink in this working-class bar? The reader must infer that Anne is asking Chauvin to relate a possible story for them that will perhaps occur in the same café. The changing pink colors of the sunset, the child's disastrous music lessons, the arrival of the foundry workers in the café, and one or two other motifs are constantly repeated, but like the symbol of the magnolia flower they resist interpretation, though one intuits that the flower has to do with Chauvin's desire. We remain detached from Anne, the central character. We do not "know" how it is that Anne "dies" at the end, though she says Chauvin has killed her: "It's done" [C'est fait] (84). We soon realize that the answers are not in the text, and we can choose to undertake to infer them, to enter into the very work of signification, or not. Many readers have of course been fascinated by this challenge, whereas others find the esthetic experience to be too unsettling. All the pleasure is in the process, in the feeling that one is approaching knowledge without ever arriving at it.

In *The Ravishing of Lol V. Stein,* the first narrator, Jacques Hold, a male friend of Lol's, attempts to provide a certain amount of psychological explanation of Lol, the object of his and our shared fascination. But there is a crucial link or connection that it is impossible for Jacques, the reader, or even Lol to make, and this concerns the missing event that precipitated Lol into her mysterious state of madness ten years earlier. Lol was abandoned by her fiancé, Michael Richardson, at a ball in their hometown. Richardson left without a word to follow the powerful seductress Anne-Marie Stretter, who, in an interesting variant of the abandonment plot, is a somewhat older woman who has brought her own daughter to the same ball.

I think it is legitimate to read *The Ravishing of Lol V. Stein* as a questioning and reevaluation of the traditional Sapphic plot. Duras presents her own specific take on that plot and relates it to both her concern with abuse of power, here with reference to men and women, and also to the ways in which the plot perpetuates the anonymity or interchangeability of women and hence their lack of differentiated identity. Lol is a long-term survivor of the catastrophe of the abandonment plot. Since the night in the ballroom, Lol has moved to another town, married, and had children. Ten years later she returns to S. Thala to live, but she is radically changed. She is passive, colorless, and empty, and her old friend Tatiana Karl and Tatiana's lover, Jacques Hold, find that she has never been able to understand the event that changed her life, the substitution in her fiancé's affections of another woman. Nor has she ever felt the expected pain. In his attempt to investigate and get a "hold" on her, Jacques becomes the narrator of her story. And it is not an innocent investigation, as we soon realize, for his need to understand Lol includes the need to control her and to penetrate her body in order to understand/possess the blank that Lol has become, if necessary against her will.

Hold experiences infinite frustration in his project of domination. The problem is that although Lol seems compliant, pleasant, even yielding, this passivity is not the traditional passivity of the female participant in the traditional plot. Rather, Lol is passive because she has somehow been voided by her experience, so that nothing she says can be taken as the truth about her, since there is no longer any truth, any person there to be understood. Lol's absence extends to the scene in which he physically penetrates her, after the two have returned together to the ballroom in S. Thala, where Lol is still unable to understand, to *feel* anything. The passage is a sort of condensation of the problematic of the novel:

> I am obliged to undress her. She won't do it herself. Now she is naked. Who is there in the bed? . . . Stretched out, she doesn't move. She seems worried. She is motionless, she stays where I have placed her. She follows me with her eyes around the room as if she didn't know me as I undress in turn. Who is she? The crisis has come. . . . She . . . probably remembers that she is here, with Tatiana Karl's lover. But all of a sudden she begins to doubt that identity, the only one she has recognized, the only one she has desired at least since I have known her. She asks, "Who is it?" She . . . asks me to say it. I say, "You could be Tatiana Karl, for instance."

> [Je suis obligé de la déshabiller. Elle ne le fera pas elle-même. La voici nue. Qui est là dans le lit? . . . Allongée elle ne bouge pas. Elle est inquiète. Elle est immobile, reste là où je l'ai posée. Elle me suit des yeux comme un inconnu à travers la chambre lorsque je me déshabille à mon tour. Qui est-ce? La crise est là. . . . Elle . . . se souvient sans doute qu'elle est là avec l'amant de Tatiana Karl. Mais voici qu'elle doute enfin de cette identité, la seule qu'elle reconnaisse, la seule dont elle s'est toujours réclamée du moins pendant le temps où je l'ai connue. Elle dit "Qui c'est?" Elle . . . me demande de le dire. Je dis: "Tatiana Karl, par exemple."] (187–88)

In this passage Duras is building her critique of the male literary tradition, of which the abandonment plot for women is an example, as a form of domination. Jacques Hold's narrative project is in fact unacceptable in the terms of the very novel he is narrating, despite the fact that he has presented all his information to the reader in an apparent act of good faith in the first part.[7]

Although Michael Richardson's choice of Anne-Marie Stretter as a replacement for Lol V. Stein is in fact a banal event in the traditional love story, here it becomes both the cause and effect of Lol's madness. If women are interchangeable, they are by definition denied a self, a subjectivity. And hard as she tries, Lol cannot fully imagine her annihilation as a subject, any more than one can dream one's own death. Yet she has been driven mad by the apprehension of this truth: choices are made arbitrarily, and individuality is a lie. She tries at the end of the novel to become the narrator, choosing a triangle of her own including herself, Tatiana, and Jacques. If she fails, it is not for the same reasons that Jacques does. Her narrative is not a counterpart to Jacques's, for her problem is different: her very lack of a definite identity makes domination an impossible project, and she remains locked in the unresolved grief of her lost love object, which, when she possessed it, had conferred on her the illusion of individuality. The real basis of Lol's madness is her conviction, after the abandonment, that all women are anonymous.

Here we are at the heart of Duras's psychic work of her middle age. If these women characters are blanked out, it is because it is impossible for Duras to confer an individuated identity on them. As a consequence, though they may survive or even reverse the Sapphic plot for women, they do not have new stories of their own. Dependent upon the sexual love of men as their only real source of intimacy, dissatisfied with its limitations and vulnerable to abandonment, they relive the fundamental problem of being the Other and of desire for fusion that begins with the mother but informs all subsequent heterosexual relationships as well. Duras said that when writing this book, she too experienced a feeling of madness and actually screamed out loud (*Places*, 102). I think it plausible that Lol is mad because she cannot accept what is in fact *unacceptable*: that women are not differentiated, that they therefore cannot be understood intellectually or deeply loved, and that the abandonment plot becomes an inevitability for them or they become prostitutes in the negative sense. If Jacques's frustration and the implicit critique of his violation of Lol constitute a fierce criticism of his desire to dominate and control, and hence of the plot, they are at the same time a refusal of a psychic situation in which many women find themselves, even if, at this moment in her life, Duras cannot yet provide her character with another kind of feminine subjectivity.

The dynamic in *The Ravishing of Lol V. Stein* is again one of inference on the reader's part and an active involvement in an investigation that is like a detective story. But unlike the suspenseful detective novel, these novels of Duras do not resolve their mysteries at the end, and the reader remains locked into these powerful texts in an endless process of looking for the answer. The novels of this period (*Moderato cantabile, The Rav-*

ishing of Lol V. Stein, The Vice Consul) became in the minds of many readers the embodiment of Durassian style and of the Durassian woman. But I would again plead for consideration of Duras's later characters, narrative structures, and writer-reader dynamics, before concluding that her "femininity" can be defined on the basis of the works of this single period of her life. The radical reinscription of the feminine of these texts was a point along a developmental continuum that is fully revealed only when the effects of aging are taken into account. It is far from clear that Duras was ultimately satisfied with the different economy of pleasure these works may have represented for many readers.[8]

Selous believes the structure at work in these blanked-out works is either Freudian or Lacanian fetishism, although both Sigmund Freud and Jacques Lacan refer only to men in their writings on this subject. It is the male child's refusal to accept the mother's "castration," and hence her desire for the father, that causes him to transfer his attention onto another object and avoid the question of the presence or absence of a phallus. Selous astutely observes that the psychic mechanism at work here is available to both sexes. She defines the structure of fetishism as "one in which a knowledge which requires the end of one attitude and a shift of position on the part of the subject is avoided or disavowed, by means of the substitution in the place of that knowledge of an object which screens or blocks it, thereby allowing the subject to retain an ambiguous position and obviating the need for an unwelcome shift" (147). Sharon Willis reminds us that Roland Barthes has already likened the suspense story, of which the detective story is a variant, to the structure of the fetish, and she adds: "This reading of suspense resembles the structure of the fetish, the suspension of the look, the reading, and the telling on the point of the threatening disclosure" (141). These texts are offered to the reader as fetishes, and finally, in the cases of Lol V. Stein, Anne-Marie Stretter, or Alissa in *Destroy, She Said* (1969), the woman herself becomes the central blank, that which cannot and must not be told, in the story.

Duras represents her own desire by means of such texts because the anxiety produced by the woman's identification with power or with its lack is too great to be confronted. Instead, it remains an obsession, forever binding the plot of the text, and preventing the relationship of full identification with or by the reader that would come with an unbinding, a final disclosure. The fetishized woman figures, as in the case of Anne-

Marie Stretter in *The Vice Consul,* can be powerful in their capacity to seduce and stimulate desire, as fetishized women in other social representations almost always are. Anne-Marie has already driven one man to suicide. But ambivalence surrounds her assumption of that power over others, and the very nature of sexual power over men is called into question as the fetishized figures themselves are shown to be both powerful and helpless. This power is the only one traditionally accorded to women in French fiction, after all, and while women readers of these fetishized images of desirable women may feel empowered by them, they simultaneously feel inadequate, as women always do when confronted by any culturally determined, idealized portrait of desirability. The fact that so many women have felt fascinated by these Durassian women bears witness, I think, to the complex ways in which we all concentrate on representations of feminine beauty, even as we are forever uncertain that we can ourselves ever correspond, or, even if we could, that such desirability could ever truly and meaningfully empower us.

Duras's work from 1979 to 1995 takes us beyond the fetishized images of women into a dynamic of greater intimacy with the reader. The process gathers momentum slowly and is fully under way by the time she reintroduces herself as narrator, subject, and object of a man's desire in *The Lover* and, in a sense, fetishizes herself when she says, "Look at me." In still later works, Duras also tells different stories, for if the shell of a traditional plot remains in *The Ravishing of Lol V. Stein, The Vice Consul,* or the film versions of the latter (*India Song* and *Sa Voix de Venise dans Calcutta désert,*) it no longer structures the stories except as an object of scrutiny and criticism, as in *The Ravishing.* While some familiar narrative stereotypes remain in Duras's work (women of leisure without material concerns who are involved only with the pursuit of love, faraway places, hotels, resorts, murders, and suicides), they become detached and are reorganized into other stories.

Older but Not Invisible

Marguerite Duras walked onto the scene of her own creation in the company of Gérard Depardieu in her film *The Truck* [Le Camion] in 1977. She was soon to turn back to writing, and already in this film all emphasis is on the written word: the two actors simply read their scripts, which Depardieu had not even seen before. The camera moves between the dark room where the young truck driver and the elderly woman passenger are reading their parts aloud, and the industrial Paris suburb through which the truck is moving in the somewhat displaced story.

The woman does much of the talking in the script; the man listens, half comprehending, more than half bored. When he first picks her up, he asks her no questions about herself, a point that Depardieu found strange, as Mary Lydon relates in "L'Eden Cinéma": "'He doesn't ask her who she is?' Gérard Depardieu inquires, and Duras replies, 'No, he doesn't wonder who she is. . . . He has nothing to do with a woman who is getting on in years. . . . (She is) small. Thin. Gray. Ordinary. She has that nobility of the ordinary. She is invisible'" (165; *Le Camion* 64). The supreme irony of this film lies in its rendering visible and unforgettable this woman of sixty-three. None of the famous actresses originally considered for the part could have presented such a physically ordinary image as Duras herself, and yet she is by 1977 a famous writer and filmmaker, and thus she is listened to, if not by the truck driver, at least by her spectators. At the end, for instance, she repeatedly makes the somewhat unexpected pronouncement that the world can "get lost" or "go to hell," and in her commentary on the script she adds: "That's the only politics" (*Le Camion* 74). She is experiencing a liberation from the felt need to choose a political alignment that had characterized her early years. The destructive impulses of 1968 had furthered this distancing, and while they awakened her feminist consciousness to a far greater degree than in most French women and restored her pride in claiming her "Creole" origins, none of this awareness would any longer lead her to political action. About *Le Camion,* she adds that the older woman is euphoric in her conviction that she is free at last from a quest for meaning in her life (81), and this freedom occurs simultaneously with Duras's acceptance of self-revelation in the film. Perhaps the two are causally connected: no longer feeling shackled by the binary political dilemma of her early years and having acquired her own identity in French society, she can present herself in her own name and in her own terms. In other texts of the same period there are even more clearly articulated statements of an acceptance of an absurd position outside the immutable facts of power abuse in society. Thus in *Cahiers du cinéma,* "Les Yeux verts," a fascinating collection of short meditations, statements, and photographs published in 1980, Duras concludes her piece "I wanted to say this especially to you" [Je voulais vous le dire à vous] by situating herself at last outside the "vast stupidity" of believing that there can ever be justice or progress in political terms (23).

Duras's sexual identity was mutating during this period of intense personal solitude. She was sixty-five by 1979 and alone, both in Neauphle and in her seaside apartment on the Norman coast at Trouville. *The Ship "Night"* [Le Navire Night] and her three short pieces about Aurélia Steiner allow us to trace the evolution of a late-life femininity inseparable from her new relation to the reader. For once Duras enters her own work with *Le Camion,* she is there to stay. It is true that she becomes clearly recognizable only with *The Summer of 1980* [L'Eté 80], but in *The Ship "Night"* there is already the play between "I" and "she" in which "I" is clearly a woman narrator. This narrator replaces the masculine and increasingly ignorant or absent narrator of the 1960s.

Like *Le Camion, The Ship "Night"* aggressively obliges the reader to recognize the primacy of words. Here we witness a passionate love relationship that lasts for several years and is conducted entirely over the telephone. What is missing, and what words must compensate for, is the lovers' physical knowledge of each other. A young man works as a switchboard operator on the night shift. He happens upon a young woman from the suburb Neuilly, who tells him she has black hair (later she sends a photo in which it is blond), is a medical student, and is terminally ill with leukemia. Finally, the young woman marries another man whom she does not love, and the telephone relationship ends. Although the woman offers opportunities for the man to discover her name and actually to see her, she sets these up as clues he must follow like other Durassian detectives. Yet each time, this man fails to investigate, revealing an obvious preference to remain in ignorance and hence separated from her. Only in these conditions, he clearly believes, can they love.

This story is preceded by notes on the failure of an original filmed version of "*Le Night.*" The story is thus framed by Duras's own voice and given credibility by her statement that the telephone love is a true story, recounted to her by a close friend. As we turn the page to begin reading the main text, a kind of autobiographical referentiality has already been established, and inevitably the "I" who opens the story appears to be Duras, along with her friend Benoît Jacquot, with whom she is traveling in Greece. They miss their rendezvous in a museum, and "je" comments frequently on the man's fears and failure to love. Within this second frame, she again assumes the narrative position and tells Jacquot and the reader the telephone love story.

Readers familiar with Duras immediately recognize this technique of stories in counterpoint, which can sometimes be an act of self-creation made possible by identification with another woman or couple. In *Hiroshima mon amour,* for instance, a model is established for the reexperiencing of a painful past experience in order to understand and correct it. A similar device is used in *Moderato cantabile,* and I think we are entitled to regard these identifications as therapeutic for these heroines. But again, there are distinctions to be made with the passing of time. In the earlier works, seeing the other is self-knowledge sought by the woman; one woman is replaced by the other in "a velvet obliteration of one's own person" (56), as Lol puts it. But now that the narrator is a woman, perhaps even Duras, and the narratee a man, the principal function of these stories within a frame becomes essentially didactic; that is, the woman sets out to communicate not only a story but a truth about separation and connection as well. Durassian texts from here on are often addressed to a particular narratee, more or less precisely identified, and they are increasingly insistent on the will and the need to establish a love relationship through words, as in *The Ship "Night."* Usually, the context is one of a connection that is denied sexual fulfillment through the body, either by physical absence, by absence of desire, or because such fulfillment would be socially unacceptable.

The Summer of 1980

One could speculate, as Frédérique Lebelley does, that the resort hotel facing the sea at Trouville, near the delta of the Seine where it flows into the English Channel, was chosen by Duras because it immersed her in memories of her early life and reconciled her to them at last. It was here at all events that Duras developed a new cycle of stories, which together form a kind of "universe," like that of the Lol V. Stein cycle. But these are later, and they include her and the student from Caen, Yann Andréa, in an increasingly confessional mode.

At age sixty-six, Duras consented to receive a visit from one of her vast number of admirers for whom she had become something of a cult figure. Yann was twenty-seven and terribly intimidated, despite the intimate exchange of letters that had preceded her acceptance. She embraced him at the door with the same erotic passion she had always known. He stayed with her and remained until her death in March 1996, bound by a strange, nameless love that could find no physical outlet after their second night, because Yann is gay.[9] Although Duras may have felt bitter about this (Lebelley 276), what emerges most often in her work is a reiterated certainty that the relationship between them is real love. Just as the Sapphic plot is concerned with power relations, most relationships with men recalled the fear of vulnerability that had begun in childhood. But by the time Yann Andréa entered her life, Duras had achieved, by self-expression in writing and cinema, an identity that distinguished her from her fetishized heroines; she had also gained a kind of power in relationships that quietly but definitively rectified the imbalances that had begun with the illusion that a woman could take real power only by sexual means and thereby avoid the prescribed plots.

All her stories were still about love; only the plots were different. I think it is obvious in the context of the other great loves of her life (her brother Paul, her Chinese lover), about whom she had not yet had the courage to write, that the "impossibility" of living these loves within any accepted social order or within any known plot for a woman's life was the very condition of their intensity. Marguerite had loved her brother in a forbidden passion, which had to remain outside any social arrangement but which already suggested to her the limitations of such arrangements; Joseph had pointed the way out of the plot proposed by the mother in *The Sea Wall*. The Chinese lover in *The Lover* made it possible for her to live, at privileged moments, a story outside the family script with its confusing power issues, but the traditional plot was impracticable for them. With Yann Andréa, a relationship again existed outside any recognizable plot, and a new intimacy became possible through Duras's writing.

In *The Summer of 1980*, written as a journalistic diary for the newspaper *Libération* at the request of Serge July, a relationship is in the process of becoming. July had sought a commentary on the political events of the summer, which in fact proved to be quite major: the Olympic Games in Moscow, famine in Uganda, Hurricane Allen, the Red Brigades' strike on a train station in Bologna, but above all the birth of Solidarity in Gdansk. Duras produces this commentary but relates it to "vous" for whom "je," as subject, is writing. She also introduces a story in counterpoint, a pair of "doubles" for herself and Yann: a six-year-old child in a summer camp and his eighteen-year-old counselor. The girl falls in love with the child, passionately and sensually. This device allows Duras to say a great many things about her love for Yann that she was not yet ready to make entirely public, and to create others.

"A year ago, I sent you Aurélia Steiner's letters" [Il y a un an, je vous envoyais les lettres d'Aurélia Steiner] (*Summer* 63), writes Duras making an extended analysis of how the act of writing relates to loving Yann. This room in her apartment facing the sea, she claims, is the one in which they *would have* made love, had that been possible; thus it is their room in her mind: "I gave you Aurélia. I addressed myself to you at those moments so that you might have the responsibility of Aurélia's birth, so that you might be there, between myself and her, so as to be the very cause of her existence . . . as, in the same way, you might have been the cause of my total silence if we had, for instance, made love . . . and Aurélia's words would not have existed, but only ours" [Je vous ai donné Aurélia. Je me suis adressée à vous dans ces moments-là pour que vous receviez la charge d'Aurélia naissante, pour que vous soyez là entre elle et moi à ce moment-là, cela afin d'en être presque la cause même . . . comme, de la même façon, vous auriez pu être la cause même que je n'écrive rien si par exemple nous nous étions aimés . . . et ces mots d'Aurélia ne seraient pas venus au jour, mais seulement encore les nôtres] (64). She gives Aurélia and herself to him in an image of childbirth in which he is both father and midwife (65).

Interestingly, if they were sexual lovers, she would be unable to write, in part, Duras clearly feels, because men don't want their women to write, to the point where a clever woman conceals her writing from her lover (*Ecrire,* 19). But there is also the fact that writing replaces, absolutely and perfectly, what cannot be lived. Duras is very much afraid of a man's ability to silence a woman, as we shall see in *Emily L.,* and she is afraid that Yann will upset the delicate power adjustments that have made this relationship possible: "In the same way, I give you Gdansk . . . For . . . the joy of Gdansk can only be known in one place: one which is not contaminated by power" [De même je vous donne Gdansk . . . Car . . . on ne peut connaître le bonheur de Gdansk que dans un seul lieu, celui qui n'est pas contaminé par le pouvoir] (*Summer* 64–65). This "place" outside society's power arrangements is the one she shared with her brother, with her lover, and now with Yann; it is the space in which women and the powerless dwell.

Ordinarily a silent space, Duras as writing subject revalorizes it and paradoxically gives it a voice: "I think that Gdansk is above all about silence, that silence contains Gdansk, its miraculous newness" [Je crois que Gdansk porte avant tout sur le silence, que le silence est le contenant du tout de Gdansk, sa miraculeuse nouveauté] (73). Gdansk is to her the most important event of the summer. Because it represents the audacity of the powerless against the powerful, it makes a perfect gift for Yann.

Beyond the Limits of Autobiography

During the cure that interrupted the writing of *The Sickness unto Death*, Yann provided care for Duras night and day and lived on the edge of despair. Duras's alcoholism had progressed to the point where her doctors could no longer predict with certainty whether she would survive a radical severance from the red wine on which she subsisted. She and Yann kept the hospitalization and treatment a secret from everyone, even her son. Yann spent the days with her and the sleepless nights alone in the apartment in the rue Saint Benoît. Duras's ordeal involved physical suffering but also an even more intense and debilitating mental disorientation, including hallucinations and delusions that persisted for weeks after her discharge from the hospital. Afterwards, she was unable to remember much of what she had experienced. But Yann had been taking notes every day, recording her words and actions and his own feelings. Out of this bedside journal came his book *M.D.* Duras encouraged him to write it and then encouraged the publication of this revelation of herself as aged and infirm. Together they produced an authorized exposure ("se faire voir") with all the details of her illness—comic, sordid, or moving: how she dribbled her food, held onto the wall when she walked, was taken to the toilet by Yann and bathed by him, her strange and terrifying hallucinations. Duras told Pivot in his *Apostrophes* interview that she admired *M.D.*, which indicates to me her willingness to "tell all" about herself to a far greater extent than most writers. *M.D.* functioned for Duras as a kind of autobiography, one in which being "seen from the outside," as in a photograph, becomes constitutive of identity: as in Lacan's mirror stage, the self or, as with Yann, the intimate Other, acts as a "photographer" and the object of the representation experiences herself as an Other. The same device is at work in *The Lover* and in *Emily L.*, as we shall see.

It is hard to imagine a greater degree of confidence and trust than the one that must have existed between Duras and Yann in order for him to have played this role even episodically. Despite whatever frustration Duras had felt or was to feel about Yann's sexual preference, it is clear in this testimony of his love that they had achieved a kind of caring that both were able to express in words and in the writing of books about each other. One morning, early in her hospital stay, the nurses found Duras sleeping naked on a towel in the bathroom. She would not eat; she could not watch television or integrate any news about the outside world. Yann's presence was all that was left. He says: "In that room you are more and more alone. You know I am there, close to you, that it has been so since the summer of 1980. . . . You are my absolute preference, inevitable from now on" [Dans la chambre vous êtes toujours encore plus seule. Vous savez que je suis là, près de vous, il en est ainsi depuis l'été 1980. . . . Vous êtes ma préférence absolue, désormais inévitable] (Andréa 45). Duras's worst fear was that she would no longer be able to write. Later, in her interview with Pivot, she admits her relief at finding her "nature" intact after the cure. Yann's belief in her identity and his ability to reassure her that she would remain who she was, a great writer (77), also reveal their importance to each other.

Afterwards, Duras was of course catapulted to a new level of international fame with the publication of *The Lover* in 1984. As early as 1977, she had in fact returned to the family romance in her play *L'Eden cinéma*, a title which has been interpreted in various ways, for it was presumably the silent movie theater where Madame Donnadieu played the piano, but in fact this is not the explanation, as Duras told Pivot. In French, "faire son cinéma" is close to the English "theatrics." It indicates a kind of melodramatic carrying-on that was characteristic of Marie Donnadieu.

This reworking of the material of *The Sea Wall* does in fact emphasize the mother's anger and potential for verbal violence in the same rather dubious Eden on the Plain. Paradoxically, the mother herself sits silent on the stage throughout the play. Suzanne and Joseph and Monsieur Jo and the others speak *about* her. But the mother's angry letter to the cadastral agents now contains her personal intention to kill them, words that had belonged to Joseph in *The Sea Wall*. Tremendous tension is created by this display of anger on the one hand, with its implicit identification with the other victims, all Indochinese, who are to commit the murder, and, on the other hand, the closing words again spoken by Joseph in his address to these victims: "White, she was white. Even if she loved you. Even if her hope was the same as yours and even if she mourned the children of the Plain, she remained a foreigner in your country. . . . She will be buried in the colonial cemetery in Saigon" [Blanche, elle était blanche. Même si elle vous aimait. Même si son espoir était le vôtre et si elle a pleuré les enfants de la plaine, elle est restée une étrangère à votre pays . . . Elle sera enterrée dans le cimetière colonial de Saïgon] (*L'Eden cinéma* 154).

Not until *The Lover* does the mother survive her experience and move on to another life beyond the Plain, as Marie Donnadieu actually did. Yet here, autobiography and perhaps a change in Duras's understanding of her mother do begin to inflect the course of the fiction by means of a theatrical device: at the moment of her "death," the character of the mother stands up and walks to the cot on which she will "play dead," her eyes wide open to the audience, "witnessing, alive, the staging of her death" [La mère, donc, se prête, vivante, à la mise en scène de sa mort] (*L'Eden cinéma* 151)

Important years in Duras's life had passed between 1977 and 1984. In *The Lover* as in *Emily L.* (1987)—the first about the family and the original question of subject formation, the second about an ongoing sense of subjectivity through writing—Duras both represents and enacts her late-life discovery of an identity that transcends the binding antinomies of her earlier life. Mature age and the seeking of intimacy through disclosure and, if necessary, apart from sexual intimacy, further encouraged by the bond with Yann Andréa, had led her to a sense of herself as individuated but deeply connected to an Other. As I have noted, this is an identity and a concept of subjectivity that differs radically from the male psychoanalytic model, according to which the process of maturation is roughly defined as increasing separateness and independence from others. In *The Lover*, we witness the fleeting and endlessly undertaken viewing of the self by the self in the sudden awareness, as in Lacan's mirror stage, that the self is an Other, an individual. But this image only occurs in intimacy.

In *The Lover*, the mirror is replaced by the photograph and its tropes. Originally, the text was to have been an accessory to a photographic biography of Duras by her son Jean Mascolo, a professional photographer. It was to have been entitled "The Absolute Photograph." But Duras lost sight of this project and even invalidated it by announcing early on that the truly important photograph, the one in which she might really have recognized herself, was never taken (16–17). And we realize that if it had existed, this book would not have been written: it is itself the missing photograph. Duras uses two pronouns here because she is writing the "photo" in which the first-person narrator ("je") creates herself through the writing and sees herself as one sees an object, from the outside ("elle").

Marguerite's love affair at age fifteen with a twenty-seven-year-old son of a Chinese millionaire had never been disclosed before, not even to her brothers. Even with the lover himself, words about their feelings were never exchanged. All communication between them occurred through their exchange of sexual pleasure and their physical awareness of each other (121). In her interview with Pivot, Duras hypothesizes that this very silence may have been the reason the Chinese lover from Cholen eclipsed all the others in her life. Now, at seventy, it is time to tell the story, to gather up the dispersed parts of herself from her various other works, all of which contain some autobiographical fragments: the Chinese suitor, Anne-Marie Stretter, the Beggarwoman, the sea wall. The "story of (her) life" may not exist, but she confesses all the same to a need to discover the reason this early period of her life always remained her primary source of inspiration. She needs to *tell* about the Chinese lover, and in the writing to achieve the resolution of her childhood dilemma within the family and within the colony. This powerful sexual experience had led her out of the family and to the decision to become a writer (126). But words are in fact the medium of transformation that the sexual experience only allowed her to intuit. When she wrote this book, Duras considered that all her early resentments were resolved once and for all and all her accounts settled; even her older brother, whom she holds strictly responsible for the death of the younger brother, is forgiven.

It is entirely possible to reconstruct the story of *The Lover* even if the text is not linear and to know the central female character, even if, like Anne-Marie Stretter, she enjoys being a sexual object for men. She is double: a fetish but also a narrator, who evolves psychologically and by the end can stand outside herself and her family, precisely because of the experience with the lover. When *The Lover* became a runaway best seller, certain critics, accustomed to a certain notion of the *nouveau roman* as ideologically radical, noted that in *The Lover* there is a return to "readability," that is, to a kind of representation that is familiar and reassuring. Some even went so far as to see a banal love story, which they dubbed "Saigon by night." In a more subtle reading that nevertheless echoes some of these complaints, Mireille Calle-Gruber notes that *The Lover* does indeed tell us a story in a way that the texts of the 1960s could not, or would not, do: "with *The Lover,* the power relationship is reversed. Whereas before, the Durassian text was dominant, formed an irreducible network of its own references, forcing the reader to get involved or remain outside . . . now the text becomes dependent on the power, and on the limitations, of the reader" [avec l'Amant, s'inversent les rapports de force. Là où, dominant, le texte durassien formait un réseau irréductible, contraignant le lecteur à s'y prendre ou à rester étranger . . . s'inscrit à présent une certaine dépendance du texte soumis au pouvoir, et aux limites, du lecteur] (Calle-Gruber 109). Like Selous, Calle-Gruber is sensitive to the fact that what has changed here more than anything else is Duras's relationship to her reader, though Calle-Gruber is critical of this filling in of the blanks, and of this kind of relationship. But I see no reason not to shift the ground of the argument in such a way as to privilege disclosure, which is characteristic of the late-life writing of women as well as men, rather than to regard self-revelation as a step backwards in an author's aesthetic or intellectual evolution.

Nor do I hesitate to call *The Lover* a love story, even if it is not a simple one and even if, as Calle-Gruber explains, the title of the book is misleading primarily because the Chinese lover is in fact not a real protagonist in the story. We know little about him, and the narrator is not even sure she loves him until she is on the ship going to France. What is essential in the afternoons spent with him is the way the girl experiences the pain of her family relations and finally the way she comes to feel about herself. Calle-Gruber describes how the narrative "je" becomes, in some key passages with the lover, the third person "elle:" "(The lover) is a *means,* a *passage.* . . . His new narrative function lies in the relation among the three terms Je/Il/Elle, *where the relationship itself is inscribed,* and where one plus one, according to a different logic, equal three. This third term "elle" is a product that is still coming into being, it is change, otherness, that occurs when Je and Il are put together" [L'amant est *faire-valoir,* pro-

ducteur pour la partenaire de valeurs et de significations nouvelles. . . .
C'est un rapport à trois termes qu'instaure la nouvelle fonction narrative:
Je/Il/Elle, *où la mise en relation s'inscrit aussi;* où il est dit que la mise
ensemble de deux éléments n'est jamais opération blanche et où un plus
un, selon une logique autre, font trois. Ce troisième terme "Elle" constitue un produit en devenir: l'altération, l'altérité, dans la mise en-
semble] (116). The triangular structure, the fusion and subsequent individuation that were impossible with the mother, are figured here. It is
also sketched out in the portrait of the narrator's friend Hélène Lagon-
elle, whose name recalls "elle," and whom the narrator desires. Or rather,
she desires to watch her lover making love to Hélène, with whom she
identifies, in what is yet another way of seeing herself from the outside
(92). For at the height of her sexual pleasure, where opposites meet and
are effaced, the narrator loses consciousness and at the same time observes that this loss of self as a subject is born: "He looks at her. . . . he
discerns less and less clearly the limits of her body, which is not like other
bodies, it is not finite, in the bedroom it continues to grow, it is still
without definite shape, always becoming, not only where he sees it but
elsewhere as well, out of sight . . ." [Il la regarde . . . il discerne de moins
en moins clairement les limites de ce corps, celui-ci n'est pas comme les
autres, il n'est pas fini, dans la chambre il grandit encore, il est encore
sans formes arrêtées, à tout instant en train de se faire, il n'est pas
seulement là où il le voit, il est ailleurs aussi, il s'étend au-delà de la
vue . . .] (121).

Where opposites merge, a third term can emerge. Entering into this
relationship enables the narrator to escape the otherwise inescapable
contradictions in the mother's relation to the society of which I have
spoken. Writing will be for the narrator the text that we have in our
hands, an overcoming of the impossible choice in the privileging of the
oxymoron: "Sometimes I know this: that if writing is not all things confounded, vanity and void, then it is nothing. If it is not, each time, all
things confounded into one by its essence unnamable, it is nothing
but advertisement" [Quelquefois je sais cela: que du moment que ce
n'est pas, toutes choses confondues, aller à la vanité et au vent, écrire ce
n'est rien. Que du moment que ce n'est pas, chaque fois, toutes choses
confondues en une seule par essence inqualifiable, écrire n'est rien que
publicité] (15). This is a fusion that is productive of identity and genera-

tive of meaning. "Elle" is a subject born in relationship, autonomous but not separated from the other.

Within the fiction of *The Lover*, words are abandoned in favor of sexual communion when the narrator says, "And that's what you say when you let words become acts" [quand on laisse le dire se faire] (55). In *The Lover from the North of China*, Duras at seventy-seven admits that she becomes a "novelist" again (12). There are important differences in this late re-working of the material it had taken her so long to disclose. Now that she has made the central revelation about the Chinese lover, and particularly in view of the public's gratifying reception of it, she is more at ease. Originally intended to be a film scenario, this new version is deliberately fictional in certain ways. The lover goes to visit the mother in order to pay off her son Pierre's gambling debts, which have ruined her. In this scene, the narrator is not even present. This scene and several others offer an imagined, idealized version of this love, a re-vision of the Chinese lover as a beneficent force against the older brother's evil and a re-vision of the mother as well. The lover and the mother arrive at a perfect understanding, from which Pierre is ostentatiously excluded. In front of Pierre, the lover tells the mother that he loves her daughter but cannot marry her because she is white; he explicitly states that they are lovers (127). The mother accepts all these truths. She finds the lover charming.

This mother of course contrasts sharply with her other incarnations, but the reader knows that this is the realm of wish-fulfillment, and as such it illuminates Duras's experience and tells us what she has come to value by age seventy-seven. The most striking difference between this version and *The Lover* is this emphasis on *telling,* as in the scene between the lover and the mother, as "acts become words" after a lifetime of silence. A certain euphoria surrounds such confessions and disclosures. At the beginning, the narrator openly questions the mother about her preference for Pierre, and the mother understands her pain and decides to send him back to France (*China* 29). The girl confesses to her mother that her love for Paul is more than intense, clearly implying that it is incestuous, and although both of them lower their eyes in shame, the mother accepts this too (30). Identification seems possible between them at last. Between the lovers, there is much conversation and storytelling. The lover's role as a kind of savior who stands outside the rest of the society of the colony is shown in his generosity toward the mother as well as by the dinner scene, in which he describes the compartments constructed by his father as innocent of any exploitative purpose (30). The lovers laugh and talk together as he tries to know her better, by explicit request (29). This ideal of intimacy through words takes us far from any preceding version, in which silence among all the characters, including the lovers, was the strict rule.

Emily L.

Power struggles did occur between Duras and Yann in the few years that followed. In her frustration, Duras went so far as to condemn homosexuality in general (*Le Matin* November 1986). Yann dutifully typed her manuscripts in the mornings, fled from her, and returned in the evenings to revile her in crises of fury. Once, while attacking her for writing in a manner he considered excessive, he called her "the whore of the Norman coast." Her response was to write a short work by this title (1986): the more he attacked her, the more she wrote. In 1987, Duras again found the way to bring him close to her by means of her writing in *Emily L.,* which Lebelley calls her "siren song" (329). In this blend of autobiography and fiction, the changes brought about by aging reached their culmination (Ladimer, "Space" 61–71). We find the clearest example of the Durassian writing subject who only exists in relationship but who discovers, in relationship, a "second self" that can be apprehended "from the outside" in writing. Duras also addresses the question of what it has meant historically and personally to her to be a woman writer.

Emily L. is an account of an experience that occurred between the author/narrator "je" and her male companion "vous" in the short space of a late afternoon and evening in June 1986. The action consists of their conversation in the bar of a café in the coastal town of Quillebeuf, and their observation of an English couple they see there and around whom the narrator constructs a fabula in which the English woman is a writer. In fact, the choice of the name "Emily" is later explained by Duras's borrowing of a poem by Emily Dickinson, "The Secret Wound," which is ascribed to this twentieth-century British character. *Emily L.* creates an autobiographical pact in that the narrator clearly identifies herself as the author (14). And as in *The Lover,* there are several references to her childhood in Indochina (46–48, 53). The setting in the Norman coastal town near Trouville and Le Havre, as known to the reader through her writing, confirms the referential effect.

Yet *Emily L.* is also fictional. It makes a "fictional pact" with the reader by the inscription "novel" on the cover, and the title seems to indicate that the principal character is not the narrator but the English woman and that we are not dealing with autobiography at all. In fact, Duras again privileges the literary imagination over memory as a means of knowing the self, here actually emphasizing the paradoxical need for distance and fiction if one is to tell the truth (cf. *La Vie matérielle,* 106–7). As in *The Lover from the North of China,* she authorizes a reading that "takes both autobiography and fiction together in their status as text" (Miller, "Women's Autobiography" 271). In this case, it is in the space *between* the autobiographical "je" and the other, fictional woman that Duras will once again embark on the project of telling us who she is.

The narrative is a constant plying between the space of the frame (the verifiable experience of the narrator at Quillebeuf) and the fabula (the imagined story of the English woman). In *Emily L.*, the narrator's story with "vous" is doubled, though imperfectly, by the story she creates for the English Emily and her companion and husband, the Captain. The English couple has been stranded in Quillebeuf after a breakdown of their yacht. Thus they are in a position of enforced idleness, in a sense imprisoned, and isolated from everyone else. Their isolation is emphasized by the fact that parts of their dialogue are given in English.

As she watches them, the narrator is fascinated, without knowing why; she is dazzled, an effect that is rendered by images of blinding whiteness (*Emily L.* 20). Under this spell, she begins to see the other woman as herself, in the facts of her description that correspond to Duras's biography: Emily is older than her companion, as Duras is older than hers; each is nearing the end of her life; Emily is also an alcoholic; each depends on a man and is depended upon by him; both members of the couple fear the other's death. Emily appears to be a typical Durassian woman: virtually asleep, half mad, her body suggestive of death. She has an intense gaze and power of perception despite her almost total physical passivity. But it seems to me that in the story that is created for Emily by the narrator, her passivity is now explained by certain facts of her history, for she is, or was, a woman writer.

In the first of several self-reflexive acts, the text describes the circumstances of its own genesis as the narrator, turning towards "vous" from the contemplation of Emily, says she has decided to write "their story" (21), though it will have to be an indirect account, part of something larger.

The man asserts there has been no story, nothing between them (23). She does not deny this absence or emptiness at the center of her projected story, but accepts it and suggests that it is possible to speak *around* the silence, the unsayable essence of their love, which the man believes to be an absence of relationship (24). Recurrent images of emptiness remind the reader of this complexity, as does a later statement about the story's "resistance to being told as evidence of its essential nature" (61). The blanks in this narrative are quite different from those of the 1960s. They do not act as a barrier to understanding for the reader, for the narrator's role will be precisely to help "vous" and all of us to understand what they mean. Throughout *Emily L.,* it is the oxymoron that seems to suggest not a simple opposition or coexistence but rather the existence of a third term that, like the love between the narrator and "vous," cannot be *said* but only *shown.* This love between them, then, is like the narrator's writing self that emerged in *The Lover,* in the circumstance of making love but also of escaping the dualistic confines of family and society. Connection is necessary to the constitution of the self, they are part of a single phenomenon, and writing is both the cause and the effect of connection.

Emily and the Captain are voyagers who have spent much of their lives sailing the seas of the Far East, as we learn when the daughter of the *patronne* of the café says to the Captain: "So, is it true that you travel all the time?" [Alors, comme ça, vous voyagez tout le temps?] (37). This apparently innocent request for information is perceived as shocking and scandalous by the Captain and the onlookers; the incident is described as a "crisis" (38). Yet even after excusing herself, the young woman persists in wanting to know. In the end, the Captain describes their itinerary, but the near-collision between the powerful Captain and the spunky girl is reproduced on the river between a gas tanker and a little ferryboat. The incident reveals the stakes of the narrative as political, sexual, and having to do with discursivity and its laws. That there are such laws and repression is made clear not only by the Captain's behavior but also by the indifference that the narrator generalizes to "vous" (50). We understand that the narrator's real fear is of "vous," that she is prevented from writing by this man because of a fear that "resembles a belief in a prohibition against writing" (57). Here as elsewhere, Duras has put a love story at the center of what is also, necessarily, a matter of politics and power.

Yet the writing is imminent. It is the Captain who begins the narration of Emily's story, as he believes she wants him to do: "Every evening I must speak a little for her, in her place" [Il faut bien, chaque soir, un peu, pour elle, à sa place, parler] (71). But the narrator challenges his understanding of his wife and substitutes her own imagined story about her. This story is organized around two texts written by Emily. Shortly after the death of Emily's newborn daughter, she writes a poem one winter afternoon, which the Captain finds and reads: "The Captain had the sensation of having been stabbed by the truth. Of having been mistaken about his wife, of living with a stranger" [Le Captain avait eu le sentiment d'être poignardé par la vérité. De s'être trompé sur la personne, de vivre avec une inconnue] (83). He burns the poem, an act that determines the course of their lives. Its loss or absence becomes an "emptiness" at the center of the fabula.

The poem "Winter Afternoons" is itself structured around an emptiness in the center. It consists of three parts, of which the first and third are clear, the second mostly crossed out and unfinished. The subject is the strange red and yellowish light that filters through the nave of a cathedral and oppresses. In the clear parts of the poem lie certain explanations:

> In the clear spaces of the writing she was saying that the wounds made by the sharp rays of the sun were inflicted on us by heaven. That they left no trace nor any visible scar, in our flesh or in our thoughts. *That they wounded us and soothed us. That their meaning was elsewhere. Elsewhere and far from where one might expect.* That these wounds foretold nothing, confirmed nothing that could be taught or that might have been a provocation in the very realm of God. *No, it was rather the perception of the ultimate difference: the one that is inside at the center of meaning.*

> [Dans les régions claires de l'écriture elle disait que les blessures que nous faisaient ces mêmes épées de soleil nous étaient infligées par le ciel. Qu'elles ne laissaient ni trace ni cicatrice visible, ni dans la chair de notre corps ni dans nos pensées. *Qu'elles ne nous blessaient ni ne nous soulageaient. Que c'était autre chose. Que c'était ailleurs. Ailleurs et loin de là où on aurait pu croire.* Que ces blessures n'annonçaient rien, ne confirmaient rien qui aurait pu faire l'objet d'un enseignement, d'une provocation au sien du règne de

Dieu. Non, il s'agissait de la perception de la dernière différence:
celle, interne, au centre des significations.] (85, emphasis mine)

Ambivalence is produced by the antithesis "wound" and "soothe," both of
which are refused in favor of an inexpressible third term, which is missing, silent, "elsewhere," beyond (or before) any rational representation
("nothing that could be taught") or binary contest ("provocation in the
very realm of God"). And here as in the frame, the unsayable around
which the text is organized is a sacred knowledge, revealed in a cathedral
by means of divine light. This is consistent with Duras's use throughout
her work of a terminology including God and the divine to represent the
supreme value of the communion between self and other.

The poem is also about the limits of representation and about the
space of the unrepresentable, or that which has been described by
French theoreticians following Jacques Derrida and Jacques Lacan as
the space of the "feminine." This space, "elsewhere and far from where
one might expect," is what Alice Jardine has called a "search for that
which has been left out, de-emphasized, hidden, or denied articulation
within Western systems of knowledge" (*Gynesis* 36). This "feminine,"
then, is a discursive effect. While Duras takes no position with respect to
these or any theoreticians, nor with French feminists in any consistent
way, she has always been concerned with the limits of the representable
in writing, and in certain late works including this one, she seems to
indicate that, to the space coded as feminine by a shared collective discourse, the speech of women maintains its own specific relation.

But it is important to stress that Duras does not propose an essentialist, conventional definition of women and their writing as incoherent or
irrational. She does not resign herself to silence; at most, hers is a
second-degree silence, as she explains in the passage about writing
"around" the silent space in the center, and of course the successful
writing of *Emily L.* testifies to the reality of a woman writing consciously
and purposefully in the mother (or father) tongue. For Duras, the special
relationship of women to the limits of language has to do instead with
their lived experience, which has enabled them to explore the unspeak-
able of love in part because they have been denied the public experiences
of speaking and writing. In his destruction of the poem as a crime (82),
the Captain is reacting not only to the discursively defined femininity it

represents but also to his wife as a "sexually gendered subject in a socially gendered exchange."[10] For throughout Duras's work, it is almost always a woman who finds herself in a position of powerlessness, even when issues of race, culture, class, or nationality are also at stake (Marini 27).

The second of Emily's texts is a letter to the caretaker of the family estate. He feels a certain complicity with Emily against the Captain, who has kept Emily in an unending voyage in the South Pacific partly, he suspects, in order to keep her from discovering her growing fame. One summer, he reveals to Emily that her work has been published. She is pleased, but she questions the caretaker about the poem "Winter Afternoons" and is inconsolable to learn that it is missing. She begins to wonder whether she actually wrote the poem after all or merely imagined doing so. The caretaker allows her to make the assumption that this fantasy was part of her "madness" of the past.

Emily kisses the caretaker in a moment that is "as long as a love affair" [un temps aussi long que celui d'un amour] (121). He tells her he would have sent the poem to the publisher even in its incomplete form, and he names her "Emily L." (120). Emily approves of this name substituted for the patronym (133), which generalizes her experience to all women ("elle") and lends it a symbolic dimension. Three years later, she takes a letter to the family lawyer, which she would like him to send to the caretaker after reading it himself. Emily asserts that she is "unfaithful" to her husband, in that the caretaker has become her "identity," the place within herself where she is receptive to love, where she sees herself "from the outside," since she is now forbidden to achieve this identity through her writing.

An extended hermeneutic act follows the letter, calling attention to its status as a *mise-en-abyme* for the book itself. "Vous" complains that the letter is incomprehensible, that it would be out of place in a book (136). The narrator agrees, admitting that the letter seems "foreign" to the rest, and then says, "I loved you with a fearsome love" [Je vous aimais d'un amour effrayant] (137), directing his interpretive effort towards their relationship and openly acknowledging the symbolic nature of the story: "You will learn of the existence of the feeling between us from outside your life. . . . You won't know until the day when you transform this situation *in your turn* into a book, or another relationship" [Le sentiment, vous en apprendrez l'existence de l'extérieur de votre vie . . . Vous

ne saurez plus rien. Jusqu'au jour où cette situation, vous la trans-
formerez *à votre tour* dans un livre ou dans une relation personnelle]
(138, emphasis mine). Writing now becomes her lover, that which allows
for the emergence of an "intersubjective self. The need for this other
lover has resulted from the impossibility of making contact between the
man and the woman, for the narrator and her fearful companion as for
Emily and the Captain. Just as the Captain's silencing of Emily led to her
love with the caretaker, so this text has been written in response to the
insistence that she *not* write (26), which she experiences as an obstacle:
"*You* are what keeps me from writing" [Ce qui m'empêche d'écrire, c'est
vous] (56). And yet by choosing to write in the text "around" the inexpressible center of their love, she has created another intersubjective
space, this one between herself and "vous," and she has established the
essential communication with him that had been lacking.

As I have suggested, the autobiographical act takes place here in the
intersubjective space between two: between the narrator and Emily, between the narrator and "vous," and between Emily and the caretaker in
the fiction. Thus the experience of selfhood takes place once again outside the limits of a separate, distinct identity. The narrator/woman must
lose herself in fusion before she can acquire the subjectivity necessary to
the telling of her own story. Duras in her late-life writing remains "at
the dangerous confines of (her) psychic life" (Kristeva 263). I think Duras
would have agreed that she dwelled at the confines of a certain kind of
subjectivity. But aging worked to make her conscious of her supreme
need for intimacy, so that she was able to leave behind the paralyzing
aspects of her fear of fusion and the confusion about her identity that
had haunted her since early life. Her subjectivity always depended on an
intersubjectivity, but perhaps this is less dangerous psychologically than
Kristeva believes. Duras and her women characters evolved substantially
after the 1960s and 70s, and yet most analyses, including Kristeva's,
tend to focus on the works of those decades and assume a static reality
for Duras's universe. Perhaps the "confines of our psychic lives" are too
confining for some of us as we move into old age, and we may need to
turn, as Duras did, towards conventional or unconventional relationships that afford greater intimacy than the ones we knew as young
adults.

CONCLUSION | chapter 6

I have talked about the way in which defining one's gender is a lifelong project, never accomplished, never abandoned. I have also speculated about how it felt to be old and a woman in French society and about how these three writers in particular experienced their notoriously marginal situations in late life. By middle age, each confronted in a fairly explicit manner the question of how to live as an aging woman, and each found an original answer. Beauvoir's first response was to investigate herself intellectually, and as preparation for her long autobiography she produced an intellectual analysis of femininity that was to become one of the founding texts of the century. Colette began to write about the necessity of abstaining from the traditional, youthful heterosexual role and even from its written plots, directing her creative and erotic energy into writing itself. Duras wrote at length about herself at the opposite position: she presented herself in her writing as an older woman whose eroticism had changed very little in her seventies, and she actually became even more revealing of herself in *The Lover* than she had been in her earlier work. Thus all three were actively engaged in recreating their femininity and their eroticism until the end. Beauvoir reminds us in *The Coming of Age* that sexuality is an orientation towards the world, a point of view and a lasting set of impulses and sensual relationships. Sexuality is related, though not reducible to, touching and being touched.[1] So even if the rules of the sexual game or plot had to be redefined after menopause, these women writers all found an important place for intimacy and sensuality in their postmenopausal years.

If Colette and Simone de Beauvoir began their middle age in anguish and uncertainty, by their sixties (as in the case of Beauvoir) or seventies (as in the case of Colette), they felt relieved from the incessant worry about physical attraction that had burdened them before. Interestingly, both continued until the end certain practices that American women writers might have been expected to abandon: Colette never allowed anyone, not even Goudeket, to see her in the morning before she had applied her makeup, and Beauvoir painted her nails bright red and wore lipstick to match (Simons 204). I have often wondered whether this was in any way related to their being French, and finally I think that it is. Even if French culture offers a more narrow spectrum of available options for aging women and may expect them to "disappear" in sexual terms, it is nonetheless true that all women of all ages are encouraged to remain esthetically pleasing to others, or, as the French themselves would say, *coquette*. This expectation remains true long after physical attractiveness has ceased to be the principal source of power to women in society, as Beauvoir and Colette recorded in the work of their thirties, forties, and fifties, with increasing levels of anxiety.

Duras did not record the same anguish about the physical changes of her middle and late age. She did attribute the sharp increase in her consumption of alcohol to her solitude, as male lovers, who had been constantly present in her life through her fifties, finally left the picture. At around the same time, she stopped caring about her physical appearance to the point of going only rarely to the hairdresser's and always wearing the same outfit, which came to be known as the "MD uniform": a light-colored turtleneck, a dark skirt of medium length with a dark vest, and short, comfortable boots. Part of the originality of her late-life eroticism, which continued to solicit active participation from men, lies in its capacity to survive in spite of Duras's disregard for social norms for physical appearance. In her latest autobiographical writing, she appears to believe that her writing, when addressed to her lover, has more amorous potential than her body and can even function as a substitute.

Going beyond rigid dichotomization of sex roles changed these women's lives, of course, and it also changed their writing in both narrative and stylistic terms. In each case, moving beyond this dichotomization meant reworking the two sides of a primal dilemma concerning traditional femininity, a task that could only be fully accomplished in age. Beauvoir had to forge a position for herself as a woman outside of *both* traditional gender constructs, male and female, since both had been understood by her in a way that seriously devalued femininity and its supposed attributes: passivity, dependence, the probability of being abandoned, and a rather unusual equivalence between aging and femininity. Originally inherited from her mother and the bourgeois milieu of her girlhood, her first understanding of gender unquestioningly endorsed certain male stereotypes, all of which are echoed in the early work of Sartre in his distinction between immanence and transcendence. Beauvoir actually produced two kinds of writing: her novels, *A Very Easy Death,* and certain restricted portions of her autobiography, and the rest of her chronicle, which she called her "autobiography," though it contained very little personal reflection on the events recounted. Between these two kinds of writing a distinction emerged: in certain novels and stories, she worked through her problem in accepting her own femininity and also changed her notion of that femininity. Beauvoir's construction of another, less stereotyped femininity that she could accept was accomplished over a lifetime, particularly in her older years, despite the fact that age necessarily brings a certain degree of dependence on others. Beauvoir differed from most elders in that she seemed to have had more difficulty "detaching" from life and people, because of her morbid, lifelong fear of death, but her relative silence on the subject of death towards the end of her life may indicate that she had at last achieved a kind of serenity, undoubtedly furthered by her relationship with Sylvie Le Bon, in which she felt that she was at last allowed a certain measure of dependency.

Colette's primary descriptive or narrative figure was the paradox, another uneasy representation of two. The traditional notions of femininity she encountered as a very young woman in Paris, which were necessary for her to assume, conflicted in some ways with the sense of herself she had developed in girlhood. Never completely comfortable with her new role, and especially after her break with Willy, she returned gradually to a more autonomous, authoritative, and authorial idea of womanhood. She endowed her women characters with the right to look at their objects of desire and to see, as she herself did in her writing. Always sensitive to the fragility of gender identities imposed by society, she privileged the paradox, reminding her reader constantly that things are not always what they seem to be. These paradoxes were sometimes explicitly associated in her writing with sexuality itself, as in *The Pure and the Impure* or the playful story *Bella Vista*. Historically the first of these women to experience a change in her womanly identity with age, and the first to assume her aging consciously and to make of it an explicit theme in her work, Colette chose renunciation of the love of men as she aged, first in her work *Break of Day* and then in her life. After the first, passionate phase of her marriage to Maurice Goudeket, as she felt herself to have grown "too old," she changed the nature of their relations. But another kind of bond, without precedent for Colette, had developed between them, so that despite her self-imposed abstinence from sex, her late life was filled with intimacy and trust. The intense sensuality of her late work bears witness to the way in which she redirected her eroticism into her art.

Duras figured the dichotomy that had conditioned her perception of womanhood in terms of oxymoron. This original perception was fraught with tension and ambivalence, because identifying fully with the model of femininity presented by her mother meant identifying with a series of internally contradictory roles and characteristics: her mother had been a victim of colonialism, but she was also, in her daughter's eyes, guilty of colonial indifference and exploitation. Duras finally found the means to transcend this problem, which involved nothing less than her sense of identity. By means of her writing she gained access, like the girl in *The Lover,* to a position beyond these dualities where she enjoyed greater wholeness and subjecthood. But this liberation was dependent on her identity as a writer, which could only have emerged with such force in the late years of her productive career. If Colette constantly strove to be in the authorial position of the one who *sees* (*voir*), Duras's project was to learn to see *herself,* and, simultaneously, to *give herself to be seen* (*se faire voir*) by the reader. The term borrowed from familiar French, which usually denotes an act of prostitution, here describes instead Duras's disclosure of herself by means of publication and, purged of its ordinary negative connotations, it renders all the intensity and intimacy of her experience.

Several variables (though there may be others) appear to be necessary to a sense of satisfaction with one's lot in old age: the capacity for intimacy and trust, a measure of control over one's life, a high degree of adaptability, and the ability to live in the present. As mentioned in chapter 2, one might have expected the issue of adaptability to be more difficult for these French women than for Anglo-Americans in that the virtual absence of Second Wave feminism might have left them relatively inexperienced, as they approached middle and old age, in assuming unexpected roles. Again, their personal marginality rescued them from a common cultural fate, and Colette and Duras were able to undergo startling transformations several times in their lives before old age, and then again in old age, partly because these were imposed on them by their circumstances (Indochina in the case of Duras; the disaster of marriage to Willy and having to support herself afterwards in the case of Colette). Beauvoir did everything possible to ward off change in her personal life, as we have seen, insisting on the unchanging nature of her relationship with Sartre and arranging her personal life so as to limit change rather radically. But after the age of forty, which she considered crucial, much the way other woman have sometimes considered menopause, she began for the first time to dare to be different. Her love affair with Nelson Algren was the first of its kind she had known since the first year she had spent with Sartre, and it occurred when she was forty-four. Then the tremendously supportive relationship with Sylvie Le Bon, which allowed her to accept her own need for dependency, and the related change in her ability to accept her mother's dying with compassion were major breaks with her past.

For all three of these French writers, writing itself and the working through of the problems relating to it seemed to be their way of learning about themselves and how to live in the present. For Colette and Beauvoir, writing about their own aging provided a form of therapy not available in a society that resolutely turned its back on issues related to women's aging and in which talking about such issues, starting with menopause, was extremely rare, even among women. All three turned increasingly to autobiography in various forms, and away from recognizable versions of the abandonment love plot for women, as they grew older. The role of autobiography may have been different for them than for many male writers: these women were seeking self-understanding as well as self-representation, and each felt the need to tell her own story over and over. Beauvoir of course produced many volumes devoted to her own story, as well as *A Very Easy Death,* and towards the end of her life she was finally able to confide more complex personal meditation on the events she related and more revelation of their personal significance to her. Colette and Duras actually entered their texts as characters and created new, frankly hybrid forms between autobiography and fiction. Disclosure and its corollary, a new form of trust, characterized all three in their way of feeling about their readers after long years of a more distant relationship with them.

As French women and heirs to the French tradition, Colette, Beauvoir, and Duras were required to wait for fame until middle age. All three began writing relatively young, but despite the nomination of *The Vagabond, She Came to Stay,* and *The Sea Wall* for the prestigious Prix Goncourt, none received this prize or any other while she was still young. Unconsciously, perhaps, they may have been considered by their French public as descending from a line of older women writers, or "grandmothers" of literature, which had included Madame de Sévigné and Madame de Staël, but of which George Sand had been the most celebrated example. In France, this model for middle-aged and old women was perhaps the only positive, empowering one available. That it existed at all may account to some extent for how these three women of letters were able to achieve serenity in their old age, after the difficulties of leaving youth behind.

It is also true that these three writers all had strong, imposing mothers who were active in their own old age. While this was undoubtedly part of the reason that the mother-daughter bond was even more difficult and determining in their young and middle years than in the lives of many other women writers, in advanced age Colette, Beauvoir, and Duras appear to have been empowered by the model of their mothers' strength. Coming to terms with their mothers in each case meant allowing contradictory feelings to coexist rather than attempting an impossible resolution or choice.

Finally, despite Colette's arthritic pain, Beauvoir's deeply rooted fear of decrepitude, and Duras's ill health, all appear to have experienced a certain amount of joy at the end of their lives. In their late experiments with style, there is often something playful: Colette wrote the adventures of her extraordinary, sensual imagination, pretending to go on a hike into the country in *The Evening Star;* Beauvoir introduced her dreams in all their irrationality into her otherwise dry autobiography; Duras invented a kind of fairy tale involving a shark and a little boy in *The Summer of 1980* and reworked it at length in *Yann Andréa Steiner.* They seem to offer proof of what Carolyn Heilbrun astutely notes in her "Introduction" to *A Certain Age,* that "age, too, has its dreams" (xix). One could tentatively conclude that even in their isolation from any discourse about aging, they were contributing all the same to the invention of "a new female linguistics that will sound strange when one or two of us speak it, but not when we all talk the delights of aging" (xvii).

Plus ça change . . . ?

The status of women in France is changing today, though it is still not clear to most Anglo-American observers exactly where it is heading. There has been a vast increase in the number of women employed outside the home, and almost all professions are now theoretically open to them. As elsewhere, but much more than in the United States, most women continue to manage their homes and families without significant help from their men. This places a heavy burden on working wives and mothers, and forces other women to choose to have only one child or no children at all. Nevertheless, it will be interesting to see how these important changes in women's lived experience are inscribed in fiction and film.

At this writing, the traditional plot is alive and well in France. The recent paperback *The Abandoned Woman* [La Femme abandonnée] is an especially interesting example: reworking the Balzacian text of 1832 by the same name, Madeleine Chapsal changes the plot only slightly in the end. In Balzac's version, the beautiful Claire de Beauséant, who is about thirty and abandoned by her first lover, falls in love again with the twenty-three-year-old Gaston de Neuil, and lives with him in perfect bliss for ten years. The young man's mother eventually recalls him to his duty to family and society by insisting that he marry a young heiress, and he succumbs to her pressure. Claire is immobilized forever by an all-consuming grief. Afterwards, unable to forget Claire, Gaston tries desperately to return to her, but she absolutely refuses even to talk to him. He kills himself with his revolver. In Balzac's version, the man realizes the horrible error he has made in turning away from the one great love of his life. There are indications that he simply does not possess enough sensitivity even to merit a creature as noble as Claire, who embodies feminine beauty, ability to love, and capacity to suffer. But Claire, in the end, is left to suffer and to die young, because, as Balzac points out, to yield to Gaston after he had left her would have been to compromise her honor. In her betrayed and helpless state, armed with her honor, she is the perfect image of feminine beauty.

In the modern reworking of this plot by Chapsal, an author of popular fiction, the heroine is better prepared for the second betrayal. She has presumably learned her lesson from the first one, but we may also speculate, it seems to me, that she has learned a great deal from reading the literary production of the preceding several centuries. So when the young heiress arrives in town, the forty-year-old mistress does not wait for what she believes to be the inevitable marriage: she leaves the man first. Afterwards, he goes through with the marriage because he has no objection to present to his family, and then, miserable and bored, he tries to return to his mistress, as in the original. And again, he ends by killing himself. Here, "Fanny" is also left suffering and alone, but with the additional enormous irony that it is she who brought about the separation because of her certainty that the plot could proceed in no other way. It is possible to see progress here, in that the man's behavior is no longer depicted as entirely programmed and that he is capable of love. Instead, the author portrays the woman as programmed in that she has so perfectly internalized the abandonment plot, which she has in fact experienced, that in her legitimate desire to defend herself she misinterprets reality. Thus I find this reworking sad and discouraging, in much the same way I found the variant in *The End of Chéri* to be frustrating. Léa does not suffer for the rest of her life after Chéri leaves her, and it is Chéri who kills himself instead of the woman, but this ferocious revenge is accomplished only at the cost of Léa's monstrous new appearance and manner.

Colette made her greatest progress towards breaking out of the constraints of this form of fiction when she abandoned it altogether, rather than when she attempted to alter its details, as we can see in a work like *Break of Day* or *The Evening Star* and in her more general move towards less fictional production in late life. Age and detachment from the heterosexual game were important to the stylistic evolution of all three of the writers we have considered, especially Colette and Simone de Beauvoir. Duras was able to imagine new forms of fiction in her old age, as in *Emily L.* or *Yann Andréa Steiner,* in which she mingled elements of fiction and autobiography, or in *The Summer Rain.* Beauvoir finally produced "Misunderstanding in Moscow," which went further than any other work in this body of fiction in reimagining a livable relationship, based on different assumptions about their respective social and sexual roles, between a woman and a man. And as we might expect by now, they are both in their sixties when this happens.

It is a hopeful sign that the canon of great works taught at the secondary school and university levels is beginning to change. In the 1990s, the curriculum taught in the *collèges* (junior high schools) and *lycées* (high schools) is finally showing some responsiveness to the individual situations and inclinations of young readers, to the point of including more contemporary texts and certain texts by French-speaking authors outside of France and by women(see Houdart 7–20). But I have found no written evidence of a desire to include texts by women as an explicit goal. The aging of the French population is receiving important coverage in the press (see *Le Monde* 3), and sociologists note that "generational analysis often replaces social class analysis" (3); some claim that new relations among the generations in French society have been responsible for more social change than changes in relations between men and women ("Les Nouvelle promesses" 10–11). The woman of forty has entered this discourse, at least once in a while,[2] but there are relatively few specific books or articles in the press devoted to the evolution of the menopausal or postmenopausal woman, apart from those that celebrate the new, youthful eroticism of women on hormone replacement therapy.[3] Nor is there the same interest as in the United States or Great Britain at this point in personal testimony from individual women on these themes. It is clear that the widespread acceptance and administration of synthetic hormones have all but eliminated the notion of a life change specific to women: menopause, in the words of the *Nouvel observateur,* has been all but erased. Like the birth control pill, hormone replacement therapy is regarded as a liberation and a blessing to women, who will now be able to enact with greater ease their own desire and their wish to remain desirable objects in their relationships with men. There is little need felt for any change in the discourse around gender and aging, and once again it is usually men who control its terms. Pierre Simon succinctly summarizes the management by endocrinologists and other doctors of the woman's midlife experience when he says, "Don't offer them flowers, gentlemen. Offer them estrogen!" (*Nouvel observateur* 12).

Nevertheless, it is interesting that two pieces of fiction by women writers published in 1996 give us the beginning of a new, positive perspective on understanding and accepting the changes of menopause, rather than simply attempting to mask them. In her story "Menopause," Marianne Servouze-Karmel describes a fifty-year-old banker, Suzanne, who very consciously suffers from physical and emotional symptoms of menopause. For her, the crisis most directly concerns her childlessness, for now she will never have a child, and her other family members are dead. After she observes from her window the nervous breakdown of another fifty-year-old woman, the resulting night of insomnia ends with her determination to be the child she never had and to offer maternal care to herself. She will find a lover and seek ways to relate to young people that will satisfy her emotional and physical needs. In *The Woman in Blue* [La Dame en bleu], Noëlle Châtelet's attractive, chic, fifty-two-year-old character Solange follows an elderly woman in the street and adopts her slower rhythm and style of life. She buys clothing appropriate to an elderly woman, reserves the use of a room in a home for elders, and drops out of her fast-track job. During her long afternoons, she learns to empty her mind and merge peacefully with her surroundings. She finds pleasure with a male companion who does not expect her to be seductive. She is happy, and when in the end she re-enters the world of her age cohorts, we know that menopause and aging will no longer have the power to frighten her. Both "Menopause" and *The Woman in Blue* are apocalyptic tales, as though their authors are aware that they are appropriating a discourse on menopause and charting new territory. Both optimistically present the resolution of lifelong fears that comes with self-understanding. Solange and Suzanne are positive images of menopausal women.

I think the long historical absence of this kind of discourse in French society invites us to consider the writing of Beauvoir, Colette, and Duras as feminist. It took a great deal of courage to talk or write openly about women's sexuality and behavior, and all three were ahead of their time in doing so. It is true that Colette refused to assume the epithet "feminist," but for a French woman, the term has always had connotations of militancy and potential social violence, for the reasons discussed in chapter 1, and it is hardly surprising that a woman born in 1873 should refuse the term. Duras would not join ranks with feminist activists in collective action after 1968, but we have seen that it was always difficult for her to adhere officially to a common cause. She nevertheless proved in *Les Parleuses* and in her film *Nathalie Granger,* which portrays in detail the hour-by-hour experience of two women friends in their home, and in many other texts, that she experienced the company of her women friends as empowering, especially during her fifties. In a manner typical of French feminists, she was intent on discovering what she considered to be the specificity of woman's nature, but she differs from most French writers in her awareness of women's exclusion from many arenas of social and political life and in her willingness to talk about it.

What is true of aging women writers in France is true for women writers everywhere, though to varying degrees. Colette, Beauvoir, and Duras, all popular, widely read authors, were genuinely transgressive in their respective times. They called into question certain of the clichés of gender difference that for so long not only governed the representation of women in French literature but also made it very difficult for them to express themselves within it in their own voice. Going beyond these dichotomizations allowed for self-expression at last, and therefore for disclosure and deeper intimacy. These are, as we have repeatedly seen, requisites for continuing growth and renewal in age. Betty Friedan's notion of "personhood," which requires the accentuation of *personal* differences rather than a binary division of society into two fixed gender roles, is an especially problematic notion for the French, since it calls into question some of the rigid distinctions that have structured French art and society. Yet I can't help feeling that Friedan is right to say that "successful aging" requires this "personhood of age," and that more traditional femininity, based as it is on a kind of seductiveness and physical attractiveness that is specifically characteristic of young women, is bound to fail with age. The same thing is true, of course about traditional, youthful masculinity, and older men often experience many of the same kinds of problems in attempting to remain seductive in youthful terms.

The specificities of the French tradition, the long-standing rigidity of its social and literary spaces reserved for men and for women, and the examples of the three women discussed here suggest how high the stakes of reimagining aging will really be in any and all societies. They point to the need for an ultimate recognition of personal freedom and personhood that will be inevitably and inextricably linked to the recognition of the value of other differences among people: race, ethnicity, sexual preference, and gender.

NOTES

Introduction

1. Aging was of course experienced differently in preceding centuries. In addition to the dramatic increase in life expectancy for women, from forty-six to almost eighty (in both France and the United States) since 1900, we can now expect a different quality of aging, and this fact must necessarily alter some of our perceptions of earlier eras. Betty Friedan describes this in *The Fountain of Age*: "While the maximum life span has remained fixed at 100 years, the accelerated decline which used to mark aging sets in at a later age. Thus, the view of gradual aging must be displaced by the concept of "a vigorous adult life span followed by a brief and precipitous senescence" (p. 99, quoting G. Labouvie-Vief, "Intelligence and Cognition," p. 506). The three writers I discuss remained lucid and fully functional until very near their deaths, but at least some of the anxiety and depression they experienced along the way can be attributed to an earlier cultural

mythology of long, unrelieved, and inevitable decline of all the faculties that came with age.

2. Among the women writers who have used the term "invisible" to describe themselves as suddenly devoid of interest to those around them are Doris Lessing, in *The Summer Before the Dark,* pp. 179, 186, and Marguerite Duras, in *Le Camion,* p. 64. Both writers present older women characters who sense that others, especially men, no longer engage with them even in conversation in the same way as when they were younger, and sometimes even fail to notice their physical presence.

3. For illustrations of the demographic shifts in France since 1860 as projected through the twenty-first century, see Bernadette Veysset-Puijalon, ed., *Etre Vieux,* p. 200, and Henri Péquignot, *Vieillesses de demain,* p. 20.

4. Marguerite de Navarre appears in the general collection *Conteurs français du XVIème siècle,* as do Louise Labé in *Poètes du XVIème siècle* and Marie de France and Christine de Pisan in *Poètes et Romanciers du Moyen Age.*

Chapter 1. The French Legacy to a Woman of Letters

1. I am primarily concerned in this chapter and elsewhere not with an essentialist notion of femininity but with the gender of actual writers and with what it has meant to be a "woman" as a socially constructed identity in France at particular times in history, considered in an economy of difference with socially and culturally constructed men.

2. Toril Moi, in her book *Simone de Beauvoir: The Making of an Intellectual Woman,* maintains, as I do, that French intellectuals even now have done relatively little to divest themselves of this blindness. She says: "In my experience, intellectuals who attempt to challenge dominant aesthetic and philosophical canons in France are few and far between. In spite of considerable recent efforts to promote texts by women and francophone authors, the French in the 1990s remain overwhelmingly committed to a Jacobin notion of a centralized and universal aesthetic canon. It is no coincidence that the three major French feminist theorists in the 1970s and 1980s (Cixous, Kristeva, and Irigaray) never stray from that canon in their selection of literary and philosophical texts either, just as it is not entirely fortuitous that every major French theoretical trend since the 1960s (Tel Quel, deconstructionism, postmodernism) has been perfectly content to remain within the confines of the accepted literary tradition" (196).

3. Although we now think of "Sapphic" as synonymous with lesbian/homosexual, Sappho has in fact only rarely been defined as a homosexual writer in the four centuries of French preoccupation with her. Questions of possible deviance from the social order were simply erased.

4. That the plot had been internalized by real women as well as fictional ones

is demonstrated by the dramatic deaths of certain prominent women for love, most notably Julie de Lespinasse, a *salonnière* of considerable reputation, well educated and well regarded, but who took an overdose of opium because of a disappointment in love.

5. This split was internalized by French women as well as men, and it has resurfaced in our time in the writings of certain French feminists advocating "une écriture féminine." These women believe as firmly as their male forebears in the connection between their female body and their writing, although they have chosen to celebrate this connection and practice their art as a form of feminist revolution, whereas earlier women writers had chosen to imitate men in order to be artistically credible.

6. At present, it would appear that the current of thought intent upon repressing consciousness and representation of gender difference, while perpetuating *la différence* in social practice, has once again won out. A recent theoretical essay on French women and feminism, contained in *Women's Words* [Les Mots des femmes] by Mona Ozouf, has elicited considerable controversy in scholarly circles on both sides of the Atlantic. In November 1995, the journal *Le Débat* published a series of reactions to Ozouf's text, explicitly raising several questions: Are French women really interested in "emancipation"? Is it appropriate to think in terms of an opposition between American feminist "differentialism" (the belief that we need to consider the difference between the lived experience of women and men, even as we assert that there is a more fundamental identity common to all human beings) and French "universalism" (the notion that it is only useful to consider experience and identity without reference to gender difference in any formal literary or philosophical discussion)? (*Le Débat* no. 87, November–December 1995, 117–46). The term "differentialism" now belongs to the Anglo-American feminists, because they insist on describing the new academic discipline that they have founded and the differences they have experienced. Many French thinkers, in contrast, agree with Ozouf that to dwell on such differences is inappropriate at least for them, since the French have found a singularly pleasant and peaceful way of reconciling the differences between the sexes in one harmonious whole in which women, like men, stand only to gain. The articles that follow represent various positions with respect to these polarities. In general, American scholars challenge Ozouf's concept of French femininity as an acceptance of difference that is never experienced as limiting. They call into question the notion of a specific French "genius" in the matter of relations between the sexes, pointing out that numerous French women throughout history have raised their voices in a common complaint against their lack of civil rights, the very complaint heard in other countries. What seems most striking in this journalistic debate is the shared acceptance of "national alignments" and culturally based dissent on these issues.

Le Débat managed to focus and make explicit the differences that had been implicit, if not manifest, in the consciousness of French and Anglo-American women writers.

Chapter 2. Reconciling Femininity and Aging

1. Woodward, *Aging and Its Discontents* (192, 193), quoting Sigmund Freud, *Standard Edition of the Complete Psychological Works* (hereafter *SE*) 5:457.

2. Lyotard 40, quoted by Woodward 156.

3. I include Betty Friedan's latest work, *The Fountain of Age*. Friedan is certainly hard to categorize, which is entirely to her credit; I think of her as somewhere between a social historian and a sociologist.

4. There is considerable speculation among aging theorists from the sciences on the physiological bases of changing gendered behavior among the elderly. In a discussion of Gutmann's observation that the behavior of each gender takes on characteristics of the other but that women especially evolve a new, more complex gender identity, James P. Henry remarks that Gutmann's implication is that these may be part of a healthy, programmed set of neuroendocrine and other physical changes, rather like whitening of the hair or menopause. Henry states, "Although the mechanisms of these changes that Gutmann describes so eloquently remain to be determined, it is likely that they involve effects of hormones on subcortical regions" (289–90). Other studies are simultaneously lending credence to the notion that environmental conditions can affect hormonal levels by means of a feedback mechanism in response to specific situations, long recognized in the case of certain stress-related syndromes. More than anything, this phenomenon points to the interconnectedness of the body and the environment in producing behavior, and would not reduce the specificity of aging women's gendered behavior to physiological factors alone. See Anke A. Ehrhardt, "The Psychology of Gender," p. 90.

Chapter 3. Colette: Inventing the Way Back

1. Their biography is an attempt to debunk certain myths about Colette as a powerless victim, which is a worthwhile project, but in their refusal to be guided by the work, Francis and Gontier have overstated their arguments. They have, for example, exaggerated the importance of possible Martiniquais ancestors on Sido's father's side of the family, and they have made no mention at all of Colette's pain in her relationships with men and the frustration she experienced. They also do not engage the issue of the reasons Colette wrote so little about her real life, if it was indeed so radically different in orientation and emphasis from her fiction. Finally, there is no analysis of Colette's felt need to reengage with her mother in her late works. The project is entirely ascribed to the early influence that the

writing of the nineteenth-century socialist thinker Charles Fourier had on Sido, which Colette was trying to claim for herself as a justification for her scandalous past. The link to Fourier is an interesting one, but it is not sufficient in my view to account for Colette's preoccupation with her mother in midlife.

2. For an excellent analysis of the importance of this shift in perspective in Colette's work, see Marcelle Biolley-Godino's study *L'Homme-objet dans l'oeuvre de Colette*.

3. Miller also notes in "Woman of Letters" other clear departures from the Ovidian Sapphic plot made by Colette in *The Vagabond*. In part three of the novel, Renée leaves Max alone in Paris to accompany her acting troupe on a tour of France, promising to return and marry him. Thus she leaves him waiting for her, and Miller comments: "Unlike the classical model glorified by Ovid in the *Héroïdes*, according to which the woman waits as the man appears, disappears, and sometimes reappears, her life suspended between waiting rewarded and waiting forever installed; here the man waits in the position of the feminine although in the dialogics of the couple his identity finally is located within a conventional masculinity" (243). This separation becomes the occasion of Renée's letter writing to Max, and thus of her return to writing. The fact that she is writing *letters*, rather than the fiction she had written in the past, enables Colette to connect this production to a feminist epistolary tradition that constitutes a pro-test against the Ovidian tradition: "Against the erotic paralysis of a Portuguese nun, Renée Néré, like Graffigny's Zilia and Riccoboni's Fanny Butlerd, will write her way out of the standard plots" (248).

4. See Danielle Deltel, "Le Scandale soufflé," 151–65.

5. This is the conclusion also reached by Yannick Resch in her study of the woman's body in Colette, *Corps féminin, corps textuel*.

6. A *New Yorker* piece entitled "Medical Notes: The Third Age," by Francine DuPlessix Gray, seems to epitomize a popular misconception about the aging Colette's feelings about her own and other women's aging. Gray points to *The End of Chéri* and *Break of Day* to support her claim that, like Martha Graham, Louise Nevelson, and Isak Dineson, Colette's female characters were unambiguously serene as they aged. Her description of Léa conveys the grotesque transformation I have noted, but Gray does not detect ambivalence in the text. I think it is essential to accept the fact that Colette felt pain and anxiety along the path that led her to her late-life serenity and that without such conflict she would not have forged her own individual late femininity, rich with the continuing, complex co-existence of renunciation and the desire to possess.

7. Hirsch points to the fact that it finally became possible to turn back to the mother in the imagination in part because maternity was no longer an uncontrol-lable force: the era of contraception and lower infant and maternal mortality had

arrived. Colette had become the mother of a daughter, but her identification with this role seems to have been held to a strict minimum; in any case, her daughter rarely finds her way into Colette's literary production, and Colette makes no apologies for this. It was not a question for these writers of becoming mothers themselves but rather of reconciling their very different lives with their own mothers' so that the latter could be "incorporated into the daughter's vision" (97). In Colette's case, as a French woman twice divorced by the 1920s, the question of real difference from her mother's life was further exacerbated and even harder to bridge; for Sido, although most unhappily married (and then widowed) a first time early in life, had had no possibility in France of divorce or separation in the 1860s, nor had it crossed her mind.

8. Much of the following material on the three novels previously appeared in Ladimer, "Moving Beyond Sido's Garden."

9. This very useful insight helps to explain that much of the imagery in all three novels can be seen as an extension by the man's consciousness of the woman's physical attributes to the environment. The man's body and sentiments as the narrator presents them are also projected onto the surroundings, as in the following passage from *La Chatte,* in which Alain, suffering from the stifling heat of the high-rise apartment, is figured as an aged tree, a dying remnant of a lost garden: "Three aged poplars, remnants of a beautiful garden that had been destroyed, waved their tops at the level of the terrace, and the vast Parisian sun, dark red, stifled in humidity, descended slowly behind their thin stalks that were losing their sap" (842).

10. In "From One Identity to Another," Julia Kristeva sees the representation of the self in the field of language as an artificial construct, distinct from the bodily experiences of the child: "the subject is merely the subject of predication, of judgment, of the sentence" (130). When the speaker says "I," she/he assures a momentarily fixed, alienated identity based on a "freeing" of the fluid, unbounded self with the field of language. Symbolic language requires this fixity in order to impose its order, its unitary conventions, on the inchoate flow of reality. Thus it is in acquiring language that the speaking or writing subject loses the immediate experience of its ever-changing drives and impulses and its sense of being merged (Kristeva's "semiotic"), although these feelings do recur. It is primarily language that enables the subject to establish firm differentiation between self and object. But in these passages, Jean has not yet acquired symbolic language. He expresses his feeling of being merged in the verbs of flight, while the changing play of impulses and feelings within him is figured by the rapid sequence of euphoria and dysphoria and by his fluid progress from one to another, a fluidity that is also emphasized by the smooth motion of flight.

11. In the United States, several feminist psychoanalysts have spoken to the

difference in women's personality that results from their different experience of the pre-Oedipal relationship. Nancy Chodorow has provided such an explanation in *The Reproduction of Mothering*. For Chodorow, all children are originally either sexually undifferentiated or "matrisexual" (164). The (heterosexual) mother unconsciously projects herself onto her daughter, with whom she feels continuous, while regarding a son as an "other." This process enables sons to differentiate themselves from their mothers and to establish separate identities. Girls, in contrast, have great difficulty in our society with differentiation and individuation. Uncertainty about the boundaries between a mother's and a daughter's self persists to a greater or lesser extent into adulthood.

12. Julien Benda, *Belphégor* (Paris: Emile-Paul Frères, 1924), (quoted in Sarde, *Colette libre et entravée* 437).

13. Two years earlier, with *Le Toutounnier,* she had studied the "cure" provided by the retreat in following Alice when she returns to the home where she was raised with her three sisters. Alice's husband has died after a period of estrangement. The *toutounnier* is a sort of old couch or sofa on which the sisters like to lounge and talk; the word is akin to baby talk and comes to signify a haven for Alice. With her sisters, she does experience a cure, but while there is certainly a sympathetic portrayal of this intimacy among women and of their strength, there is also an ironic distance: Alice, once cured, will only go on to other loves. In this respect, apart from the compelling warmth of the gyneceum, *Le Toutounnier* differs little from a very early story in *Tendrils of the Vine*, "The Cure," in which "Colette" consoles her suffering friend Valentine and foretells the successive stages of her recovery. At the end, "Colette" is not surprised, but rather resigned, when Valentine only wants "another love."

Chapter 4. Simone de Beauvoir: On Becoming a Woman

1. A number of critics have claimed that the only truly intimate text produced by Beauvoir, despite her lengthy memoirs, is the story of her mother's death in *A Very Easy Death*. While I certainly agree that this work is among her most personal (in fact, I believe it inaugurated a new stage in her psychic development and writing), I do not feel that it is the only one. The first part of *All Said and Done*, "Malentendu à Moscou," certain passages in *The Coming of Age* (in which Beauvoir freely allows herself to express her personal feelings about aging), parts of the character Anne's journal in *The Mandarins*, and even the epilogue to *The Force of Circumstances* have the same genuinely personal, "worked through" quality as the story of her mother's death. I should emphasize that I am not talking here about what Toril Moi calls Beauvoir's "personal writing," that is, her journals and letters that constituted a writing of "disavowal" of her distress over Sartre's

behavior towards her. Moi is right to say that for the most part these are mechanical, uninteresting texts, including large parts of the memoirs that are transpositions of these journals. But there are exceptional passages even in this "personal writing," as indicated above. I agree with Moi's claim that for Beauvoir, both fiction and autobiography communicate through "non-knowledge," as distinct from the essay form, and that both are equally suited to convey the "ambiguity" of reality (247).

2. H. M. Parshley, cited by Deirdre Bair p. 433: "She certainly suffers from verbal diarrhea. I have seldom read a book that seems to run in such concentric circles. Everything seems to be repeated three or four times but in different parts of the text, and I can hardly imagine the average person reading the whole book carefully."

3. A valuable discussion of this subject can be found in Michèle Le Doeuff's *Hipparchia's Choice: An Essay Concerning Women, Philosophy,* and in Toril Moi's chapter "Freedom and Flirtation" in *Simone de Beauvoir: The Making of an Intellectual Woman.*

4. It was at this point, when she suddenly felt herself to be middle aged, that Beauvoir discovered a lump in her breast and was briefly face-to-face with the threat of literal mutilation. When she told Sartre about it, he too interpreted it as somehow related to the times, telling her in all seriousness (and somewhat callously) that in any case they would probably all die soon in an atomic war.

5. Toril Moi offers an interesting interpretation of the different functions within Beauvoir's writing of the letters and diaries as distinct from the other forms destined for publication. The diary functions, according to Moi, to allay her severe bouts of fear and depression: "In Simone de Beauvoir's works the very appearance of the form or genre of the diary signifies emotional anguish. . . . When she feels more receptive to the outside world, she gets on with her other writing, leaving her journal aside. Such swings of mood often happen within very short spaces of time" (245). In *The Mandarins,* Anne's journal is certainly the space of confession of fear of loneliness and depression, while Henri's third-person account is focused on the outside world and is *relatively* euphoric, even though he too suffers intellectual anguish and unhappiness with women. Combining the two already familiar means of expression within one novel was undoubtedly Beauvoir's way of including her entire range of experience at that time, which is of course of uncertain or undecidable gender when considered in its totality.

6. See also Bianca Lamblin, *Mémoires d'une jeune fille dérangée,* for a scathing and often convincing indictment of Sartre and Beauvoir's joint seduction and betrayal of her in the immediate prewar period.

7. André Billy, "Tristesse du vieillissement féminin," *Le Figaro,* Feb. 5, 1968, quoted in Bair 527.

Chapter 5. Marguerite Duras: Love and Intimacy at Eighty and Beyond

1. Kathleen Woodward, *Aging and Its Discontents*, 169. Woodward also provides a reference to a more familiar view of the aged woman's face in "Arenas of Visibility: Representations/Older Women/Self-Representation" in *Feminist Collections*. She begins this review with a description of the October 1992 issue of *Life*, whose cover story was "Can We Stop Aging?" Woodward remarks: "The accompanying image—of a woman—was designed to elicit the shock with which aging is received in the United States. The cover photograph was a closeup of the face of a (once) beautiful woman, white, her face bifurcated technologically down the middle, the right half of her as she is today, an old woman, the left half as she was some fifty years before. The message so clearly sent by this mass-mediated representation of woman was that aging is a catastrophe, that it is a scandal particularly for women. . . . Tellingly enough, this woman remained only an image, a frightening lure for readers to turn to the story inside (written by a man) in which we learn nothing about her life, her experience, her subjectivity. Indeed she is never mentioned." I must admit that I have trouble imagining such a magazine cover in France, but only because of its capacity to shock visually, which might be considered in poor taste. The fear to which it plays is certainly powerful nevertheless. It is also equally likely that the old woman would be totally obscured from the actual text of the article, suddenly "invisible" when the thrilling sight of her degradation was over. It is in this social context that we need to consider Duras's writing about her own face. She provides us with the subjectivity that was lacking in the article and by this gesture provides a glimpse of the originality of her feelings about herself in old age.

2. In terms of the aged woman's face as seen in French literature, certain negative images are already familiar, including those we have seen in the works of Simone de Beauvoir or Colette. Among the most interesting created by a male writer is Honoré de Balzac's description of the fifty-year-old Marquise d'Aiglemont, who had originally been the "Woman of Thirty," and who created a reputation for Balzac as the first portraitist of the beauty of the middle-aged women in *La Femme de trente ans;* the age of thirty was, in the 1830s, the end of true youth and the beginning of middle age. Surely his description of Julie d'Aiglemont at thirty is appreciative. He considers her experience and self-possession as translated into bodily attributes of grace and refinement that make her more attractive than in her first youth. But by the time the unhappily married Julie reaches fifty, her face reflects a life of suffering and guilt, and appears "even older" than it is. At the end of her life and of the novel, she is undergoing the final punishment for having tried to find happiness "in a romanesque life, outside of society's received

ideas, and far from her mother." Thus Balzac's sensitive and original understanding of many women's plight in marriage is confronted with his intransigent moral position, and the reflection of a woman's character in her lined, aged face is more ambiguously connotated than at age thirty. At fifty, Julie's wrinkles are attributed, like Duras's, to her experience of passion, but love has "tortured her features" with exaggerated and yet eloquent wrinkles that make her "sublime in horror, beautiful in melancholy, or magnificent in calm" (1201, 1206).

3. In my view, the two biographies written before Duras's death, *Marguerite Duras* by Alain Vircondelet and *Marguerite Duras ou le poids d'une plume* by Frédérique Lebelley, attempt little separation between fact and fiction, based as they are in large part on Duras's own writing, which is simply presumed to be about herself. Neither one relies much on interviews with Duras. These biographies, quite different from each other in several ways, represent more than anything two individuals' interpretations of Duras's life as seen through her work, and for me their interest lies in these readings. Their way of proceding by interpreting the writing rather than by conducting interviews is hardly surprising, in that Duras was still alive at the time of their writing and it is rare to find a biography of a person in France who is not already dead. In 1998, Laure Adler was the first to publish a biography, *Duras*, after the writer's death in 1996. Adler had conducted interviews with Duras for several years before her death and had access to substantial archival material through Duras's son Jean Mascolo. Adler explicitly attacks the problem of writing the biography of someone who constantly reinvented herself through her fictional writing, confusing truth and fiction in her own mind as much as in her readers'. This initial admission of the inextricable weave of truth and fiction does much to enhance the credibility of her account, and one finds in this book a wealth of detail about Duras's personal circumstances that was missing in the others. Adler rightly asserts that "while writing a biography from a chronological and historical perspective, [she] also had to observe one absolute principle: what remains of Marguerite Duras is her writing" (Pierre Lepape in *Le Monde*, August 26, 1998, qtd. in "The Heart of the Matter," Manchester, England, *Guardian Weekly*, September 27, 1998: 18). All the same, some readers will find that Adler surrendered too readily to a certain sensationalism surrounding the account of the Chinese lover, Duras's role in the Resistance, and in particular her relationship with Charles Delval, alias Rabier, as presented in *The War*. In these instances, Adler confronts Duras's multiple accounts of these parts of her life with "facts" that discredit these accounts or reestablish a rigid boundary between biography and fiction that the writer transgressed in a more or less deliberate attempt to make herself more acceptable or attractive to her public. Duras emerges from Adler's scrutiny as more ambivalent about collaboration than has generally been thought and less clearly a member of the French Resis-

tance. It would also appear, from Adler's version, that the Chinese lover was in fact never a real lover at all but that he remained much like Monsieur Jo of *The Sea Wall*. In the end, however, the reader's conclusion must remain the same: Duras's own consciousness of these experiences is available to us, and perhaps to her, only through her writing.

4. Joseph is present throughout part 1 and at the end of the novel. Before the trip to the city, Suzanne follows him into the forest in a remarkable passage in which the forest, ordinarily a dangerous place for a young girl, is reworked in marine terms, recalling the ocean that has destroyed the mother's life but which is here safely under Suzanne's possession and control. In Joseph's company, it becomes a place of freedom, fulfillment, and pleasure. "The vines and the orchids, in a monstrous invasion, supernatural, bound the entire forest together and made it into a compact mass that was as impenetrable and stifling as the depths of the sea. . . . The forest slept under this vast ramification of orchid basins full of rainwater and in which were the same fish as in the swamps of the plain" (158).

5. See Nancy Chodorow, *The Reproduction of Mothering*.

6. It is important to remember that *The Lover*, which contains the explicit connection between Duras's brother Pierre and the evils of fascism, was not published during her mother's lifetime. Duras in fact made an effort to protect her mother's privacy, waiting until after her mother's death to rework the story of *The Sea Wall* in *L'Eden cinéma*. But in Duras's first novels, *Les Impudents* and *La Vie tranquille*, Pierre sensed in the stifling family milieu, which many compared to the near-madness of Mauriac's depictions of French family life, an attack on himself or at least the potential for one. He was of course not wrong.

7. Martha Noel Evans recognizes in *Masks of Tradition* that his search for Lol's truth is primarily an attempt to dominate, even if his rhetoric is one of love (138).

8. The curious text *The Sickness unto Death* [La Maladie de la mort], written in 1981 and published in 1982, may well be Duras's own critique of her "fetishized" women who can only maintain a relationship of sterile fascination with the reader. Such women, especially given the problems Duras discusses elsewhere, only increase the alienation of the sexes and the frustrating difference in experience that the sexual act alone cannot overcome. The story is addressed to a man called "vous," who, presumably inspired by Yann, suffers from his inability to love women and, in an effort to "know" the feminine, has "rented" a sleepy young woman for a few days spent in bed in a room by the sea. The woman sleeps almost all of the time, but when she does awaken, she speaks to the man in terms that reveal her contempt (48). In fact, he has realized that she is right, in a startlingly ambiguous passage in which the narrator admits that the sickness of death is fomented in the woman's body and imposed by her (38). Yet the narrator is not the

woman, is not "she." She is elsewhere, a third person watching this blanked-out woman who secretes this illness and this man who is incapable of love because he suffers from it. According to Maurice Blanchot, the ambiguity of these statements about the woman betrays a fundamentally uneasy relation between the text and its author: "a strange passage which leads us almost too suddenly to another version, to another reading: 'the sickness of death' is not the sole responsibility of the man who refuses to know the feminine or, even if he knows it, refuses to become familiar with it" (Maurice Blanchot, La Communauté inavouable 65). Blanchot is correct to feel that the woman is also responsible, because it is in fact the man who makes all the efforts, asks all the questions, attempts to elucidate the mystery of the sexes, whereas the woman does literally nothing but sleep and condemn. There would seem to be a critique here, not only of the man who cannot love but also of the typical "Durassian woman," the last to appear in the Durassian corpus and from whom the narrator is clearly separating.

9. After making love on their first night together, according to the account in Yann Andréa Steiner, Yann told her that her body was "incredibly young" (31). Duras adds: "I hesitated before publishing that sentence." She says that she couldn't help writing it and that she often writes things she doesn't fully understand. Laughing, she tells Yann that her Chinese lover said the same thing to her when she was fourteen (31). This appears to be the only clear reference in her work to the way the age difference between them might have affected Yann in terms of physical response. Obviously, when she was fourteen her body was "incredibly young" to the twenty-seven-year-old lover. Here, Yann is also twenty-seven, but she is sixty-six. Is this a form of denial of her own aging? Or has she really experienced the changes brought by aging as negligible to the desire another might feel for her? I am rather inclined to the latter conclusion, however astonishing it may seem, for one difference between this reference to her own aging and the ones made by other female authors I have read in both French and English is that she fearlessly addresses it to the young man she is making love with, not in a confessional act to the reader alone.

10. Nancy K. Miller, "The Text's Heroine: A Feminist Critic and Her Fictions," pp. 49–50. Miller used these terms in a debate with Peggy Kamuf about the relationship of writing to the body and the problem of gender in writing. In response to Kamuf's assertion that feminist criticism is merely "cosmetic modification on the face of humanism and its institutions," Miller makes a statement of particular relevance to the suppression of Emily's poem: "Moreover and implicitly, to code as 'cosmetic' and to foreclose as untimely, discussions of the author as a sexually gendered subject in a socially gendered exchange is to be too confident that nondiscursive practices will respond correctly to the correct theory of discursive practice."

Chapter 6. Conclusion

1. As Margaret Forster observes in her essay "How Was It for You?" Germaine Greer's view of sexuality in the life of postmenopausal women as expressed in her book *The Change* is only partly correct. Greer denies that sexuality continues to count, a position Forster finds exaggerated. She asserts instead that it does not disappear but rather plays a role that is *different,* as our writers clearly illustrate. Greer and Forster are both talking about genital sexuality and the sex act, whereas I have tried, following Beauvoir, to expand the notion to include sensuality, intimacy, and one's sense of oneself as a gendered being. In this larger sense especially, sexuality continues to play an important role.

2. For example, in Claire Fleury's article "Rude Cap pour les femmes," the author notes that there are two kinds of forty-year-old women: a majority, who are depressed by the physical signs of aging, the approach of menopause, and the fear of loneliness, and those who consciously address the question, come to terms with it, and experience new energy and contentment.

3. See Pierre Simon, M.D., *La Femme de quarante ans ou le sacre de l'été,* and also the dossier "Femmes: La Révolution de la quarantaine," devoted to the new woman of forty.

BIBLIOGRAPHY

All translations from French are mine unless otherwise noted

Primary Sources

Beauvoir, Simone de. *Les Belles images* (The beautiful pictures). Paris: Gallimard, 1966.

———. *La Cérémonie des adieux* (Adieu: A farewell to Sartre). Paris: Gallimard, 1981.

———. *Le Deuxième sexe* (The second sex), I, II. Paris: Gallimard, 1949. Translated by H. M. Parshley, New York: Vintage, 1974.

———. *La Femme rompue* (The woman destroyed). Paris: Gallimard, 1967.

———. *La Force de l'age* (The prime of life). Paris: Gallimard, 1960.

———. *La Force des choses* (Force of circumstance) I, II. Paris: Gallimard, 1963.

———. *L'Invitée* (She came to stay). Paris: Gallimard, 1943.

———. *Lettres à Sartre 1940–1963* (Letters to Sartre 1940–1963). Paris: Gallimard, 1990.

———. "Malentendu à Moscou" (Misunderstanding in Moscow). In *Roman 20–50: Revue d'étude du roman du XXème siècle*, no. 13, June 1992, 137–88. Paris.

————. *Mandarins* (The Mandarins) I, II. Paris: Gallimard, 1954.

————. *Mémoires d'une jeune fille rangée* (Memoirs of a dutiful daughter). Paris: Gallimard, 1958. Translated by James Kirkup. New York: Harper and Row, 1959.

————. *Une Mort très douce* (A very easy death). Paris: Gallimard, 1964.

————. *Tout comte fait* (All said and done). Paris: Gallimard, 1972.

————. *La Vieillesse* (The coming of age). Paris: Gallimard, 1970.

Colette, Sidonie Gabrielle. "Bella-Vista." In *Oeuvres* III, edited by Claude Pichois, 1097–1145. Paris: Gallimard, Bibliothèque de la Pléiade, 1991.

————. *Le Blé en herbe* (The ripening seed). In *Oeuvres* II, edited by Claude Pichois, 1185–1270. Paris: Gallimard, Bibliothèque de la Pléiade, 1986.

————. *La Chatte* (The cat). In *Oeuvres* III, edited by Claude Pichois, 809–91. Paris: Gallimard, Bibliothèque de la Pléiade, 1991.

————. *Chéri*. In *Oeuvres* II, edited by Claude Pichois, 717–828. Paris: Gallimard, Bibliothèque de la Pléiade, 1986.

————. *Claudine à l'école* (Claudine at school). In *Oeuvres* I, edited by Claude Pichois, 7–218. Paris: Gallimard, Bibliothèque de la Pléiade, 1984.

————. "L'Enfant malade" (The sick child). In *Gigi*. Paris. Hachette, 1960. Translated by Antonia White. In *The Collected Stories of Colette*, edited by Robert Phelps. New York: Farrar, Straus and Giroux, 1983.

————. *L'Etoile vesper* (The evening star). Paris: Fayard, 1986. Translated by David Le Vay. New York: Bobbs-Merril, 1973.

————. *Le Fanal bleu* (The blue lantern). Paris: Fayard, 1987. Translated by Roger Senhouse. New York: Farrar, Straus, 1963.

————. *La Fin de Chéri* (The end of Chéri). Paris: Flammarion, 1983.

————. "Flore et Pomone" (Flora and Pomona). In *Oeuvres de Collette*. Vol. 3. Paris: Flammarion, 1960.

————. *Julie de Carneilhan*. Paris: Fayard, 1941.

————. "Le Képi." In *Le Képi*. Paris: Fayard, 1943.

————. *La Maison de Claudine* (My mother's house). In *Oeuvres* II, edited by Claude Pichois, 967–1084. Paris: Gallimard, Bibliothèque de la Pléiade, 1986.

————. *Mes Apprentissages* (My apprenticeship). In *Oeuvres* III, edited by Claude Pichois, 981–1076. Paris: Gallimard, Bibliothèque de la Pléiade, 1991.

————. *La Naissance du jour* (Break of day). In *Oeuvres* III, edited by Claude Pichois, 277–371. Paris: Gallimard, Bibliothèque de la Pléiade, 1991. Translated by Enid McLeod. New York: Farrar, Straus and Cudahy, 1961.

————. *Paris de ma fenêtre* (Paris from my window). Paris: Editions du milieu du monde, 1944.

————. *Sido*. In *Oeuvres* III, edited by Claude Pichois, 495–550. Paris: Gallimard, Bibliothèque de la Pléiade, 1991.

————. *Le Toutounnier*. In *Oeuvres* III, edited by Claude Pichois, 1215–71. Paris: Gallimard, Bibliotheque de la Pléiade, 1991.

————. *La Vagabonde* (The vagabond). In *Oeuvres* I, edited by Claude Pichois, 1067–1232. Paris: Gallimard, Bibliothèque de la Pléiade, 1984.

————. *Les Vrilles de la vigne* (Tendrils of the vine). In *Oeuvres I*: 959–1063. Paris: Gallimard, Bibliothèque de la Pléiade, 1984.

Duras, Marguerite. *L'Amant* (The lover). Paris: Editions de Minuit, 1984.

————. *L'Amant de la Chine du nord* (The lover from the north of China). Paris: Gallimard, 1991.

————. *Un Barrage contre le Pacifique* (The sea wall). Paris: Gallimard, 1950.

————. *Le Camion* (The truck). Dir. Marguerite Duras. Perf. Marguerite Duras and Gérard Depardieu. D. D. Productions, 1977.

————. *Dix heures et demie du soir en été* (Ten-thirty on a summer evening). Paris: Gallimard, 1960.

————. *La Douleur* (The War). Paris: P.O.L., 1985.

————. *Ecrire* (Writing). Paris: Gallimard, 1993.

————. *L'Eden cinéma*. Paris: Mercure de France, 1986.

————. *Emily L*. Paris: Editions de Minuit, 1987.

————. *L'Eté 80* (The summer of 1980). Paris: Editions de Minuit, 1980.

————. *L'Homme assis dans le couloir* (The man sitting in the corridor). Paris: Editions de Minuit, 1980.

————. *India Song*. Dir. Marguerite Duras. Gallimard, 1973.

————. *La Maladie de la mort* (The sickness unto death). Paris: Editions de Minuit, 1982.

————. *Moderato cantabile*. Paris: Editions de Minuit, 1958.

————. *Le Navire night* (The ship "night"). Paris: Mercure de France, 1979.

————. *Les Parleuses* (Women speaking). Paris: Editions de Minuit, 1974.

————. *La Pluie d'été* (The summer rain). Paris: P.O.L., 1990.

————. *Le Ravissement de Lol V. Stein* (The ravishing of Lol V. Stein). Paris: Gallimard, 1964.

————. *Le Vice-Consul* (The vice consul). Paris: Gallimard, 1966.

————. *La Vie Materielle* (Material life). Paris: P.O.L., 1987.

————. *Yann Andréa Steiner*. Paris: P.O.L., 1992.

————. *Le Yeux bleus cheveux noirs* (Blue eyes and black hair). Paris: Editions de Minuit, 1986.

————. "Les Yeux verts" (Green eyes). *Cahiers du cinéma* no. 312–13 (June 1980).

Duras, Marguerite, and Michelle Porte. *Les Lieux de Marguerite Duras* (Places). Paris: Editions de Minuit, 1977.

Secondary Sources

Adler, Laure. *Duras*. Paris: Gallimard, 1998.

Andréa, Yann. *M.D.* Paris: Editions de Minuit, 1983.

Apostrophes: Bernard Pivot rencontre Marguerite Duras. L'Institut National de l'Audiovisuel and Les Editions du Seuil. France 2 (Antenne 2), Paris. Sept. 28, 1984.

Bair, Deirdre. *Simone de Beauvoir*. New York: Simon and Schuster, 1990.

Balzac, Honoré de. *La Femme de trente ans*. Vol. 2. Editions de la Pléiade. Paris: Gallimard, 1976.

Banner, Phyllis. *In Full Flower: Aging Women, Power, and Sexuality*. New York: Vintage, 1992.

Bart, Pauline. "Why Women's Status Changes in Middle Age: The Turns of the Social Ferris Wheel." *Sociological Symposium* 3 (fall 1969), 1–18.

Barthes, Roland. *Le Plaisir du texte*. Paris: Seuil, 1973.

Biolley-Godino, Marcelle. *L'Homme-objet dans l'oeuvre de Colette*. Paris: Klincksieck, 1972.

Blanchot, Maurice. *La Communauté inavouable*. Paris: Editions de Minuit, 1983.

Butler, Judith. "Sex and Gender in Simone de Beauvoir's *The Second Sex*." *Yale French Studies*, edited by Hélène Wenzel, 72 (1986): 35–49.

Butler, Robert N. "The Life Review: An Interpretation of Reminiscence in the Aged." *Psychiatry: Journal for the Study of Interpersonal Processes* 26 (1963): 65–76.

Calle-Gruber, Mireille. "Pourquoi n'a-t-on plus peur de Marguerite Duras." *Revue des sciences humaines* 202 (April–June 1980).

Chapsal, Madeleine. *La Femme abandonnée*. Paris: Editions de Poche, 1994.

Châtelet, Noëlle. *La Dame en bleu* (The woman in blue). Paris: Stock, 1996.

Chodorow, Nancy. *The Reproduction of Mothering: Psychoanalysis and the Sociology of Gender*. Berkeley: University of California Press, 1978.

Le Débat. No. 87 (November–December 1995): 117–46.

Deguy, Jacques, ed. *Roman 20:50* 13 (June 1992).

DeJean, Joan. *Fictions of Sappho 1546–1937*. Chicago: University of Chicago Press, 1988.

Del-Bono, Jean Laurent, and Philippe Sollers. "L'Idole des jeunes." *Le Nouvel Observateur* 1526 (June 1994): 18–22.

Deltel, Danielle. "Le Scandale soufflé: Le Paradoxe dans l'écriture de Colette." In *Colette, Nouvelles approches critiques*, edited by Bernard Bray. Paris: Nizet, 1986.

Ehrhardt, Anke A. "The Psychology of Gender." In *Gender and the Life Course,* edited by Alice S. Rossi. New York: Aldrine, 1985.

Erikson, Erik. *The Life Cycle Completed: A Review.* New York: Norton, 1985.

Evans, Martha Noel. *Masks of Tradition: Women and the Politics of Writing in Twentieth Century France.* Ithaca, N.Y.: Cornell University Press, 1987.

"Femmes: La Révolution de la quarantine." *Le Nouvel Observateur* (May 2–8, 1996): 4–12.

"Les Femmes en France dans une société d'inégalité." *Report to the Minister of Women's Rights,* March 1982.

Fleury, Claire. "Rude Cap pour les femmes." *Le Nouvel Observateur* (June 16–22 1994): 11.

Ford, Marianna."Spatial Structures in *La Chatte.*" *French Review* 58 (1985): 11.

Forster, Margaret. "How Was It for You?" In *A Certain Age: Reflecting on Menopause,* edited by Joanna Goldsworthy, 151–52. New York: Columbia University Press, 1994.

Francis, Claude, and Fernande Gontier. *Colette.* Paris: Perrin, 1997.

Freud, Sigmund. *Standard Edition of the Complete Psychological Works.* 24 vols. London: Hogarth Press, 1953–1974.

Friedan, Betty. *The Fountain of Age.* New York: Simon and Schuster, 1993.

Gilbert, Sandra M., and Susan Gubar. *No Man's Land: The Place of the Woman Writer in the Twentieth Century.* Vol. 1. New Haven: Yale University Press, 1988.

Giroud, Françoise and Bernard-Henri Lévy. *Les Hommes et les femmes.* Paris: Olivier Orban, 1993.

Gray, Francine DuPlessix. "Medical Notes: The Third Age." *The New Yorker.* March 4, 1996, 186.

Greenberg, Jay E., and Stephen A. Mitchell, eds. *Object Relations in Psychoanalytic Theory.* Cambridge: Harvard University Press, 1983.

Gubar, Susan. "Sapphistries." *Signs* 10, no. 11 (1984): 43–62.

Gullette, Margaret Morganroth. "Creativity, Aging, Gender: A Study of Their Intersections, 1910–1935." In *Aging and Gender in Literature,* edited by Anne Wyatt-Brown and Janice Rossen. Charlottesville: University Press of Virginia, 1993.

———. *Safe at Last in the Middle Years: The Invention of the Midlife Progress Novel.* Berkeley: University of California Press, 1988.

Gutmann, David L. "Beyond Nurture: Developmental Perspectives on the Vital Older Woman." In *In Her Prime: A New View of Middle-Aged Women,* edited by Virginia Kerns and Judith K. Brown. South Hadley, Mass.: Bergin and Garvey, 1985.

Heilbrun, Carolyn. "Introduction." In *A Certain Age: Reflecting on Menopause,* edited by Joanna Goldsworthy. New York: Columbia University Press, 1994.

————. *Writing a Woman's Life.* New York: Norton, 1988.

Henry, James P. "The Archetypes of Power and Intimacy." In *Emergent Theories of Aging,* edited by James Birren and Vern L. Bengston. New York: Springer, 1988.

Hirsch, Marianne. *The Mother-Daughter Plot.* Bloomington: Indiana University Press, 1983.

Houdart, Violaine. "Des Discours officiels aux copies d'élèves: Les valeurs dans l'enseignement du français depuis 1880." In *Le Français aujourd'hui: La littérature et les valeurs* (Revue de l'Association française des enseignants de français), no. 100 (June 1995): 7–20.

Jardine, Alice. "Death Sentences: Writing Couples and Ideology." In *Critical Essays on Simone de Beauvoir,* edited by Elaine Marks. Boston: Hall, 1987.

————. *Gynesis: Configurations of Women and Modernity.* Ithaca, N.Y.: Cornell University Press, 1985.

Jung, Carl G. *The Structures and Dynamics of the Psyche.* Translated by R. F. C. Hull. New York: Pantheon Books/Bolingen Series 20, 1960. (First printed in 1931.)

Kerns, Virginia, and Judith K. Brown, eds. *In Her Prime: A View of Middle-Aged Women.* South Hadley, Mass.: Bergin and Garvey, 1985.

Kristeva, Julia. "From One Identity to Another." In *Desire in Language,* edited by Leon Roudiez. New York: Columbia University Press, 1980.

————. *Soleil noir: Dépression et mélancolie* (Black sun: Depression and melancholy). Paris: Gallimard, 1987.

Labouvie-Vief, G. "Intelligence and Cognition." In *Handbook of the Psychology of Aging,* edited by J. E. Birren and K. Werner Schaie. New York: Van Nostrand Reinhold, 1985.

Ladimer, Bethany. "Colette: Rewriting the Script for the Aging Woman." In *Aging and Gender in Literature,* edited by Anne Wyatt-Brown and Janice Rossen, 243. Charlottesville: University Press of Virginia, 1993.

————. "Moving Beyond Sido's Garden: Ambiguity in Three Novels by Colette." *Romance Quarterly,* vol. 36, no. 2 (May 1989): 153–164.

————. "The Space of a Woman's Autobiography in *Emily L."* *Dalhousie French Studies,* spring-summer 1990, 61–78.

Lafayette, Madame de. *La Princesse de Clèves.* Translated by Nancy Mitford. London: Penguin, 1988.

Lamblin, Bianca. *Mémoires d'une jeune fille dérangée.* Paris: Balland, 1993.

Larnac, Jean. *Colette, sa vie, son oeuvre.* Paris: Krâ, 1927.

Le Doeuff, Michèle. *Hipparchia's Choice: An Essay Concerning Women, Philosophy.* Translated by Trista Selous. Oxford: Blackwell, 1991.

Lebelley, Frédérique. *Marguerite Duras ou le poids d'une plume.* Paris: Grasset, 1994.

Lessing, Doris. *The Summer Before the Dark.* New York: Vintage, 1983.

Lobel, Edgar, and Denys Page. *Poetarum Lesbiorum Fragmenta.* Oxford: Clarendon Press, 1955.

Loevinger, Jane. *Ego Development.* San Francisco: Jossey-Bass, 1976.

Loevinger, Jane, and, B.C. Neugarten. *Middle Age and Aging.* Chicago: University Press of Chicago, 1968.

Lottman, Herbert. *Colette.* Paris: Gallimard, 1990.

Lydon, Mary. "L'Eden Cinéma: Aging and the Imagination in Marguerite Duras." In *Memory and Desire,* edited by Kathleen Woodward and Murray M. Schwartz. Bloomington: Indiana University Press, 1986.

Lyotard, Jean-François. *Just Gaming: Conversations.* Minneapolis: University of Minnesota Press, 1985.

Marini, Marcelle. *Territoires du féminin avec Marguerite Duras.* Paris: Editions de Minuit, 1977.

Marks, Elaine. "Lesbian Intertextuality." In *Homosexualities and French Literature,* edited by George Stambolian and Elaine Marks. Ithaca, N.Y.: Cornell University Press, 1979.

———. "Transgressing the (In)cont(in)ent Boundaries: The Body in Decline." *Yale French Studies,* edited by Hélène Wenzel, 72 (1986): 181–200.

Le Matin. November 1986.

Meillassoux, Claude. *Maidens, Meals and Money.* Translated by Felicity Edholm. New York: Cambridge University Press, 1981.

Miller, Nancy K. "The Anamnesis of a Female 'I': In the Margins of Self-Portrayal." In *Colette: The Woman, the Writer,* edited by Erica Eisinger and Mari McCarty. University Park: Pennsylvania State University Press, 1981.

———. *Bequest and Betrayal: Memoirs of a Parent's Death.* New York: Oxford University Press, 1996.

———. *Subject to Change.* New York: Columbia University Press, 1988.

———. "The Text's Heroine: A Feminist Critic and Her Fictions." *Diacritics* 12 (1982): 1–2.

———. "Women's Autobiography in France: For a Dialectics of Identification." In *Woman and Language in Literature and Society,* edited by Borker McConnell-Ginet and Furman, 271. New York: Praeger, 1980.

Moi, Toril. *Simone de Beauvoir: The Making of an Intellectual Woman.* Cambridge, England: Blackwell, 1994.

Ozouf, Mona. *Women's Words: Essay on French Singularity.* Translated by Jane Marie Todd. Chicago: University of Chicago Press, 1997.

"Les Nouvelles promesses du désir" (New promises of desire). *Le Nouvel Observateur* (May 2–8, 1996): 101–11.

Péquignot, Henri. *Vieillesses de demain.* Paris: J. Vrin, 1986.

Peyre, Henri. "The Tragedy of Passion in Racine's *Phèdre*." In *Tragic Themes in Western Literature,* edited by Cleanth Brooks. New Haven: Yale University Press, 1955.

Relyea, Suzanne. "The Symbolic in the Family Factory." *Women's Studies* 8 (1981): 283–97.

Resch, Yannick. *Corps féminin, corps textuel.* Paris: Klinksieck, 1973.

Sarde, Michèle. *Colette libre et entravée.* Paris: Stock, 1978.

———. *Regard sur les Françaises.* Paris: Stock, 1983.

Sartre, Jean-Paul. *Being and Nothingness: An Essay on Phenomenological Ontology.* Translation and introduction by Hazel E. Barnes. New York: Philosophical Library, 1956.

Schwartzer, Alice. *Simone de Beauvoir aujourd'hui: Entretiens.* Paris: Mercure de France, 1984.

Selous, Trista. *The Other Woman: Feminism and Femininity in the Work of Marguerite Duras.* New Haven: Yale University Press, 1988.

Servouze-Karmel, Marianne. *Ménopause et autres récits,* (Menopause and other stories). Paris: Attique, 1996.

Simon, Pierre. *La Femme de quarante ans ou le sacre de l'été* (The woman of forty, or the rites of summer). Paris: Hachette, 1996.

Simons, Margaret A. "In Memoriam." In *Simone de Beauvoir: Witness to a Century. Yale French Studies,* edited by Hélène Wenzel, 72 (1986): 204.

Staël, Madame de. *Corinne ou l'Italie.* Paris: Gallimard, 1985.

Veysset-Puijalon, Bernadette, ed. *Etre Vieux.* Paris: Autrement, 1992.

"Vieux, riches et biens portants." *Le Monde: Dossiers et documents* (September 1994): 3.

Vircondelet, Alain. *Marguerite Duras.* Paris: Editions François Bourin, 1991.

Willis, Sharon. *Marguerite Duras: Writing on the Body.* Chicago: University of Illinois Press, 1987.

Woodward, Kathleen. *Aging and Its Discontents: Freud and Other Fictions.* Bloomington: Indiana University Press, 1991.

———. "Arenas of Visibility: Representations/Older Women/Self-Representation." *Feminist Collections* 4, no. 5 (winter 1993): 2–5.

———. "Simone de Beauvoir: Aging and Its Discontents." In *The Private Self: Theory and the Practice of Women's Autobiographical Writing,* edited by Shari Benstock. Chapel Hill: University of North Carolina Press, 1988.

———, "Youthfulness as Masquerade." *Discourse* 11, no. 1 (fall–winter 1988–89): 119–42.

Wyatt Brown, Anne, and Janice Rossen, eds. *Aging and Gender in Literature.* Charlottesville: University Press of Virginia.

INDEX